Lost Causes of Motoring

By the same author:

THE MOTORING MONTAGUS:

The Story of the Montagu Motor Museum

Lost Causes of Motoring

by

LORD MONTAGU OF BEAULIEU

Research by Michael Sedgwick

A MONTAGU MOTOR BOOK
NEW SERIES

CASSELL · LONDON

CASSELL & COMPANY LTD
35 Red Lion Square · London W.C.1
and at
MELBOURNE · SYDNEY · TORONTO
CAPE TOWN · AUCKLAND

———

Set in 10 on 11 point Baskerville type and
printed in Great Britain
by photolithography
Unwin Brothers Limited
Woking and London
766

CONTENTS

R. W. Plenderleith (Royal Scottish Museum), R. A. Pope, J. R. Rice-Evans, John Rowland-Hosbons, G. R. J. Seary, J. A. Shutler, F. Sidebotham, R. C. Symondson, A. I. Tarby (University Motors Ltd.), G. H. K. Taylor (Thomson and Taylor Ltd.), Alistair Thomson (Royal Scottish Museum), D. B. Tubbs, G. A. Upton, G. R. Volkert, C. C. Wakefield and Co. Ltd., Major H. M. Weir, G. F. Westley (Airflow Streamlines Ltd.), R. Walton (Avon Bodies Ltd.), C. K. Wigram, T. Wood (Wood and Lambert Ltd.).

I should also like to thank all others who answered my appeals for information and wrote in to volunteer their assistance or to lend photographs or literature. It would take a whole book to name them all. And finally I should like to thank my publishers, whose generosity in the matter of deadlines has enabled us to include a lot more information than would otherwise have been possible.

MONTAGU

This book is dedicated to all those, famous or forgotten, who pioneered the motor car.

AUTHOR'S NOTE

THE adjectives 'Veteran', 'Edwardian', 'Vintage' and 'Post-Vintage Thoroughbred' will often be found in these pages, applied to cars or to periods. They were devised by the Veteran Car Club and the Vintage Sports Car Club as convenient labels. The 'Veteran' period extends from the earliest days of the motor car up to the end of 1916. 'Edwardian' is a subdivision of 'Veteran', covering cars built between 1905 and the close of the period. 'Vintage' cars were built between 1917 and the end of 1930, and the phrase 'Post-Vintage Thoroughbred' is applied to certain cars of the 1931–40 era which, by reason of their fine qualities, stand out from the mass of their contemporaries.

ILLUSTRATIONS

ILLUSTRATIONS

ACKNOWLEDGMENTS

R. W. Plenderleith (Royal Scottish Museum), R. A. Pope, J. R. Rice-Evans, John Rowland-Hosbons, G. R. J. Seary, J. A. Shutler, F. Sidebotham, R. C. Symondson, A. I. Tarby (University Motors Ltd.), G. H. K. Taylor (Thomson and Taylor Ltd.), Alistair Thomson (Royal Scottish Museum), D. B. Tubbs, G. A. Upton, G. R. Volkert, C. C. Wakefield and Co. Ltd., Major H. M. Weir, G. F. Westley (Airflow Streamlines Ltd.), R. Walton (Avon Bodies Ltd.), C. K. Wigram, T. Wood (Wood and Lambert Ltd.).

I should also like to thank all others who answered my appeals for information and wrote in to volunteer their assistance or to lend photographs or literature. It would take a whole book to name them all. And finally I should like to thank my publishers, whose generosity in the matter of deadlines has enabled us to include a lot more information than would otherwise have been possible.

MONTAGU

This book is dedicated to all those, famous or forgotten, who pioneered the motor car.

AUTHOR'S NOTE

THE adjectives 'Veteran', 'Edwardian', 'Vintage' and 'Post-Vintage Thoroughbred' will often be found in these pages, applied to cars or to periods. They were devised by the Veteran Car Club and the Vintage Sports Car Club as convenient labels. The 'Veteran' period extends from the earliest days of the motor car up to the end of 1916. 'Edwardian' is a subdivision of 'Veteran', covering cars built between 1905 and the close of the period. 'Vintage' cars were built between 1917 and the end of 1930, and the phrase 'Post-Vintage Thoroughbred' is applied to certain cars of the 1931–40 era which, by reason of their fine qualities, stand out from the mass of their contemporaries.

...e real obscurities are missing, but it lists forty-...
...vhich were independent financial entities, and w...
...akable for anything else. Go back a little further...
...ve a staggering picture, for in that year the bu...
...y, the choice of 105 makes, all of them British...
...ufacture, ranging in size from the Austin Seven a...
...angovers to the 7·4-litre Rolls-Royce 'Silver Gho...
...ay never have existed save on paper, and there...
...doubt if the Ensign 'Magnetic' (or the Chelsea-bu...
...etic with the same 'electro-magnetic transmissi...
..., for that matter) ever reached the production li...
...he 11 h.p. Adamson had twin-belt drive, the Blac...
...t-lived venture by the well-known East Yorkshi...
...e Marseal an early effort by D. M. K. Marend...
..., anon), the Stoneleigh a discreet and none-to...
...by Armstrong-Siddeley into the light-car marke...
...ck a London product which remained upon th...
...ne suspects, as an entry in the *Buyers' Guide*—...
...h vehicles emanated from the most unlikely place...
...vhich boasted a mechanical kick-starter, hailed fro...
...om Stamford, and the N.P., as its initials implie...
...agnell, where it was made in the works of Salmon...
...eers of low-priced convertible coachwork. Thi...
...tally, was again turning out motor cars in th...
...after Salmons-Tickford was acquired by the Davi...
...ut instead of the staid and undistinguished N.P...
...h the highly successful and individualistic Aston...
...ondas—a rare instance where the age of standard-...
...red a more interesting product.
...anced student will delve deeply into the obscurer...
...ey fluttered briefly across the scene in the face of a...
...from birth by ever-fiercer competition. Faced with...
...as W. R. Morris, who never feared to slash his...
...uire the source of his components if the supply...
...drying up, the small independents withered and...
...ise was often accelerated by the defensive action of...
...s, who purchased the firms who made their engines,...
...odies, for no assembly plant can survive when there...
...assemble. Some have mild technical interest, others...
...uccessful appearances in the competition world, but...
...must be regarded as engaging side-issues.
...k at the forty-two makes that were available in

INTRODUCTION

EVERY present has its past.

The study of motoring history is a new science, because it is only since the late war that men have come to look upon the motor car as something with a history. It has been argued that the technological background of the internal combustion engine has been fully documented by three generations of learned scientists, and this I will concede. But so often their findings, though vital to the specialized seeker after knowledge, have been dry as dust, and have failed to take into account the numerous and diverse applications of those technical theories, and the personalities, simple and complex, plain and colourful, who have devoted their lives and their capital to the furtherance of the internal combustion engine.

My father was one of these. He did not design cars, nor did he engage in the motor industry, other than as a director of a number of companies, but from the age of thirty-one until his death in 1929, he drove cars, he wrote about them, and he championed the cause of their owners and drivers in both Houses of Parliament. More than this, he founded *The Car Illustrated*, and in conjunction with this venture he issued a series of Montagu Motor Books, dealing with a variety of subjects: the improvement of the road system, good driving, and advice to travellers. Perhaps the most famous of these was a series entitled *Cars And How To Drive Them*. These were not manuals in the modern sense, for in those days most motorists, whether they sometimes drove themselves or not, employed a full-time chauffeur; but they represented excellent advice to anyone wishing to 'learn the ropes' on a particular model. They were invaluable in those pioneering days, when nothing was standardized, and a right-hand lever might actuate a brake, the gear-change, or simply a sprag; when makers' handbooks were a rarity, and properly equipped service stations the exception rather than the rule.

Lost Causes of Motoring is the first volume of a new series of Montagu Motor Books issued in my father's memory, with the object of dealing with all aspects of motoring throughout the years. It is hoped to issue two titles a year, and I should like to point out that, to be historical, a volume need not deal with the remote past. Motoring history did not stop with a bang in 1930; it is being made today and will continue to be made, as long as there are roads, and free people to use them.

I hope that by doing this I am performing a service to the community which may help to repay my debt of gratitude to all those who by their enthusiasm and understanding made possible the building-up of the Montagu Motor Museum. Nor is it my intention that my contribution shall stop here, for it is also my aim to establish Beaulieu as an historical research centre for motorists and motoring enthusiasts the world over, to which end I am setting up a reference library open to the public.

To these enthusiasts, I offer *Lost Causes of Motoring* as an endeavour to fill one of the gaps in the history of our movement.

MONTAGU

INTRODUCTION TO SECOND EDITION

HISTORY is constantly being made, and even some of the Lost Causes described in this book have reappeared on the scene since 1960, both Lea-Francis and Trojan having been active in the field of private-car production. *Lost Causes of Motoring* aroused great interest when it was first published; and numerous readers have written to me with helpful suggestions and criticisms of my interpretation of history. Many of these letters drew attention to obscure points of history that can elude even the most diligent researcher. I have therefore decided to revise and bring up to date the story of the Lost Causes, incorporating all the fresh information I have been able to amass.

Beaulieu, March 1966   MONTAGU

Ration

'I woul

NOWADAYS, we take
with a combination
to our everyday mo
there was. Road tra
appreciation of this i
interest in old cars to
Vintage events, but
pioneers who helpec
mainstay of her exp
name is perpetuated
thirty others have fall
of them.

A random glance
industry reveals that
—Lagonda—which
similar figures for Fr
But will these statis
will not, for even the
ing industrial group
—accounts for no fe
units and not many
nents of the Big Five
of the remainder and
partly or wholly fo
therefore attained to
of *marque* names, a
motoring journalists
Italianate shapes i
another.

To gain a fair pic
when individuality
Guide of 1930. This,

B

one or two of t
makes, most of
not readily mist
1924, and we h
had, theoretical
design and man
a few cyclecar h
Some of these
serious reason to
15·9 h.p. Magr
across air space'
Of the oddities,
burn was a sho
aircraft firm, th
(of whom more
successful essay
and the Whitlo
scene—largely,
late as 1936. Su
The Horstman,
Bath; the Pick f
from Newport P
and Sons, pior
factory, inciden
nineteen-fifties,
Brown group, b
there came fort
Martins and Lag
ization has fathe

Only the adv
cars of 1924—th
slump, doomed
such opponents
prices or to ac
showed signs of
died. Their dem
their bigger riva
gearboxes, and h
is nothing left to
made fleetingly s
in the main they
When we loo

1930–31, however, we can see how Britain's motor industry has changed. Twenty of the names listed in 1930 are still listed in 1966, but of these only Alvis, Rolls-Royce and Rover can claim continuity of descent from birth. Of the others, Hillman, Humber, Vauxhall and Wolseley had already succumbed to the pressure of big business before 1931. Aston Martin, Lagonda, Bentley and Frazer-Nash, it is true, still stand for all that is best in their particular fields, but the first one is now part of a large engineering group, Lagonda production was suspended in 1964, the Frazer-Nash is only in token production, and, while no one could deny the superb quality of the workmanship that goes into a modern Bentley, it would be equally hard to refute the assertion that only its radiator grille distinguishes it from the corresponding Rolls-Royce.

For the rest, little more than the names survive. Worthy vehicles though modern B.M.C. products are, it is too easy to divide them into watertight groups, not by make, but by classification, as small touring cars, large touring cars, sports cars and luxury cars. History, incidentally, repeats itself: in 1908 when Clément and Gladiator had amalgamated, and Austin had undertaken the assembly of the latter's products for the British market as a sideline, unkind correspondents in *The Autocar* were writing pungent letters asking what the differences were between the three makes. The names of Sunbeam and Singer are still perpetuated by the Rootes Group, and their reputation has not suffered—but they owe their continued existence to sentiment plus the need for variations, *de luxe* and sporting respectively, on the immortal 'Minx' theme. Under the aegis first of Sir John Black, then of Leyland Motors, Standard and Triumph, who amalgamated in 1945, contrived to preserve a degree of individuality until the name of Standard was dropped in 1963, though at one stage the commodity sold in Britain as a Standard Ten was retailed to the Americans as a Triumph. Realism also demands the admission that the present Triumph company is thrice removed from the famous and still highly successful motor cycle firm which launched into car manufacture in 1923. After the divorce of the car and motor cycle interests in 1936, not even Donald Healey could keep the car side off the rocks, and in 1939, after a year of near-bankruptcy, it was acquired by the Sheffield steel firm of Thomas W. Ward Ltd., coming under Standard's control some five years later.

What has caused this? In a simple word, rationalization. The small firms came into being on a sellers' market, and many of them were little more than assemblers and trimmers of parts manufactured elsewhere. When Big Business slashed its prices, these small 'manufacturers' could only follow suit by skimping quality, and the British public has always clung earnestly to its fleshpots in the face even of post-war austerity—as witness the keen demand for two-tone colour schemes, radios, heaters, and overdrives, which items are costly, and carry the burden of cumulative purchase tax. They could not buy their components more cheaply, since reduced costs were dependent on unattainably higher sales, so they had the choice of abandoning assembly for manufacture, branching out into other fields of commerce, or going out'of business. Morris had earlier taken the first course, and certain of the true manufacturers, notably Trojan, were to take the second; but the majority lacked the capital or foresight and faded quietly away. Some of them took an unconscionable time a-dying: the Calthorpe was moribund by 1927, but lingered on in the *Buyers' Guide* till 1932; while others, like drowning swimmers, bobbed up forlornly, at intervals, under different control or a different *marque* name. Thus two abortive Invicta companies kept the name, which had in effect fizzled out in 1933, alive after a fashion for another sixteen years.

These comments must, in the main, apply to the firms which specialized in 'the mixture as before', a species of family touring car which grew smaller with the years. It could be typified in 1912 or thereabouts as a '15/20 h.p.', of 2½ to 3 litres capacity, endowed with a long-stroke monobloc four-cylinder engine. Twelve or so years later, it had shrunk into an '11·9' with a 1½-litre four-cylinder unit, a three-speed gearbox, and a ponderous touring body whose impressive all-weather equipment sent the weight soaring and the gear ratios dropping away to abysmal depths. By 1934, this type of car was as dead as the dodo, and its sponsors' spiritual successors were either exploring other fields, or toying with small sports cars possessed of close-ratio remote-control gearboxes, soup-plate instruments and proprietary engines. Others sought to exploit the joys of a cheap American engine in a light chassis, thus placing themselves in the rarefied atmosphere which surrounds the specialist manufacturer.

The specialist manufacturer's problem was a different one. He had to decide either to go the whole hog, or to abdicate. The position of this gentleman in the Golden Age of 1910–14 was secure: large-scale production was a thing of the future, as far as Great Britain was concerned, and consequently manufacturers could afford to market large ranges embracing everything from a near-cyclecar to vast 'sixes' of nine and ten litres capacity. No maker ever adopted so down-to-earth an attitude as the late Lord Austin, yet in 1910 he was offering seven models, ranging from the diminutive single-cylinder Seven to a monstrous white elephant in the form of a 121 × 127 mm. six-cylinder Sixty—and Austin's brief period of financial insecurity lay a good ten years ahead! Everyone was a specialist; so much so that somewhat of a furore was occasioned in 1908 by Straker-Squire's announcement that in future they would concentrate on one model only—a 14/16, incidentally, on the same general lines as our hypothetical '15/20'.

After the war, the specialists went to town. Rolls-Royce quietly went on making the 'Silver Ghost', but Lanchester, Napier, Leyland and Ensign in this country, together with such firms as Farman and Hispano-Suiza in France, Isotta-Fraschini in Italy, and Duesenberg in the United States, launched into an energetic programme of large, complex and costly motor cars. In the immediate post-War boom, there were plenty of profiteers who were willing to spend £2,000 on a chassis alone, and double their investment with one of the specialist coachbuilders. Slightly lower down the scale came Sunbeam, Humber, Argyll, Arrol-Johnston, Crossley, and their competitors, who were turning out large and medium-sized touring cars of excellent quality. Alas, the market for these steadily dried up, and slowly the ranks of the specialist producers withered. Some firms, like Humber, sold out early on, and bought themselves peace, success, and ultimately honour. Others, like Lanchester, held on almost till too late; while Sunbeams obstinately refused to cater for the popular market, and died slowly and painfully. Napiers scuttled unreservedly, and went on to build successful multi-cylinder aero-engines of fearsome complexity. Arrol-Johnston, by this time encumbered with the equally insecure Aster Engineering Co. Ltd., embarked upon a spree of unprincipled escapism. Already wedded to the commercially unsuccessful Burt-McCollum single sleeve-valve engine, they plunged wildly into the straight-eight field, and that was that!

The straight-eight principle stalks like some sinister skeleton through the story of the Lost Causes. Cecil Clutton has drawn a fascinating parallel in *The Vintage Motor Car Pocketbook* between the incidence of the small 'six' and the intervention of the Official Receiver. While no one would refute the element of truth in Mr Clutton's thesis, there is to my mind a far closer relation between the eight-in-line and the bankruptcy courts. Of the firms who toyed with this impressively lengthy power unit in Britain, only Daimler emerged scatheless. Among the last engines evolved by Lanchester,

Hillman and Sunbeam as independent entities were straight-eights. Belsize (1925), Arrol-Aster (1929), and Hampton (1930) breathed their last to the silken purr of eight cylinders in line, while Wolseley, Alvis and Triumph did nothing to enhance their bank balances by excursions into this sphere. The firm of Lenaerts and Dolphens, sponsors of the Beverley-Barnes, built nothing else for nine years, and only one of their cars has survived, while when we come to review the unhappy saga of the Jam Factory at Maidenhead, we shall again meet the straight-eight. That this theory is no illusion is borne out by the fact that, of America's Big Three, only Chrysler listed such a machine in the Vintage era, General Motors abstaining till 1931; while Henry Ford would have none of it at any time.

Of those who changed their tune, Lagonda went the whole way, concentrating on specialist sporting vehicles, and survived a bankruptcy in 1935. Crossley elected to take the opposite course, and plunged into the manufacture of some truly dreadful small cars with proprietary i.o.e. engines and preselector gearboxes. Rovers, still a highly respected and independent firm, nearly succumbed to the same dread disease, but saner counsels prevailed after two years of unmitigated frightfulness, and the firm was able to face 1934—the year of recovery—with a range of excellent, if uninspired cars and a handsome profit. Talbot, under the aegis of Georges Roesch, started to build specialist cars in 1927, and would undoubtedly have survived but for the deadweight of the conservative Sunbeam company, and the moribund Darracq works at Suresnes.

There are then, in effect, three basic causes for failure: lack of capital, an unrealistic policy, and the systematic production of really undistinguished cars. A lamentable case of the last was B.S.A., who espoused first a 'cheap' variation of the Daimler, and subsequently a depressing front-wheel-drive small car which, alas, matched a high degree of technical ingenuity with a total lack of performance. Well-deserved success in the motor cycle field kept the B.S.A. cars alive ten years longer than they merited, and, but for the bombing of Coventry, they might have survived still.

While purists would insist on the inclusion of such firms as Bentley, Riley, Vauxhall and Wolseley in this book, we must, in fairness, exclude them. For all the loud protests of the Old Brigade, men have been known to forsake a '4½' in old age for a Derby or Crewe-built Bentley, and the same people who bought the old long-stroke 'Big Four' Riley later bought the B.M.C.-built 'six'. The decline of the Vauxhall was a gradual process, too, the connecting link being the six-cylinder 20/60 of 1928. It would be fair, however, to include in our terms of reference the two genuinely defunct offshoots of Riley; the Riley Engine Co., who built a large machine called the Riley Seventeen in 1923, and Autovia Cars Ltd., who launched an equally unsuccessful vee-eight some thirteen years later. The Wolseley, though it has lost its individuality over the years, still caters for the same public as it did before Lord Nuffield acquired the company in 1927.

The true dead-ends, however, are complex in their own right. Star of Wolverhampton produced cars under the names of Starling, Stuart and Briton, the latter pursuing an independent existence up to 1929. Crossley allied themselves with the Willys-Overland empire, and assembled their products in their Stockport plant, finally adding to their collection the car side of the A.J.S. motor cycle business; while the ramifications of the Invicta story, as we shall see, are fearsome.

Another engaging aspect of the Lost Causes is their lack of any geographical cohesion. Here there is little parallel with America, where the ascendancy of mass production from a very early date tended to centralize manufacture in established industrial areas. It is therefore a matter of moment to American historians that as late as 1921 at least one car—the Hanson—was still being made in the Deep South, whereas the smaller British firms, wedded as they were to limited production, were free to pursue the manufacture of vehicles anywhere they chose. Most big towns offered foundry facilities on a scale adequate for their purposes, and in many cases the major components were 'bought out'.

Apart from Coventry and Birmingham, Wolverhampton must rate as one of the most prolific centres of car manufacture, but the town was dogged with ill-fortune from the start. Clyno, after a meteoric rise which reached its peak about 1926, faded away three years later. A.J.S.'s short-lived car venture expired in 1933, a year after operations had been transferred to Stockport, while Star and Sunbeam were both dead by 1935. The Turner company, which had been quietly manufacturing first steam and then petrol cars since 1902, abandoned the unequal struggle towards the end of the Vintage decade. It would be unfair to class Guy among the Wulfrunian failures, for Sydney Guy saw the red light, and reverted to the manufacture of trucks alone in 1924; but even now the era of Wolverhampton bankruptcies is not over, it would seem. The late summer of 1959 saw the failure of Frisky Cars, a minicar venture originally sponsored by Henry Meadows Ltd., well known as manufacturers of proprietary power units. This little machine, incidentally, was later revived under different management.

Neither Liverpool nor Manchester was prominent as a car-manufacturing city, though the latter produced two of the better-known Lost Causes, Belsize and Crossley. The Belsize was among the pioneers, starting life as the Marshall, a pseudo-Benz, in 1897. Other Lancashire products were the Moveo, an ephemeral which appeared in Preston in 1932, and the Vulcan, Southport's contribution. Its name lingered on into the nineteen-fifties, but by this time it was neither a private car, nor even made in Lancashire. Yorkshire, by contrast, was fairly prolific of motor cars—the Bramham hailed from Leeds, the Bond (no connexion with the famous Minicar) from Brighouse, the Richardson from Sheffield, and the Jowett from Bradford. The Bell was even made in both counties, starting life in Ravensthorpe, and migrating in its declining years to Manchester, where it was sponsored by no less an organization than the Co-operative Wholesale Society. As it was offered in 4-litre form in 1924, with hand starting only, sales can hardly have been brisk, even in the unselective market of those days.

Few of Scotland's thirty-odd makes, apart from the famous three 'A's, achieved much currency, and the Belfast-built Chambers, which survived until 1930, was the only noteworthy Irish car. Lincoln had the Ruston-Hornsby, Bristol the Straker-Squire and Stroud the Hampton, while Essex products included the Clarkson steamer at Chelmsford and the Bentall at Maldon. The Castle three-wheeler emanated from Kidderminster, on the fringes of the Midlands, but neither Devon nor Cornwall put a car into production. The Victorian Lifu steam car was made in Cowes, I.O.W. Bedford produced the Adams 'pedals-to-push' car, and Aylesbury made three bids to board the bandwagon: the Edwardian Iris, the Vintage Cubitt, and the post-Hitler war Murad.

London and the Home Counties have long been the home of recondite motor cars, from Veterans like the New Orleans and James and Browne and Edwardians such as the horizontal-engined N.E.C. (made at Willesden), up to such modern obscurities as the Vale (a product, as might be imagined, of Maida Vale from 1933 to 1936), and the Powerdrive three-wheeler, which Wood Green offered in 1956. Other minicars from the London area were Denham's Coronet and Leighton Buzzard's Russon. Such Anglo-Americans as the Atalanta, Lammas, and Railton also centred round London, while in the nineteen-twenties we can find the A.B.C., Albert, Bleriot-Whippet, Ensign, Eric-Campbell, Gwynne,

Loyd-Lord, New Carden, Orpington, Palladium, Seabrook, Sizaire-Berwick, Surrey, Tamplin, Waverley, Whitlock and Windsor, which all attained varying degrees of series production in or near the Metropolis. At Herne, in Kent, Major Prescott-Westcar produced the 11·9 h.p. Westcar, a conventional 'assembled' machine, and the unit-construction Heron, which was anything but conventional, and probably helped to put the Strode Engineering Works out of business.

But perhaps the most curious home of Lost Causes was the Upper Thames. Passing the high-tide mark at Teddington, where A.V. Motors (still in business) once marketed that perilous contraption, the A.V. Monocar, we encounter A.C.s at Thames Ditton (still very much alive under the direction of the Hurlock brothers, but with a record of receivership behind them in the early nineteen-thirties), A.B.C. at Hersham (no longer making motor cars), and the factory at Staines Bridge which once made Lagondas, before reaching Maidenhead and the Jam Factory—one-time home of at least four different *marques* and now producing St. Martin's Chunky Marmalade. Nor have we finished here, for just downstream at Datchet is the ancestral home of the Jam Factory's original incumbent, the G.W.K., and on a tributary of the Thames upstream from Maidenhead is a precision engineering plant associated in 1920 with a vehicle of the depressingly communistic name of Unit No. 1. At the top of the hill which rises above Henley Reach there was born the exciting twin o.h.c. Squire, one of the legendary sports cars which enlivened the dreary nineteen-thirties; while Reading fathered the Speedwell and the H.E., the latter emanating from what later became the Thornycroft marine works at Caversham. Not far away, at Highclere, a Rutherford steam car was made in 1908. It is not until we reach Oxford that the hoodoo seems to leave us, though Oxford, one feels, would have been more appreciative of the hoodoo than the other car-making towns of the Upper Thames. The trend still continues, and 1962 saw another casualty in the form of Wraysbury's Warwick, a Triumph-based *gran turismo* which succeeded Slough's very similar Peerless.

It is curious how the car factories seemed to hug the river. The Hallford lorry and the Thames car were being made in the Port of London in Edwardian times, while further upstream could be found the Gwynne at Chiswick, the Beverley-Barnes at Barnes, and the Warren-Lambert at Richmond. Almost all are now gone, leaving Ford of Dagenham and A.C. of Thames Ditton as the sole manufacturers occupying a river frontage.

What have the defunct manufacturers left behind them? The traces are all too few, as latter-day owners of these makes have learnt to their cost. In many cases, spares continued to be available a few years after the companies' demise, when a falling demand and the high cost of manufacture caused the cars to become orphans. Even those manufacturers who forsake the production of cars for other interests are not always helpful, though Trojan remains an honourable exception. This is not to say that the cars are forgotten; clubs cater for B.S.A., Clyno, Crossley, Invicta, Jowett, Lea-Francis, Lanchester, Railton, Star and Trojan. A rally organized to celebrate the 150th anniversary of D. Napier and Son brought forth two dozen Napiers from all over the country, no mean feat in view of the fact that the firm's *total* production of private cars during their peak period—1909 to 1911—amounted to a mere 1,800-odd; while local antiquarian societies are showing an interest in their erstwhile motor industries. The last few years have seen Salisbury questing a Scout, and Lincoln a Ruston-Hornsby.

They have also left a heritage of technical development: Lanchester's disc brake and epicyclic gearbox, Napier's leadership in the six-cylinder field, the pioneer work of Argyll, Arrol-Johnston and Crossley with four-wheel brakes, and Invicta's fully automatic transmission, marketed a full six years before any other British manufacturer was prepared to take the plunge. And in this era of rationalization, even a Clyno or a Swift, perhaps two of the duller Vintage family cars, will still attract a bigger crowd than will the latest psychomatic monster in hangover pink—because it looks like a car, and could not be mistaken for anything else.

This is the story of some of these 'Lost Causes of Motoring'—their rise to fame, and their downhill slide to bankruptcy and limbo. It should be remembered, though, that these are but a few from hundreds, and that this book can only skim the surface of a wealth of motoring lore that would take years to extract from the few who know, or care to remember such vehicles. If your favourite is not included, it is for no reason other than because its inclusion might involve the production of a book at least treble the length of mine.

INTRODUCTION

EVERY present has its past.

The study of motoring history is a new science, because it is only since the late war that men have come to look upon the motor car as something with a history. It has been argued that the technological background of the internal combustion engine has been fully documented by three generations of learned scientists, and this I will concede. But so often their findings, though vital to the specialized seeker after knowledge, have been dry as dust, and have failed to take into account the numerous and diverse applications of those technical theories, and the personalities, simple and complex, plain and colourful, who have devoted their lives and their capital to the furtherance of the internal combustion engine.

My father was one of these. He did not design cars, nor did he engage in the motor industry, other than as a director of a number of companies, but from the age of thirty-one until his death in 1929, he drove cars, he wrote about them, and he championed the cause of their owners and drivers in both Houses of Parliament. More than this, he founded *The Car Illustrated*, and in conjunction with this venture he issued a series of Montagu Motor Books, dealing with a variety of subjects: the improvement of the road system, good driving, and advice to travellers. Perhaps the most famous of these was a series entitled *Cars And How To Drive Them*. These were not manuals in the modern sense, for in those days most motorists, whether they sometimes drove themselves or not, employed a full-time chauffeur; but they represented excellent advice to anyone wishing to 'learn the ropes' on a particular model. They were invaluable in those pioneering days, when nothing was standardized, and a right-hand lever might actuate a brake, the gear-change, or simply a sprag; when makers' handbooks were a rarity, and properly equipped service stations the exception rather than the rule.

Lost Causes of Motoring is the first volume of a new series of Montagu Motor Books issued in my father's memory, with the object of dealing with all aspects of motoring throughout the years. It is hoped to issue two titles a year, and I should like to point out that, to be historical, a volume need not deal with the remote past. Motoring history did not stop with a bang in 1930; it is being made today and will continue to be made, as long as there are roads, and free people to use them.

I hope that by doing this I am performing a service to the community which may help to repay my debt of gratitude to all those who by their enthusiasm and understanding made possible the building-up of the Montagu Motor Museum. Nor is it my intention that my contribution shall stop here, for it is also my aim to establish Beaulieu as an historical research centre for motorists and motoring enthusiasts the world over, to which end I am setting up a reference library open to the public.

To these enthusiasts, I offer *Lost Causes of Motoring* as an endeavour to fill one of the gaps in the history of our movement.

MONTAGU

INTRODUCTION TO SECOND EDITION

HISTORY is constantly being made, and even some of the Lost Causes described in this book have reappeared on the scene since 1960, both Lea-Francis and Trojan having been active in the field of private-car production. *Lost Causes of Motoring* aroused great interest when it was first published; and numerous readers have written to me with helpful suggestions and criticisms of my interpretation of history. Many of these letters drew attention to obscure points of history that can elude even the most diligent researcher. I have therefore decided to revise and bring up to date the story of the Lost Causes, incorporating all the fresh information I have been able to amass.

Beaulieu, March 1966   MONTAGU

CHAPTER 1

Rationalization Triumphant

'I would rather build one good car a day. . . .'
Saying ascribed to Joseph Lisle,
of the Star Motor Co.

NOWADAYS, we take the motor car for granted. Unless we are faced with a combination of ice and fog, there is little adventure attached to our everyday motoring, and only a novice would pretend that there was. Road transport has become a part of our lives, and the appreciation of this is reflected in the tremendous and nation-wide interest in old cars today. Thousands turn out to watch Veteran and Vintage events, but how many of them pause to think of those pioneers who helped to build Britain's motor industry into the mainstay of her export trade? For every one manufacturer whose name is perpetuated on the radiator grilles of the present, some thirty others have fallen by the wayside. This is the story of a handful of them.

A random glance at a current *Buyers' Guide* of the British motor industry reveals that thirty-six makes are still listed, plus another —Lagonda—which is currently dormant. By comparison with similar figures for France or the U.S.A., this is a formidable figure. But will these statistics stand close scrutiny? Unfortunately, they will not, for even the most superficial student is aware that the leading industrial group in the country—the British Motor Corporation —accounts for no fewer than eight makes, utilizing six basic power units and not many more basic structures. The remaining components of the Big Five contribute a further eight *marque* names, while of the remainder another four are dependent upon the major groups partly or wholly for the supply of mechanical parts. Variety is therefore attained to a great extent by the sentimental preservation of *marque* names, and very little more, and already responsible motoring journalists have been led astray by the similarity of certain Italianate shapes into mistaking one 1½-litre family saloon for another.

To gain a fair picture of the British motor industry in the days when individuality was triumphant, we must go back to the *Buyers' Guide* of 1930. This, perhaps, does not present the true picture, since one or two of the real obscurities are missing, but it lists forty-two makes, most of which were independent financial entities, and were not readily mistakable for anything else. Go back a little further to 1924, and we have a staggering picture, for in that year the buyer had, theoretically, the choice of 105 makes, all of them British in design and manufacture, ranging in size from the Austin Seven and a few cyclecar hangovers to the 7 4-litre Rolls-Royce 'Silver Ghost'. Some of these may never have existed save on paper, and there is serious reason to doubt if the Ensign 'Magnetic' (or the Chelsea-built 15·9 h.p. Magnetic with the same 'electro-magnetic transmission across air space', for that matter) ever reached the production line. Of the oddities, the 11 h.p. Adamson had twin-belt drive, the Blackburn was a short-lived venture by the well-known East Yorkshire aircraft firm, the Marseal an early effort by D. M. K. Marendaz (of whom more anon), the Stoneleigh a discreet and none-too-successful essay by Armstrong-Siddeley into the light-car market, and the Whitlock a London product which remained upon the scene—largely, one suspects, as an entry in the *Buyers' Guide*—as late as 1936. Such vehicles emanated from the most unlikely places. The Horstman, which boasted a mechanical kick-starter, hailed from Bath; the Pick from Stamford, and the N.P., as its initials implied, from Newport Pagnell, where it was made in the works of Salmons and Sons, pioneers of low-priced convertible coachwork. This factory, incidentally, was again turning out motor cars in the nineteen-fifties, after Salmons-Tickford was acquired by the David Brown group, but instead of the staid and undistinguished N.P. there came forth the highly successful and individualistic Aston Martins and Lagondas—a rare instance where the age of standardization has fathered a more interesting product.

Only the advanced student will delve deeply into the obscurer cars of 1924—they fluttered briefly across the scene in the face of a slump, doomed from birth by ever-fiercer competition. Faced with such opponents as W. R. Morris, who never feared to slash his prices or to acquire the source of his components if the supply showed signs of drying up, the small independents withered and died. Their demise was often accelerated by the defensive action of their bigger rivals, who purchased the firms who made their engines, gearboxes, and bodies, for no assembly plant can survive when there is nothing left to assemble. Some have mild technical interest, others made fleetingly successful appearances in the competition world, but in the main they must be regarded as engaging side-issues.

When we look at the forty-two makes that were available in

1930–31, however, we can see how Britain's motor industry has changed. Twenty of the names listed in 1930 are still listed in 1966, but of these only Alvis, Rolls-Royce and Rover can claim continuity of descent from birth. Of the others, Hillman, Humber, Vauxhall and Wolseley had already succumbed to the pressure of big business before 1931. Aston Martin, Lagonda, Bentley and Frazer-Nash, it is true, still stand for all that is best in their particular fields, but the first one is now part of a large engineering group, Lagonda production was suspended in 1964, the Frazer-Nash is only in token production, and, while no one could deny the superb quality of the workmanship that goes into a modern Bentley, it would be equally hard to refute the assertion that only its radiator grille distinguishes it from the corresponding Rolls-Royce.

For the rest, little more than the names survive. Worthy vehicles though modern B.M.C. products are, it is too easy to divide them into watertight groups, not by make, but by classification, as small touring cars, large touring cars, sports cars and luxury cars. History, incidentally, repeats itself: in 1908 when Clément and Gladiator had amalgamated, and Austin had undertaken the assembly of the latter's products for the British market as a sideline, unkind correspondents in *The Autocar* were writing pungent letters asking what the differences were between the three makes. The names of Sunbeam and Singer are still perpetuated by the Rootes Group, and their reputation has not suffered—but they owe their continued existence to sentiment plus the need for variations, *de luxe* and sporting respectively, on the immortal 'Minx' theme. Under the aegis first of Sir John Black, then of Leyland Motors, Standard and Triumph, who amalgamated in 1945, contrived to preserve a degree of individuality until the name of Standard was dropped in 1963, though at one stage the commodity sold in Britain as a Standard Ten was retailed to the Americans as a Triumph. Realism also demands the admission that the present Triumph company is thrice removed from the famous and still highly successful motor cycle firm which launched into car manufacture in 1923. After the divorce of the car and motor cycle interests in 1936, not even Donald Healey could keep the car side off the rocks, and in 1939, after a year of near-bankruptcy, it was acquired by the Sheffield steel firm of Thomas W. Ward Ltd., coming under Standard's control some five years later.

What has caused this? In a simple word, rationalization. The small firms came into being on a sellers' market, and many of them were little more than assemblers and trimmers of parts manufactured

elsewhere. When Big Business slashed its prices, these small 'manufacturers' could only follow suit by skimping quality, and the British
public has always clung earnestly to its fleshpots in the face even of
post-war austerity—as witness the keen demand for two-tone colour
schemes, radios, heaters, and overdrives, which items are costly, and
carry the burden of cumulative purchase tax. They could not buy
their components more cheaply, since reduced costs were dependent
on unattainably higher sales, so they had the choice of abandoning
assembly for manufacture, branching out into other fields of commerce, or going out 'of business. Morris had earlier taken the first
course, and certain of the true manufacturers, notably Trojan, were
to take the second; but the majority lacked the capital or foresight
and faded quietly away. Some of them took an unconscionable time
a-dying: the Calthorpe was moribund by 1927, but lingered on in
the *Buyers' Guide* till 1932; while others, like drowning swimmers,
bobbed up forlornly, at intervals, under different control or a
different *marque* name. Thus two abortive Invicta companies kept
the name, which had in effect fizzled out in 1933, alive after a
fashion for another sixteen years.

These comments must, in the main, apply to the firms which
specialized in 'the mixture as before', a species of family touring car
which grew smaller with the years. It could be typified in 1912 or
thereabouts as a '15/20 h.p.', of $2\frac{1}{2}$ to 3 litres capacity, endowed
with a long-stroke monobloc four-cylinder engine. Twelve or so
years later, it had shrunk into an '11·9' with a $1\frac{1}{2}$-litre four-cylinder
unit, a three-speed gearbox, and a ponderous touring body whose
impressive all-weather equipment sent the weight soaring and the
gear ratios dropping away to abysmal depths. By 1934, this type of
car was as dead as the dodo, and its sponsors' spiritual successors
were either exploring other fields, or toying with small sports cars
possessed of close-ratio remote-control gearboxes, soup-plate instruments and proprietary engines. Others sought to exploit the joys of
a cheap American engine in a light chassis, thus placing themselves
in the rarefied atmosphere which surrounds the specialist manufacturer.

The specialist manufacturer's problem was a different one. He
had to decide either to go the whole hog, or to abdicate. The position of this gentleman in the Golden Age of 1910–14 was secure:
large-scale production was a thing of the future, as far as Great
Britain was concerned, and consequently manufacturers could
afford to market large ranges embracing everything from a near-
cyclecar to vast 'sixes' of nine and ten litres capacity. No maker ever

4

adopted so down-to-earth an attitude as the late Lord Austin, yet in 1910 he was offering seven models, ranging from the diminutive single-cylinder Seven to a monstrous white elephant in the form of a 121 × 127 mm. six-cylinder Sixty—and Austin's brief period of financial insecurity lay a good ten years ahead! Everyone was a specialist; so much so that somewhat of a furore was occasioned in 1908 by Straker-Squire's announcement that in future they would concentrate on one model only—a 14/16, incidentally, on the same general lines as our hypothetical '15/20'.

After the war, the specialists went to town. Rolls-Royce quietly went on making the 'Silver Ghost', but Lanchester, Napier, Leyland and Ensign in this country, together with such firms as Farman and Hispano-Suiza in France, Isotta-Fraschini in Italy, and Duesenberg in the United States, launched into an energetic programme of large, complex and costly motor cars. In the immediate post-War boom, there were plenty of profiteers who were willing to spend £2,000 on a chassis alone, and double their investment with one of the specialist coachbuilders. Slightly lower down the scale came Sunbeam, Humber, Argyll, Arrol-Johnston, Crossley, and their competitors, who were turning out large and medium-sized touring cars of excellent quality. Alas, the market for these steadily dried up, and slowly the ranks of the specialist producers withered. Some firms, like Humber, sold out early on, and bought themselves peace, success, and ultimately honour. Others, like Lanchester, held on almost till too late; while Sunbeams obstinately refused to cater for the popular market, and died slowly and painfully. Napiers scuttled unreservedly, and went on to build successful multi-cylinder aero-engines of fearsome complexity. Arrol-Johnston, by this time encumbered with the equally insecure Aster Engineering Co. Ltd., embarked upon a spree of unprincipled escapism. Already wedded to the commercially unsuccessful Burt-McCollum single sleeve-valve engine, they plunged wildly into the straight-eight field, and that was that!

The straight-eight principle stalks like some sinister skeleton through the story of the Lost Causes. Cecil Clutton has drawn a fascinating parallel in *The Vintage Motor Car Pocketbook* between the incidence of the small 'six' and the intervention of the Official Receiver. While no one would refute the element of truth in Mr Clutton's thesis, there is to my mind a far closer relation between the eight-in-line and the bankruptcy courts. Of the firms who toyed with this impressively lengthy power unit in Britain, only Daimler emerged scatheless. Among the last engines evolved by Lanchester,

Hillman and Sunbeam as independent entities were straight-eights. Belsize (1925), Arrol-Aster (1929), and Hampton (1930) breathed their last to the silken purr of eight cylinders in line, while Wolseley, Alvis and Triumph did nothing to enhance their bank balances by excursions into this sphere. The firm of Lenaerts and Dolphens, sponsors of the Beverley-Barnes, built nothing else for nine years, and only one of their cars has survived, while when we come to review the unhappy saga of the Jam Factory at Maidenhead, we shall again meet the straight-eight. That this theory is no illusion is borne out by the fact that, of America's Big Three, only Chrysler listed such a machine in the Vintage era, General Motors abstaining till 1931; while Henry Ford would have none of it at any time.

Of those who changed their tune, Lagonda went the whole way, concentrating on specialist sporting vehicles, and survived a bankruptcy in 1935. Crossley elected to take the opposite course, and plunged into the manufacture of some truly dreadful small cars with proprietary i.o.e. engines and preselector gearboxes. Rovers, still a highly respected and independent firm, nearly succumbed to the same dread disease, but saner counsels prevailed after two years of unmitigated frightfulness, and the firm was able to face 1934—the year of recovery—with a range of excellent, if uninspired cars and a handsome profit. Talbot, under the aegis of Georges Roesch, started to build specialist cars in 1927, and would undoubtedly have survived but for the deadweight of the conservative Sunbeam company, and the moribund Darracq works at Suresnes.

There are then, in effect, three basic causes for failure: lack of capital, an unrealistic policy, and the systematic production of really undistinguished cars. A lamentable case of the last was B.S.A., who espoused first a 'cheap' variation of the Daimler, and subsequently a depressing front-wheel-drive small car which, alas, matched a high degree of technical ingenuity with a total lack of performance. Well-deserved success in the motor cycle field kept the B.S.A. cars alive ten years longer than they merited, and, but for the bombing of Coventry, they might have survived still.

While purists would insist on the inclusion of such firms as Bentley, Riley, Vauxhall and Wolseley in this book, we must, in fairness, exclude them. For all the loud protests of the Old Brigade, men have been known to forsake a '4½' in old age for a Derby or Crewe-built Bentley, and the same people who bought the old long-stroke 'Big Four' Riley later bought the B.M.C.-built 'six'. The decline of the Vauxhall was a gradual process, too, the connecting link being the six-cylinder 20/60 of 1928. It would be fair,

6

however, to include in our terms of reference the two genuinely
defunct offshoots of Riley; the Riley Engine Co., who built a large
machine called the Riley Seventeen in 1923, and Autovia Cars Ltd.,
who launched an equally unsuccessful vee-eight some thirteen years
later. The Wolseley, though it has lost its individuality over the
years, still caters for the same public as it did before Lord Nuffield
acquired the company in 1927.

The true dead-ends, however, are complex in their own right.
Star of Wolverhampton produced cars under the names of Starling,
Stuart and Briton, the latter pursuing an independent existence up
to 1929. Crossley allied themselves with the Willys-Overland empire,
and assembled their products in their Stockport plant, finally adding
to their collection the car side of the A.J.S. motor cycle business;
while the ramifications of the Invicta story, as we shall see, are
fearsome.

Another engaging aspect of the Lost Causes is their lack of any
geographical cohesion. Here there is little parallel with America,
where the ascendancy of mass production from a very early date
tended to centralize manufacture in established industrial areas. It
is therefore a matter of moment to American historians that as late
as 1921 at least one car—the Hanson—was still being made in the
Deep South, whereas the smaller British firms, wedded as they were
to limited production, were free to pursue the manufacture of
vehicles anywhere they chose. Most big towns offered foundry
facilities on a scale adequate for their purposes, and in many cases
the major components were 'bought out'.

Apart from Coventry and Birmingham, Wolverhampton must
rate as one of the most prolific centres of car manufacture, but the
town was dogged with ill-fortune from the start. Clyno, after a
meteoric rise which reached its peak about 1926, faded away three
years later. A.J.S.'s short-lived car venture expired in 1933, a year
after operations had been transferred to Stockport, while Star and
Sunbeam were both dead by 1935. The Turner company, which had
been quietly manufacturing first steam and then petrol cars since
1902, abandoned the unequal struggle towards the end of the
Vintage decade. It would be unfair to class Guy among the Wulfrunian failures, for Sydney Guy saw the red light, and reverted to
the manufacture of trucks alone in 1924; but even now the era
of Wolverhampton bankruptcies is not over, it would seem. The
late summer of 1959 saw the failure of Frisky Cars, a minicar
venture originally sponsored by Henry Meadows Ltd., well
known as manufacturers of proprietary power units. This

little machine, incidentally, was later revived under different management.

Neither Liverpool nor Manchester was prominent as a car-manufacturing city, though the latter produced two of the better-known Lost Causes, Belsize and Crossley. The Belsize was among the pioneers, starting life as the Marshall, a pseudo-Benz, in 1897. Other Lancashire products were the Moveo, an ephemeral which appeared in Preston in 1932, and the Vulcan, Southport's contribution. Its name lingered on into the nineteen-fifties, but by this time it was neither a private car, nor even made in Lancashire. Yorkshire, by contrast, was fairly prolific of motor cars—the Bramham hailed from Leeds, the Bond (no connexion with the famous Minicar) from Brighouse, the Richardson from Sheffield, and the Jowett from Bradford. The Bell was even made in both counties, starting life in Ravensthorpe, and migrating in its declining years to Manchester, where it was sponsored by no less an organization than the Co-operative Wholesale Society. As it was offered in 4-litre form in 1924, with hand starting only, sales can hardly have been brisk, even in the unselective market of those days.

Few of Scotland's thirty-odd makes, apart from the famous three 'A's, achieved much currency, and the Belfast-built Chambers, which survived until 1930, was the only noteworthy Irish car. Lincoln had the Ruston-Hornsby, Bristol the Straker-Squire and Stroud the Hampton, while Essex products included the Clarkson steamer at Chelmsford and the Bentall at Maldon. The Castle three-wheeler emanated from Kidderminster, on the fringes of the Midlands, but neither Devon nor Cornwall put a car into production. The Victorian Lifu steam car was made in Cowes, I.O.W. Bedford produced the Adams 'pedals-to-push' car, and Aylesbury made three bids to board the bandwagon: the Edwardian Iris, the Vintage Cubitt, and the post-Hitler war Murad.

London and the Home Counties have long been the home of recondite motor cars, from Veterans like the New Orleans and James and Browne and Edwardians such as the horizontal-engined N.E.C. (made at Willesden), up to such modern obscurities as the Vale (a product, as might be imagined, of Maida Vale from 1933 to 1936), and the Powerdrive three-wheeler, which Wood Green offered in 1956. Other minicars from the London area were Denham's Coronet and Leighton Buzzard's Russon. Such Anglo-Americans as the Atalanta, Lammas, and Railton also centred round London, while in the nineteen-twenties we can find the A.B.C., Albert, Bleriot-Whippet, Ensign, Eric-Campbell, Gwynne,

Loyd-Lord, New Carden, Orpington, Palladium, Seabrook, Sizaire-Berwick, Surrey, Tamplin, Waverley, Whitlock and Windsor, which all attained varying degrees of series production in or near the Metropolis. At Herne, in Kent, Major Prescott-Westcar produced the 11·9 h.p. Westcar, a conventional 'assembled' machine, and the unit-construction Heron, which was anything but conventional, and probably helped to put the Strode Engineering Works out of business.

But perhaps the most curious home of Lost Causes was the Upper Thames. Passing the high-tide mark at Teddington, where A.V. Motors (still in business) once marketed that perilous contraption, the A.V. Monocar, we encounter A.C.s at Thames Ditton (still very much alive under the direction of the Hurlock brothers, but with a record of receivership behind them in the early nineteen-thirties), A.B.C. at Hersham (no longer making motor cars), and the factory at Staines Bridge which once made Lagondas, before reaching Maidenhead and the Jam Factory—one-time home of at least four different *marques* and now producing St. Martin's Chunky Marmalade. Nor have we finished here, for just downstream at Datchet is the ancestral home of the Jam Factory's original incumbent, the G.W.K., and on a tributary of the Thames upstream from Maidenhead is a precision engineering plant associated in 1920 with a vehicle of the depressingly communistic name of Unit No. 1. At the top of the hill which rises above Henley Reach there was born the exciting twin o.h.c. Squire, one of the legendary sports cars which enlivened the dreary nineteen-thirties; while Reading fathered the Speedwell and the H.E., the latter emanating from what later became the Thornycroft marine works at Caversham. Not far away, at Highclere, a Rutherford steam car was made in 1908. It is not until we reach Oxford that the hoodoo seems to leave us, though Oxford, one feels, would have been more appreciative of the hoodoo than the other car-making towns of the Upper Thames. The trend still continues, and 1962 saw another casualty in the form of Wraysbury's Warwick, a Triumph-based *gran turismo* which succeeded Slough's very similar Peerless.

It is curious how the car factories seemed to hug the river. The Hallford lorry and the Thames car were being made in the Port of London in Edwardian times, while further upstream could be found the Gwynne at Chiswick, the Beverley-Barnes at Barnes, and the Warren-Lambert at Richmond. Almost all are now gone, leaving Ford of Dagenham and A.C. of Thames Ditton as the sole manufacturers occupying a river frontage.

9

What have the defunct manufacturers left behind them? The traces are all too few, as latter-day owners of these makes have learnt to their cost. In many cases, spares continued to be available a few years after the companies' demise, when a falling demand and the high cost of manufacture caused the cars to become orphans. Even those manufacturers who forsake the production of cars for other interests are not always helpful, though Trojan remains an honourable exception. This is not to say that the cars are forgotten; clubs cater for B.S.A., Clyno, Crossley, Invicta, Jowett, Lea-Francis, Lanchester, Railton, Star and Trojan. A rally organized to celebrate the 150th anniversary of D. Napier and Son brought forth two dozen Napiers from all over the country, no mean feat in view of the fact that the firm's *total* production of private cars during their peak period—1909 to 1911—amounted to a mere 1,800-odd; while local antiquarian societies are showing an interest in their erstwhile motor industries. The last few years have seen Salisbury questing a Scout, and Lincoln a Ruston-Hornsby.

They have also left a heritage of technical development: Lanchester's disc brake and epicyclic gearbox, Napier's leadership in the six-cylinder field, the pioneer work of Argyll, Arrol-Johnston and Crossley with four-wheel brakes, and Invicta's fully automatic transmission, marketed a full six years before any other British manufacturer was prepared to take the plunge. And in this era of rationalization, even a Clyno or a Swift, perhaps two of the duller Vintage family cars, will still attract a bigger crowd than will the latest psychomatic monster in hangover pink—because it looks like a car, and could not be mistaken for anything else.

This is the story of some of these 'Lost Causes of Motoring'— their rise to fame, and their downhill slide to bankruptcy and limbo. It should be remembered, though, that these are but a few from hundreds, and that this book can only skim the surface of a wealth of motoring lore that would take years to extract from the few who know, or care to remember such vehicles. If your favourite is not included, it is for no reason other than because its inclusion might involve the production of a book at least treble the length of mine.

CHAPTER 2

The Three 'A's of Scotland:
I— The Dogcart Brigade

'Recognized specialists in the construction of Motor Vehicles for the Country House.'
                                                    Albion advertisement, 1914

'We were never in a better position to produce a first-rate car.'
                Prologue to announcement of 'Victory' Arrol-Johnston, 1919

IT has been observed that Scotland's major exports are brains and whisky. Comparatively few Scots seek to extract a living from their own country, and it has always surprised me that so many of them sought to make cars there. According to A. S. E. Browning of the Glasgow Museum, who has made a serious study of the subject, some forty car manufacturers have operated north of the Border, though some, like Madelvic and Little Scotsman, were mere flashes in the pan, and others, like the Scottish Aster, are no more than names in long-forgotten lists. But in all this welter of unsifted history, the three 'A's of Scotland stand out in the same way as do the three 'P's of America—Packard, Peerless and Pierce-Arrow—for Argyll, Arrol-Johnston and Albion were the three makes which put Scotland on the international motoring map. They invariably listed their country of origin as 'Scotland', not 'Britain'; Argylls talked of 'export to England' in their press releases, and Arrol-Johnston in their racing days decked out their cars in tartan to compensate for the absence of Scottish national colours.

Private car manufacture in Scotland, after a slow start, rose to a crescendo of glory around 1907, after which it faded slowly away. In the early days, Arrol-Johnston and Albion, sharing a common ancestry, catered for the home market in its narrowest sense, while Argyll aspired for wider honours. In 1913, Albion turned firmly to commercial vehicles, leaving its two erstwhile rivals to slide down the precipice to oblivion by way of single sleeve-valves. Yet, in the main, they were not bad cars: Argylls are still remembered with affection, as is the T-head 15 h.p. Albion, while Arrol-Johnston's more conventional productions more than lived up to the solid reputation claimed for them by the factory, albeit their eccentricities lost them more money than they could afford.

The story really starts in August 1894, when one George Johnston, fired by a progressive spirit, is said to have imported a German Daimler dogcart into his native Scotland. Having learnt what he could from this primitive device, he purchased a Panhard with the sliding gearbox the following year, and in 1897 he decided to make cars himself. In partnership with Sir William Arrol, a famous consulting engineer and architect of the Forth Bridge, Archibald Coats of the famous textile family, and John Miller, he founded a firm with the infelicitous title of the Mo-Car Syndicate Ltd., and works at Bluevale, Camlachie. Most of the money undoubtedly came from Sir William Arrol, thus leading *The Car Illustrated*, for one, to assert that he was responsible for the design of the Arrol-Johnston car, but some measure of Coats support is indicated by the fact that the firm's first serious factory at Underwood, Paisley, occupied part of the Coats thread mills. Also associated with the Mo-Car project was one Dr T. Blackwood Murray, who was to leave the little group and set up on his own two years later.

Variously known in the earliest days as 'Mo-Car' and 'Arrol-Johnston', George Johnston's first cars were of peculiarly rustic aspect, if eminently suited for the rough terrain of their native Scotland. They corresponded closely with the 'high-wheelers' disseminated in America by Sears-Roebuck and others almost up to the outbreak of the first World War. Johnston used a large two-cylinder horizontally-opposed unit lying under the floor, with opposed pistons. The connecting rod of one piston worked directly on the crankshaft, and that of the other through a rocking lever. Ignition was by a low-tension magneto, and drive was by primary chain to a gearbox which on the later cars had four forward speeds. A single central chain carried the drive to a live rear axle. Cooling was furnished by a horizontal tubular radiator mounted fore-and-aft on the frame, while petrol and water tanks were mounted forward as well. The whole equipage was finished off in dogcart style with solid tyres and a varnished wood finish which emphasized the vehicle's equestrian ancestry. In spite of this, the Arrol-Johnston enjoyed some concessions to modernity. From quite early days it was steered by a self-locking and tilting wheel, though on the six-seaters any visual advantages of this were nullified by the positioning of the driver in the second row, with a whole bench of passengers in front of him. The car started from the seat, via a rope coiled round a pulley. This was connected with a pinion engaging with another on the crankshaft, and incorporated a half-compression device. Once the engine fired, a spring on the pulley re-coiled it automatically, in readiness for the next time.

Crude as it was, it undoubtedly worked. Johnston, who had experimented with electric carriages, asserted that it gave forth 'no smell, no dirt, and no vibration'. Certainly the passengers were well insulated from all of these. The Murray low-tension ignition was more reliable than contemporary trembler coils, and vibration was averted by governing these engines to 850 r.p.m.—itself quite an alarming thought in those days. Johnston even claimed to have evolved a special brand of rubber that gave as smooth a ride as the new-fangled pneumatics.

These devices continued as part of the Arrol-Johnston range until at least 1906, when a fire at Camlachie caused the firm to move into the Underwood Works at Paisley, their home until 1913. Sales were steady, if unspectacular, even though Lord Rosebery bought one in 1903. The firm made the mandatory attempts at the reliability trials of the period, never disgracing themselves, while in July, 1904, a Dr G. England Kerr, writing to *The Autocar*, spoke in glowing terms of the fleet of three—including one of the very first 5½ h.p. cars with tiller steering—which he used in his practice. This machine, said to be the fourth to leave the factory, had covered 60,000 miles in six years with no trouble, and the doctor was quite convinced that solids were the only wear for Scottish roads. At the Crystal Palace Show in 1904, the Mo-Car Syndicate were claiming that they made everything save the tyres, radiator and chains, and they were also exploring the commercial vehicle field. The 12 h.p. (108 × 165 mm.) engine was used to power a two-ton van announced in 1904, and in August of that year a fleet of sixteen-passenger charabancs in toast-rack style were plying for hire in Fleetwood, the makers claiming that the opposed-piston engine could haul all this *carrosserie* along at 12 m.p.h. In 1906, two launches were operating at Blackpool, using motors of the same type, while in June, 1905, on the eve of that first T.T. which brought Arrol-Johnston right into the public eye, the firm's advertising was still trumpeting the virtues of solid tyres, low-tension ignition and a non-automatic carburettor.

While the Mo-Car Syndicate was slowly gathering momentum, two of its members had broken loose, and on 31 December 1899, Dr T. Blackwood Murray and Norman Fulton formed the Albion Motor Company, with offices and works at Finnieston Street, Glasgow.

The initial products of the new firm reflected Mo-Car influences, and bore a close external resemblance to early Arrol-Johnstons, horizontal engines being retained up to 1903. The first car appeared in 1900. After a long and chequered career, including a period as the works service van, it ended up in 1908 in the Glasgow Museum, where it still is, while Albion No. 2 is preserved by the Royal Scottish Museum at Edinburgh. Murray brought with him his own system of low-tension magneto ignition. Engine speed was automatically governed by the Murray patent governor, and another feature of Albion design was his patent lubricator, whereby all working parts could be lubricated from the driver's seat while the vehicle was in motion, without going through all the evolutions of the then-fashionable drip-feed system.

Walter Creber's privately-entered Albion did well in the 1901 Glasgow Trials, and a year later its proud owner was reporting 9,000 trouble-free miles in eighteen months. If anything, the Albion dogcarts were an even more substantial proposition than their rivals from Paisley, as in 1904, one of the first cars was said to have run 40,000 miles at a cost of less than a halfpenny a mile; apart, of course, from going through four sets of tyres. By 1902, cars were being exported to Malaya and Siam, and the first Albion delivery vans were on the streets of Glasgow.

The story of Albion's private-car venture is one of a solid reputation steadily built up. In May 1903, the Finnieston works proved incapable of coping with the demand, and a move was made to Scotstoun, where the firm has remained ever since. Finnieston, incidentally, had not seen the last of motor car manufacture, for the works were acquired by Walter Bergius, who made a few Kelvin cars there before concentrating on marine engines, for which the Bergius Engine Company has since become justly famous.

In 1904, Albion was offering a 12 h.p. dogcart with thirty-four-inch wood wheels, exhaust-heated carburettor and Murray governor and ignition for £440, and vertical front-mounted engines were available for the first time. Curiously enough, there has been a reversion in recent years to the inclined tubular radiator mounted forward of the engine, and current Albion trucks with underfloor engines have a layout remarkably similar (in this respect alone!) to that of the first dogcarts. Nineteen hundred and four also saw a one-ton commercial chassis, but it was the last year of the dogcart era, the staple offering for 1905 being the 16 h.p. twin-cylinder (125 × 127 mm.) model, still on solid tyres, though pneumatics were soon made an option. Sixteen b.h.p. was developed at 900 r.p.m., and bodies for all standard Albions were made by Penman of Dumfries.

The following season Albions came out with a luxury chauffeur-driven chassis, the 24 h.p. (108 × 114 mm.) four-cylinder. The side chains were remarkably quiet, Albion's system of lubrication via pipes from the Murray lubricator being likened in quality to Sunbeam's famous 'little oil bath chain cases'. Dr Murray's conservatism however, was reflected in the retention of low-tension ignition, though the governor now allowed engine speeds up to 1,200 r.p.m. Chassis price was £633, and *The Autocar* commented favourably upon the car's handling characteristics—'the car steers easily and lies nicely on the road when rounding corners'. These two models represented most of Albion's private-car production, the 24 h.p. being continued until 1912, and the 16 h.p. 'twin' a year longer.

Despite the fact that the makers still recommended the use of solid tyres—which were even fitted on the new shooting-brake sold to the pioneer Scottish motorist T. R. B. Elliot in 1909—the firm's experimental department was by no means unreceptive to new ideas. In 1909, the Allen-Liversidge front-wheel brakes were tried out on a 16 h.p. van. In the same year the firm patented a slide valve, (but had too much horse sense to put it into production), and in 1911 the thrifty Scots of Glasgow, W.4, were demonstrating a paraffin carburettor, in those days a legally permitted economy, and one in which, incidentally, the Crown Agents for the Colonies showed a keen interest. Another pioneering departure was the standardization, in 1906, of a system of code-words for use when ordering new parts.

Albion, however, were finding it difficult to meet their commitments in both private and commercial fields. Their reputation now rested solidly on the country-house business, and no one could have foreseen in 1912 that the country-house itself was doomed to extinction—certainly not Albions, who were proudly proclaiming, as late as 1920, that their estate vehicles were again available for the first time since the war. A new 15 h.p. private-car chassis was announced for 1912, with a four-cylinder 79 × 127 mm. monobloc engine, unit construction gearbox and worm drive, but with the side valves in a T-head, a layout by now considered conservative. The Murray governor and lubrication system were, of course, retained, and it sold at £475, complete with Penman touring body. At the 1912 Olympia Show, the emphasis was on shooting-brakes, and a year later nothing else was displayed. Out of 554 chassis that left Scotstoun in this year, only about 150 were private cars, and in November 1913, a smart 15 h.p. coupé marked the end of the line. The 15 h.p. engine was still made, but thenceforward it was fitted in trucks alone.

It was a wise move. Today the firm is a part of the Leyland Group, yet retains a high measure of independence, and Albions are still Albions, and not a *pot-pourri* of assembled parts.

Arrol-Johnston, meanwhile, were going places. Nineteen hundred and five saw the first of those odd experiments which punctuated their whole career, and two interesting steps forward, which were to boost annual production to some 700 cars by 1907. The oddity was a three-cylinder car, available in 16 and 20 h.p. forms, which had an inclined engine mounted at the front, and cylinders of different size, the central cylinder having a larger bore in each case. Unit construction of engine and gearbox was an advanced feature. Transverse suspension was utilized and the influence of George Johnston was reflected in the retention of solid tyres. These did not survive beyond the 1905 season. On the credit side, J. S. Napier (no connection with the Acton firm) was engaged as chief engineer and a new company, the New Arrol-Johnston Car Co. Ltd. was formed under the backing and chairmanship of Sir William Beardmore, later Lord Invernairn. This, incidentally, was purely a personal connexion, and when later Beardmores entered the motor industry, they exercised no jurisdiction or control over the various Arrol-Johnston enterprises.

The immediate result of Napier's arrival was an incursion into racing, with an 18 h.p. (121 × 165 mm.) horizontal-twin car which was entered for the first 'fuel consumption' T.T. in 1905. Its designer drove it into first place, averaging 33·9 m.p.h. and 31·1 m.p.g.—a great success, though it must be confessed that Percy Northey's more conventional 20 h.p. Rolls-Royce was potentially a faster car. E. J. C. Roberts on the second Arrol-Johnston took fourth place.

These cars had forced lubrication, always an Arrol-Johnston feature, four-speed gearboxes, Hele-Shaw multi-plate clutches and wire wheels, and were put on the market in modified and detuned form. Determined attempts were made both to overcome a resistance to the horizontal engine and to persuade customers that the T.T. winner really was a stock car. Roberts' car was fitted with a coupé body, and Napier joined the craze for hill-storming by persuading both his 18 h.p. T.T. car and the less potent touring Twelve up the 1-in-3¾ gradient of Loch Striven Head. The immediate result of this endeavour was that the dynamic Captain H. H. P. Deasy took off for Scotland in one of the Martinis he was then promoting and repeated the experiment. The hill joke was satirized in the contemporary motoring press, *The Autocar* waxing jubilant when

16

A 1912 15·9 h.p. Arrol-Johnston in Cape Town, 1959

After over 250,000 miles of use, this 1926 15·9 Arrol-Johnston was still in regular use in 1959

A 24/30 h.p. Albion of 1910, now lovingly preserved by its makers

One of the first Argyll *voiturettes* of 1900–01, with De Dion engine and Renault-like lines

'Apparently a late poppet-valve Argyll,' this is in fact a 1907 14/16 h.p. model modernized in about 1912

two Arrol-Johnstons failed to make the grade from Llangollen to Glyn Ceiriog in 1907. Had the horizontal 'twins' been particularly successful either as touring or racing cars, the Arrol-Johnston story might have been very different, but the 1905 victory was a mere flash in the pan. They tried again in the 1906 T.T., but were beset by tyre troubles, Napier's speed on the second lap being a mere 17·6 m.p.h. as against the winning Rolls-Royce's 39·8 m.p.h. For the 1908 race they produced the 'raciest and smartest cars on the course', four-cylinder 105 × 127 mm. engines being favoured this year, with Rudge-Whitworth wire wheels and Doolittle detachable rims. In addition, E. H. Arnott drove a 40 h.p. car in the concurrent Heavy Car Race. Napier was unlucky: he collided with an 'uncontrolled horse' in practice, and retired on the last lap in the race itself from fuel shortage.

George Johnston, meanwhile, had transferred his allegiance to the All British Car Co. Ltd., arousing a chorus of complaint from his old firm, who maintained that people were subscribing to the new flotation in the belief that it was an Arrol-Johnston subsidiary. They need not have worried. An eight-cylinder engine very like an early Arrol-Johnston in layout was displayed at the 1907 Agricultural Hall Show, but that was the sum total of the All British Car Co.'s achievements.

By 1907 Arrol-Johnston were marketing two large 'fours', the 108 × 127 mm. 24/30 and the 143 × 152 mm. 38/45, in addition to the horizontal 12/15 h.p. 'twin'. These featured three-point suspension for the gearbox, Arrol-Johnston carburettors, dual ignition by low-tension magneto and coil, and disc clutches. Cylinders were cast in pairs, there were side valves in L-heads, and prices were £700 and £850 respectively. For 1908, only the 12/15 and 38/45 were retained, but an i.o.e. 16/25 with dual ignition, still designed by Napier, was added to the range. These three models constituted the 1909 programme as well.

The years 1907–8 saw the construction of a special car for Ernest Shackleton's Antarctic expedition. This was an air-cooled 'four' with separate cylinders, overhead inlet valves, and a Renault-style bonnet. Dual ignition was provided, and ingenious features included a snow-melter box fitted over the exhaust pipe. The engine was of Simms manufacture, and two sets of wheels—fitted respectively with wooden tyres and Dunlop pneumatics—were provided, the latter proving infinitely more successful. Prices produced a special non-freezing oil for this engine. This pioneer utilization of the motor vehicle for Polar exploration met with only moderate success, though Arrol-Johnstons gained considerable kudos thereby. My father, incidentally, was consulted on the design of this car.

In April 1909, T. C. Pullinger was appointed general manager. Pullinger had a distinguished record of service behind him in the motor industry. Starting with J. and E. Hall at Dartford, he had gravitated, via a period at Woolwich Arsenal, to the French cycle industry, serving first with Darracq and then with Duncan et Suberbie. He had also been responsible for the design of the Teste et Moret *voiturette*. An interesting aspect of his sojourn in France is that his daughter, Dorothée, who will play a substantial part in this story, came to England knowing not a word of her mother tongue! To Pullinger, who persuaded them to take up the manufacture of the 12 h.p. Berliet, Sunbeam owed their strong position in the motor industry. He had supervised the assembly of the ill-fated Weir-Darracq racers in 1904, and had enjoyed four successful years in charge of Humber's Beeston works. He undoubtedly did more than anyone to consolidate Arrol-Johnston's reputation, though one suspects that some of his whims helped to bring about the decline and fall of the company.

Four months after his arrival, a disastrous fire at Underwood demolished the repair, paint and buffing shops, as well as the tool and trimming rooms; in spite of this, the first-fruits of the new régime, in the shape of the 15·9, appeared in time for the 1909 Show. This vehicle favoured thermo-syphon cooling, with the radiator mounted astern of the engine, *à la* Renault. Otherwise it was a fairly conventional motor car, with a side-valve 80 × 120 mm. engine, high-tension magneto ignition, shaft drive and detachable wheels. In one notable respect, however, it was most advanced. Pullinger adopted front-wheel brakes on the Allen-Liversidge system, whereby the internal expanding brakes on the front wheels were operated by the pedal, and the rear wheel brakes by the hand lever. As Austin Seven owners will testify, uncoupled systems have their weaknesses, and the layout was dropped for 1912. A curious boat-tail was adopted on the touring bodies, in contrast with the horribly stodgy styling affected by Arrol-Johnston in the early nineteen-twenties.

Arrol-Johnston's touring-car designs during the remaining pre-war years were unexciting. An attempt to persuade the Courts that they held a master patent covering detachable wheels, a feature which they had pioneered, failed signally, as did Pullinger's endeavour to discourage other manufacturers from using the term '15·9' to describe their '80-bore' four-cylinder engines—one wonders what he would have thought of Ford of Dagenham's 1960 effort. In 1911, a 23·8 h.p. six-cylinder car on similar lines to the 'four', but without four-wheel brakes, joined the range: and in 1912 four-wheel brakes disappeared altogether, though, to give Pullinger his due, he did not re-adopt transmission braking either. The range was rounded out with a 69 × 120 mm. 11·9 h.p., the stroke of the 15·9 being lengthened to 140 mm. Dynamo lighting was listed as an option for 1913, and in 1914 a 15·9 tourer with electric starting and lighting could be bought for a mere £360. The six-cylinder car gave way to a four-cylinder 91 × 140 mm. 20·9. Arrol-Johnston stopped making cars early in the first World War, but a 1915 proto-type was made in the shape of a 17·9 h.p. (85 × 120 mm.) car with full electrical equipment, and a frontal radiator. It was listed at £375.

Pullinger, however, shared Coatalen's belief that racing improved the breed, and in 1911 he had entered three tuned 15·9 h.p. cars (Reid, Resta and Hodge) in the *Coupe Des Voitures Legères*. All three finished, but Reid's, the fastest car, could manage no higher than seventh place. In 1912, they tried again, fielding side-valve cars for the second time, after experiments with an overhead-camshaft engine. The 80 × 140 mm. units were cooled by frontal vee radi-ators, and the cars had five-speed gearboxes, the geared-up top endowing them, theoretically, with a speed of 117 m.p.h. at 3,000 r.p.m. One wonders. Two of the cars had side-chain drive—a curious departure—though the detachable *wooden* disc wheels were discarded in favour of the conventional Sankey steel type before the race. The shaft-driven cars had friction-type shock absorbers at the rear. In the event, they were not particularly successful, Wyse, the best performer of the team, finishing fifth. Thereafter the firm withdrew from competition work.

Meanwhile, the works had been moved in 1913 from Paisley to Heathhall, Dumfries, so as to be as near as possible to the principal export market—England. The old Underwood Works were later used by Beardmores during their vintage sally into car manufacture. The first news from the plant was another curious side-issue of the kind which Arrol-Johnston apparently found irresistible. This time it concerned electric cars. In 1913, Edison Accumulators Ltd. had been formed in London to promote the battery-electric vehicle in England, the principal directors being Colonel H. C. L. Holden, of four-cylinder motor cycle fame, and my father. The car to be mar-keted was based on the Detroit Electric—incidentally, the last electric private car to be made in series in the U.S.A.—and Arrol-Johnstons contracted to build a preliminary series of fifty. One was certainly made, differing from American prototypes in having wheel steering and the 'Renault' bonnet, and it was duly driven from Dumfries to London, with fourteen charging stops, to demonstrate the efficacy of the design. While the run from Heathhall to Manchester—156 miles—was claimed with justification to be a record for a day's journey by electric car—I do not think that the Arrol-Johnston-Edison ever got much further than the 1913 Olympia Show, and I have never been able to trace any reference to the matter in my father's papers.

For all their vicissitudes, Arrol-Johnston were well established by 1914. They had even achieved (in July 1911) a War Office order for the 15·9, and if their four-wheel braking experiments had proved abortive, at least they had been early in the field with detachable wheels. During the war they worked with Beardmore, on the evolution, from the original Beardmore-built six-cylinder Austro-Daimler, of the 230 h.p. B.H.P. (Beardmore-Halford-Pullinger) aero-engine, later to be known as the Siddeley 'Puma'. In 1915, incidentally, Pullinger put his workmen into uniform khaki overalls, with the kindly intention of preserving them from interfering old ladies and would-be senders of white feathers. Arrol-Johnston, too, were ready for the Peace with a new car. With much trumpeting, and issue of preliminary and interim catalogues, they launched their car to end all cars—the 'Victory' model.

The 'finest material' and 'the most brilliant intellects' were behind this. The designer was G. W. A. Brown, late of Clement-Talbot Ltd., who had been responsible for Percy Lambert's famous 100 m.p.h. Brooklands car, and the 'Victory' bristled with interesting features. In an era when side valves were standard wear in the medium-price bracket, it featured an overhead camshaft. While the unhappy transitional styling of 1914 still permeated makers' catalogues, it possessed what was then known as a 'streamlined' body, with a smooth line from scuttle to bonnet. When right-hand control was *de rigueur* on this side of the Atlantic, it had a central change, and a central handbrake lever, actuating, I regret to state, a transmission brake. In engine dimensions it conformed to contemporary thought, bore and stroke being 75 mm. and 150 mm. respectively: 40 b.h.p. was claimed at 2,000 r.p.m., and a five-seater tourer complete weighed a mere twenty cwt., despite a ten-foot wheelbase. At £700 it should have caught the public's fancy as did the Jowett 'Javelin' in 1947.

Unfortunately, it did not. It was a flop. Very few ever reached the public, and one which was supplied to H.R.H. the Prince of

Wales in August 1919, was quietly withdrawn from service after breaking down at Yeovil on a West Country tour. By the 1919 Show, Arrol-Johnston were offering an alternative—not, be it said at this stage, a replacement—for the 'Victory', in the shape of the dear old 15·9. This had already reverted to its 120 mm. stroke in 1914—the abandonment of the racing programme having nullified the value of the extra 20 mm.—and was now to adopt the front-mounted radiator. Otherwise it remained much as in 1914, and only a conservative 22 b.h.p. was claimed. More interesting was the claim that it 'was designed for quick production methods'. It had to be, for Arrol-Johnston had nothing else to sell in 1919. Still, it was quite well received at £645.

While Lord Invernairn's other company, Beardmore, pursued a curiously schizophrenic policy of producing three different types of car in three different factories, and later divided their time in 1923–4 between the potent Francis-designed 2-litre which took the Shelsley Walsh record and the production of taxicabs, in which industry they are still active, Arrol-Johnston went quietly down hill. Not that the cars deteriorated in quality—they remained excellent, solidly-built touring vehicles, with no performance whatsoever. Long after others had abandoned this market, they still listed 'Colonial' models. It was simply that they ceased to be competitive, and, instead of adhering to a one or two-model policy, they plunged into all manner of curious experiments.

Six-cylinderism still claimed part of their time. Practically nothing is known of either of their Vintage 'sixes', but in 1921 Hotchkiss of Coventry supplied the firm with fifty o.h.v. push-rod engines, to what purpose we shall probably never know. At the 1922 Show, furthermore, they displayed a 73 × 98 mm. two-stroke chassis, for which £630 was asked. History, however, is equally silent on the fate of this contrivance. Meanwhile, something had to be done to retrieve the 'Victory' fiasco—a number of the staff had drifted down to London, where they engaged themselves in the manufacture of the Hammond car in a factory at Finchley, but all the bits and pieces remained. So Pullinger decided to try his hand at a light car, to be made in the wartime aero-engine factory at Tongland, Kirkcudbright.

Here again it was the ensuing complication of the range rather than the car itself that brought about failure. The Galloway, as the new venture, introduced in October 1920, was named, was quite a good little car. It was based on the highly successful Tipo 501 FIAT, and the cylinder blocks were made of the melted-down back axles stockpiled for the 'Victory' cars. The supervision of the Tongland plant was put in the capable hands of Miss Dorothée Pullinger, and women were largely employed in these works. The engine followed FIAT practice in being a side-valve monobloc unit of 65 × 110 mm. (1,460 c.c.) with detachable head. The car had the central ball change used on the 'Victory', controlling a three-speed unit box, and Michelin detachable disc wheels were used. The standard body style was a 'doctor's coupé', listing at £550, and in deference to the peculiarities of the Scottish market, ease of maintenance was carefully studied. It was unkindly said that the sterling FIAT qualities were lost by cost-cutting, but owners' experiences do not seem to bear this out.

Arrol-Johnston, meanwhile, were still turning out some fifty cars a week, all 15·9s with Michelin disc wheels. *The Autocar* tried one in July 1920, and the tester experienced no feeling of fatigue after a hundred miles of Cotswold roads. The full-elliptic springs at the rear, however, left something to be desired, and the sensitive management at Heathhall duly replaced them with three-quarter elliptics for the 1921 season, being rewarded with a pat on the back from the press when the model was again tried in March of that year. The Galloway's central change was, however, criticized as being too far away from the driver—some testers are horribly hard to please!

The next three years saw Arrol-Johnston struggling to keep going. Despite the success of a 'one-make' rally at the Great Central Hotel, London, in November 1921, when Pullinger delivered a lecture and a prize was awarded to the best-kept car present, developments were limited to minor reshuffles in the range. For 1922, the 15·9 acquired a monobloc engine with detachable head, the firm now compromising with a stroke of 130 mm., while a unit-construction gearbox and semi-elliptic rear springs were further concessions to modernity. The Galloway's wheelbase was lengthened by ten inches, the power unit moved back three inches in the frame, and its American-style ball change lever replaced by a conventional central gate. Despite quite a good record in the reliability trials of the year, it was found necessary to close down Tongland and consolidate activities at Heathhall, though the Galloway Engineering Co. Ltd. retained its separate entity.

Arrol-Johnston came out with a 2,121 c.c. Fourteen and a 90 × 150 mm. (3,290 c.c.) 'Empire' model for Colonial conditions in 1924, and were rewarded by an order for one of the latter from Viscount Goschen, the Governor of Madras. This model, however, was innocent of either shock absorbers or front-wheel brakes, and was duly criticized by the press—but the 1925 cars still had two-wheel braking only. For 1925, the Fourteen was replaced by a 69·5 × 110 mm. Twelve, the four-speed box including a 17·1 bottom gear for hilly country, while compensated f.w.b. were included at a price of £360 for a tourer. The 15·9 now cost only £425, and the big 'Empire' tourer £510. There was an additional Galloway model in the shape of a Twelve, sharing the same engine as the smallest Arrol-Johnston model. The small Arrol-Johnston, incidentally, received a very good write-up in *The Autocar* in August, 1925, its ability to start off in second gear being noted, as also—a sore point this, at Heathhall—was the absence of shock-absorbers. This type, along with the 10 h.p. Galloway, was dropped in 1926, when the remaining models acquired o.h.v. heads, the blocks still being produced in Arrol-Johnston's own foundry. Front-wheel brakes, however, were available for the new season, though r.w.b. could be had as a low-cost option. Prices with full equipment were £385 for the 15·9 h.p. 'Dominion', and £275 for the 12 h.p. Galloway, which had now been brought into line with its bigger sisters and looked like a miniature Arrol-Johnston. Having now rung all the changes, the firm offered the same cars for 1927.

At this juncture the step was taken that was to spell *finis* for the Dumfries concern. In April 1927, it was announced that Arrol-Johnston had amalgamated with the Aster Engineering Co. Ltd.

To explore all the complexities of the Aster story would be a lengthy business. The parent firm, Ateliers de Construction Mécanique l'Aster, had stood second only to De Dion as a manufacturer of proprietary engines in the earliest years of the century, numbering among their customers Gladiator, Argyll and Whitlock. Aster engines had been made in England under licence since 1899, when the Begbie Manufacturing Co. Ltd. had been formed, and the Wembley works opened. Under Mr Sydney Begbie's direction, successive Aster companies had built and marketed engines of Aster design, though cars sold under this name in England in the early years of the century were, in fact, Ariès chassis with Aster engines and British bodywork. They also had a flourishing motor repair business and made Green aero-engines and generating sets, while their proprietary units reappeared on the market after the first World War, these including an exciting-sounding 65 × 150 mm. twin o.h.c. 'four'. In 1922, they decided to enter the private car market, and for the next four years they offered some very attractive luxury cars with six-cylinder o.h.v. push-rod engines of Sunbeam-like aspect, four-speed gearboxes, and cantilever rear suspension on Lanchester lines. The quality of workmanship was very high, as was the price, an 18 h.p. tourer listing at £850 in 1923. Aluminium pistons were standard, as were duralumin push-rods, and in 1924 balloon tyres and Perrot-type front-wheel brakes were available. By 1926, the original 18 h.p. car had grown into a 3,048 c.c. 21/60 good for well over 70 m.p.h., and H.R.H. The Duke of York had purchased a stylish Aster sports saloon. Bodywork, incidentally, was a strong suit with the Aster, the well-rounded lines contrasting with the angular ugliness of some of its contemporaries, while among the attractive features to be found on the individually-built bodies were electric cigar lighters in the doors, continuous winding windows and a two-way opening dickey seat for the ladies. Not many cars were made, and only two survive, to the best of my knowledge—one in Australia, and one which I have been fortunate enough to borrow for my Museum at Brighton.

For the 1927 season Asters, though still listing the 21/60, had decided to launch into the town carriage market with a big 80 × 115 mm. 24/70 with a wheelbase of 12 ft. 3 in. While this closely resembled previous productions in outward appearance, it used the Burt-McCollum single sleeve-valve engine, with certain 'improvements'. These consisted mainly of the method of actuating the sleeves via a 'wobble-shaft', a species of crankshaft mounted below the base of the sleeves, and driven from the crankshaft proper. This method of drive was quieter than the normal train of gears, but the shaft was inherently unbalanced, and consequently maximum revs. were limited to about 3,400. Above this, things were apt to happen!

As Pullinger had already retired, the Board of the combined companies consisted of Lord Invernairn and W. Lowe, representing the Scottish firm, and Mr Begbie and Mr Clench of Asters. Manufacture was centralized at Heathhall, Wembley becoming a London depot and service station. One would have thought that when the two companies joined forces, some sort of rationalization would have ensued. Nothing of the kind was to happen: Arrol-Johnston and Aster Ltd. faced 1928 with a selection of *six* different models. Of these, the 12 h.p. Galloway, 15/40 h.p. Arrol-Johnston and 21/60 h.p. Arrol-Aster had push-rod-operated o.h.v., while the 17/50 h.p. Arrol-Aster and the 21/60 and 24/70 Asters favoured single sleeve valves. Styling now followed Wembley rather than Heathhall, which was an improvement, and prices ranged from £360 for the Galloway up to £1,200 for the big Aster. The new Arrol-Aster had a free-wheel incorporated in the transmission, and was a pleasant enough car up to about 70 m.p.h., though it had

24

inherited a poor steering lock from its Wembley-built forebears.

The following year a serious degree of rationalization was at last adopted. All models except the six-cylinder Arrol-Aster and the two sleeve-valve Aster 'sixes' were dropped, but the firm proceeded to take the last step towards bankruptcy by introducing a 23/70 Arrol-Aster straight-eight. This had the same engine dimensions as the 17/50, 67·5 × 115 mm., giving a capacity of 3,293 c.c., and was an attractive-looking machine, with a '8' *motif* on the radiator and one-shot lubrication, a feature introduced on the original sleeve-valve Aster of 1927. It suffered from the same wobble-shaft weakness as its small sister.

Nothing could save the firm now. Sir Malcolm Campbell entrusted the 1928–9 reconstruction of his 'Bluebird', with which he made an unsuccessful attempt on the World's Land Speed Record at Verneuk Pan, in South Africa, to the Dumfries works, and they made an excellent job of the bodywork. A return to competition was attempted, under the direction of Mr Leverett, the London agent, and straight-eights appeared in blown form in the Alpine Trials and in several T.T.s, driven by Leverett himself, Norman Garrad and E. R. Hall. They were very pretty cars, but never notably fast. The Cozette-blown models were even catalogued and earned favourable mention for their quietness and lack of temperament. The supercharged 17/50, incidentally, recorded 72 m.p.h. and 17 m.p.g. only, even with a sensible set of gear ratios, thus showing the penalty imposed by excessive weight and a limited rev. range. In July 1929, the company went into liquidation, but for a year or so more Arrol-Asters, mainly 23/70s, continued to be made at Heathhall. Even in September 1931, when the spares department was sold to Messrs. Kryn and Lahy of Letchworth, it was stated that the Dumfries factory was still servicing cars and making 'industrial machinery'.

Of all the major Lost Causes, the Arrol-Johnston is perhaps the deadest. Heathhall now belongs to the North British Rubber Co., but Dumfries is the only town in which my appeal for information via the local press fell on sterile soil. Veteran and Edwardian examples of the breed exist in fair quantities, but the Vintage models —outside the now defunct Sword Collection—are few and far between, and interest in them seems to be non-existent. What killed this great enterprise? The hard facts seem to be that the chaotic diversity of models, the succession of odd experiments and the remarkable dullness of the standard product brought about a situation from which there was no escape.

CHAPTER 3

The Three 'A's of Scotland:
II—Marble Halls of the Single Sleeve

'Some critics have asserted that the promoters of Argyll Motors Ltd. spent too much on appearances, but the few extra hundreds required to provide a motor-car factory second to none in the world have been repaid already, and with interest, by the very advertisement that such a building is in itself.'

Argyll catalogue, 1907

THUS spake some wiseacre in the Argyll publicity department while the firm hovered at its zenith. Seven years later, he would have been howled down by a chorus of angry creditors, seeking a scapegoat for one of the most formidable and best publicized bankruptcies in the history of the motor industry. Such were the reverberations of the Argyll collapse that the excellent reputation which the cars enjoyed was swept away in an instant, the consequence being that most historians dwell at length upon the marble halls of Alexandria, and spare little thought for the thousands of cars that kept this vast barrack going as long as it did.

Argyll brochures of the 1907–8 era generally include a shot of the impressive façade of the Alexandria works in winter, with snow on the ground, and a suitably large Argyll tourer—probably a 26/30—in the foreground. This illustration looks as if it has strayed out of some diplomat's memoirs of St. Petersburg, and indeed there is a Czarist atmosphere of lost grandeur about the whole sad story. Perhaps the fascination which Argyll holds for me is inherited, for my father performed the opening ceremony at the Alexandria Works, and, as we shall see, he never lost interest in them completely.

The true story of Argyll, however, starts in an entirely down-to-earth manner. In 1897, a firm of cycle parts manufacturers in Redditch, the Eadie Manufacturing Co. Ltd., imported three çars from the Continent, a Vallée, a Mors and a Benz, and used their experience with these to evolve their own light car. Their works superintendent was a young Scotsman named Alex Govan. We know little of this Eadie prototype, but in 1899 Govan crops up again, this time on the premises of the defunct Scottish Cycle Company at Hozier Street, Bridgeton, Glasgow. Here he designed and built a light car, and cast around for a backer to launch it on the market.

In the Glasgow Museum is preserved a beautifully restored example of a very early Argyll *voiturette*, so it is possible to see in detail the lines on which the young engineer was working. Unlike Johnston and Murray, who took a large horse-drawn carriage and fitted it with a motor, Govan based his ideas closely on those of Louis Renault—though Billancourt, it would seem, did not take Bridgeton seriously enough to start proceedings for infringement. The tubular steel chassis was sprung with full elliptic springs all round, and steering was by handle-bars in the fashion of the contemporary Peugeot. Cycle-type wire wheels were fitted, and the car was powered by a 258 c.c. M.M.C.-De Dion high-speed engine with water-cooled cylinder head, power being transmitted by a leather-faced internal cone clutch to a three-speed gearbox of Govan's own design. Unlike most contemporary designers, Govan favoured shaft drive, and the footbrake was operated by the clutch pedal. The impression is of a neat little car, on which one is not constantly looking round for shafts or a quadruped.

Whether Govan was an originator or an inspired copyist, he clearly had something to offer, and in 1900 a suitable backer emerged, in the guise of W. A. Smith of the National Telephone Company, who formed the Hozier Engineering Co. Ltd. with a capital of £15,000. Argylls were in business.

It took some time for the car to catch on. The gear-change on these early Argylls was distinctly tricky, and the Southsea agent made no fewer than three unsuccessful attempts to drive a car for delivery down from London before giving up the unequal struggle and entraining the troublesome *voiturette*. For 1901, a 5 h.p. M.M.C. replaced the earlier 2¾ h.p. engine, a side gear-lever replaced the steering-column type, wheel steering was adopted, and a new radiator of characteristic design appeared. The original Argylls had four vertical tanks connected by horizontal tubes: now the position was reversed, and the two tanks were horizontal, and linked by vertical tubes, on the principle that the water, when heated, would rise into the upper tank. Argylls were said to run a hundred miles on a single intake of water. Everything, apart from the engines, was now being made at Bridgeton, special interest being aroused by the complex Govan gearbox, which was still very tricky to operate, with the added problem of a separate lever for reverse. This device remained standard equipment for several years, and was received with mixed feelings. In a 'Cars And How To Drive Them' feature in

June 1903, *The Car Illustrated*, after pointing out that these boxes needed no lubrication, observed that 'Argyll gearing differs from the Panhard, and should never be forced'—which sentiment cannot have pleased the firm of Panhard et Levassor. Mr A. H. Lindsay of Argylls (London) Ltd., told me, however, that the worst fault was the reverse pinion, which was housed in the lid of the box and *demanded regular lubrication*.

From the early days Alex Govan, unlike his conservative fellow-manufacturers in Scotland, attached great importance to two aspects of the business—competitions and publicity. He drove his own cars in all manner of events, up to a few days before his untimely death, and much of what we know of Argyll affairs during the first eight years of the company's life comes direct from the countless press releases that poured out of Bridgeton and Alexandria alike. It is true that when Arrol-Johnston tried their hand at racing under J. S. Napier's direction, the Argyll Company pontificated on the subject of unnecessary activities 'which prove nothing', but they also celebrated an *eighth* place in the 1905 T.T. with the following purple passage, typical of Argyll advertising in the Govan period:

'In the Tourist Trophy Trials, as in ALL other public competitions of a kindred nature in which the Argyll has figured, the car made an ABSOLUTE NON-STOP RUN.'

In July 1901, we see Govan at the wheel of one of his *voiturettes* in a Scottish Automobile Club run; another entrant was John Brimlow, whom we shall meet later, driving a 'Parisian phaeton', clearly one of William Stirling's confections from Granton, since Brimlow had been working for Stirling's Motor Carriages Ltd. since 1897. In the same month, Govan challenged W. McLean's Darracq to a five-mile match over the Glasgow Exhibition Track, and was beaten, but in the Glasgow Trials that September, Govan and the Argyll really arrived. The little 5½ h.p. car was described in the contemporary press as 'one of the striking features of the trials'. It stood alone in its class in losing no marks on the road section, and ascended the difficult Whistlefield Hill at 12·4 m.p.h., repeating the trip with four passengers at 4·54 m.p.h.

The 1902 models were available with 8 h.p. Simms engine and Simms-Bosch magneto ignition, or a 100 × 130 mm. M.M.C. engine of the same rating, capable of 1,500 r.p.m. Ten h.p. and 12 h.p. two-cylinder, and 16 h.p. four-cylinder cars were said to be on the way, and were actually on the market later in the year, the great J. B. Dunlop ordering a 12 h.p. car in August—he was to be a repeat customer for some time to come. Braking was conventional, though *The Autocar* found it necessary to remark that 'both brakes act either forward or reverse', perhaps with some uncanny fore-knowledge of the Bendix system!

The Argyll press department, which reported an output of six cars a week in February, and eight a week in April, had something to crow about. Despite the Boer War, Argylls were being shipped to Johannesburg, where they were said to be popular—when one considers that those two prize horrors, the M.M.C. and the Stirling, were the only other nominally British makes then represented in South Africa, the boast must have been rather an empty one. A car was driven from Glasgow to Bexhill at an average running speed of 15·4 m.p.h., and then celebrated the event by carting Bexhill's Charter of Incorporation through the streets, which may have been the first time such a charter was thus transported. A Mr J. T. Taylor of Penzance, not to be outdone, took delivery of his car at the works, and proceeded to drive it home; while Govan built himself an 8 h.p. 'sports car' with light wicker body, with which he made f.t.d. at the Scottish Automobile Club's hill-climb in June. R. C. Richie subsequently drove this same car from London to Edinburgh in twenty-two hours. An 8 h.p. Argyll also played its part in the melo-drama of Dr Lehwess and his monstrous Panhard omnibus 'Passe-Partout', acting as a tender to the big car on its round-the-world attempt. The Hozier Engineering Company backed the Argyll to go anywhere the Panhard could, but the strain proved too much for the little vehicle, which burned out an exhaust valve not far from Warsaw and fetched up on the end of a tow-rope.

For the next three years, the pace was speeded up: works exten-sions were put in hand at Hozier Street in March 1903, and the combined output for May and June was sixty-two cars. They were making fifteen cars a week in January 1904, and working night shifts in the process; while by July of that year, the certified pro-duction figures for the last quarter were given as 156 cars, in Govan's view a record for the United Kingdom. In August, it was stated that the firm had £100,000 worth of orders on their books, and, as though to clinch this assertion, a new engine works employing 300 men was opened in November. In February 1905, the directors told their agents, at the annual dinner at the Trocadero, that they anticipated an annual output of the unheard-of figure of 1,200 cars. That year the April–June production was up by sixty-four cars on 1904, this impressive volume necessitating the charter of a special train to bring the export models to London.

The range, like that of most manufacturers in those days, was fairly complicated. For instance, in February 1903, the engines available were said to be the 11 h.p. two-cylinder Clément, the 9 h.p. single-cylinder De Dion, and the 6½ h.p. Aster. Ten h.p. two-cylinder cars were being made with conventional honeycomb radiators, but the 16 h.p. four-cylinder is not mentioned again until the 1,000 Miles Trial in July, when the contestants included Argyll models of 8 h.p., 10 h.p., 14 h.p. and 16 h.p., having one, two, three and four cylinders respectively.

This point really marks the beginning of the close association with Aster, whose influence will be traceable in some Argyll engines' design right up to the adoption of the Burt-McCollum single sleeve-valve unit in 1912, though the name is not mentioned in Argyll catalogues after 1909. The 1904 range consisted of the 8 h.p. 'single' with 100 × 120 mm. De Dion engine, priced at £275, the 10 h.p. two-cylinder with Aster engine at £335; the three-cylinder 90 × 120 mm. car, for which Argylls made their own engine, at £400 —it was now more conservatively rated at 12 h.p.—and the 16 h.p. four-cylinder, fitted with an 88 × 120 mm. Aster engine, for which £550 was asked. The 'singles' and the twin-tank radiator disappeared for good in 1905, honeycomb radiators being standardized throughout the range. Metal-to-metal clutches were universal wear, save on the 10/12 h.p. 'twin', and an interesting feature was the adoption of a new type of staggered-spoke artillery wheel, said to resist side-slip and to be two and a half times as strong as the orthodox design. The three-cylinder cars were continued, as was the Aster-engined Sixteen, now known as the 16/20, but there was in addition a new big car, rated at 20/24 h.p. The engine was a 95 × 130 mm. Argyll with cylinders cast separately. The gearbox had three forward speeds and was of Govan type, and dual ignition —a feature either standard or optional on most of the later Argylls —was furnished. This car was said to be capable of 60 m.p.h.

Competition appearances continued, the controversial Govan gearbox collecting a Silver Medal in the 1903 1,000 Miles Trial, at which date Argyll advertising, with a nasty jab at the ponderous productions of the Mo-Car Syndicate, observed: 'Mere weight does not mean reliability: Argylls are scientifically designed.' In November 1904, Alex Govan read a paper to the Scientific Society of Glasgow, in which he lavished praise on such features of Bridgeton productions as coil ignition, high-speed engines, long-stroke units, thermo-syphon cooling, pneumatic tyres and live axles.

There was also a plethora of stunts. As yet the motor car had not reached that state of reliability in which long-distance runs in reverse gear could be contemplated, but one has no doubt that Govan would have been the first to promote such an attempt. The Argyll stands at the shows were a spectacle in themselves, consisting of a reproduction of a Scots double portcullis—it is a pity, in passing, that all this gimmickry has been swept away now, though it probably made a bigger hole in the shareholders' money than they would have appreciated. In March 1904, one Douglas Whitehead knocked ten hours off J. W. Stocks' John-o'-Groat's–Land's End record with an Argyll, liquidating one dog and five rabbits in the process, though two months later G. P. Mills on a 2 h.p. Raleigh motor cycle was to beat this by two hours, apparently without any carnage.

In May of that year a Mr Mitchell of Huddersfield drove a 10/12 h.p. two-seater non-stop from Glasgow to his home at an average speed of 28·5 m.p.h. The Mitchells were evidently triers, for fog alone stopped his wife from making a successful onslaught on the family record two years later, still on an Argyll. In August, E. J. Robertson Grant brought the end-to-end record down to forty-two hours five minutes, thanks to excellent advance organization. Esdaile pulled off a Silver Medal in the farcical Delhi–Bombay Trials in December, and Argylls took first and second places in the Australian Reliability Trials. Mr Harley Tarrant, incidentally, won the 'heavy class' in the Sydney–Melbourne event in April, on a 10 h.p. car. One wonders what the Australian idea of a light car was at this time! Tarrant, who held the Argyll agency, followed this success up by building a number of cars under his own name, which can best be described as crypto-Argylls. In 1905, W. R. Grimwade finished second in his class in the Australian trials, the course including eighty-nine miles of 'bad roads' (another case, I think, of Antipodean understatement). In 1906, though, he had transferred his allegiance to a 14/16 h.p. Tarrant, thus supporting local industry if not local design.

The Autocar, meanwhile, was collating evidence on the motoring habits of the medical profession, which must have heartened the Board at Bridgeton, since many doctors favoured their twin-cylinder cars, one practitioner asserting that his Argyll was cheaper to run than two horses. Others, incidentally, were less fortunate, as witness the case of the unhappy gentleman who had expended £100 more in twelve months on his belt-driven Pick than he would on horses, and expressed relief that the cars were no longer in production: he was wrong, for Picks were made at Stamford till 1925. The Argyll commercial vehicle business was also on its way up, Bryant and May buying their first 10/12 h.p. Aster-engined van in March, 1904. In December 1905, W. A. Smith, a director of the match firm, was claiming that Argylls were the most economical form of transport. Well he might, being also the presiding genius at Hozier Street! The truck department was now under the direction of John Brimlow, who had come over from Stirlings.

Nineteen hundred and six saw no major alterations to the cars, though the previous October the way had been paved for a drastic expansion of the company when an agreement was signed with the French Aster concern, under which Aster engines were to be made in the Argyll works: French engineers were to come over to supervise operations. In the same month, the firm of Argylls (London) Ltd., opened new and sumptuous premises in Newman Street, off Oxford Street, which included a motor school with instructresses for lady customers. Unlike some of the firm's more grandiose projects, this concern was run with the utmost efficiency, and offered customers a free bi-monthly engineer's report on their car, an anticipation of the 'service schemes' with which the Big Battalions sought to woo their clients in the nineteen-fifties. In May 1906, the London house instituted an Argyll Driver's Prize of £5 for the most economical performance by a car over 5,000 miles' running, the relative costings of the various models being conscientiously worked out in advance to avoid any discrimination against the bigger cars. A year later, monthly Argyll Trophies were being offered for meritorious performances by owners. The development of this powerful organization, incidentally, enabled Argylls to rent two stands at the 1906 Olympia Show, while the Argyll clientele now enjoyed their own magazine, *The Motorist*, which was, I suspect, the first publication of its kind this side of the Atlantic. A thirty-five per cent dividend was paid in 1905, and the weather was set fair for the Glasgow company.

Then came Alexandria. The vast marble halls rose rapidly: in 1905, 40,000 bricks were being laid a day. Altogether, £220,000 of the £500,000 capital available to the new concern, Argyll Motors Ltd., which had taken over the business of the Hozier Engineering Co. Ltd. in March 1905, went on the construction of this vast factory, which included a testing track and a test hill in its grounds. By April 1906, *The Autocar* was saying, with awe untinged by any note of caution:

'Nothing has been omitted that can tend to add to the comfort of the workpeople. The sanitary arrangements are above criticism, and the space

A B.S.A. three-wheeler of 1935, with air-cooled 1,021 c.c. vee-twin engine

This 1904 7 h.p. single-cylinder Alldays and Onions is the property of
G. James Allday, M.B.E., Life Patron of the V.C.C.

The Enfield 'Nimble Nine' of 1914

The De Dion 'works' of the prototype Enfield Quad

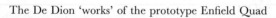

A 1924 10·8 h.p. Rhode four-seater at the summit of Beggar's Roost

Sword into ploughshare: a 1919 R.F.C.-type 25/30 h.p. Crossley tourer

This Crossley six-wheeler with the 19·6 h.p. engine was supplied to
H.M. King George V in 1929

devoted to lavatory and cloakroom accommodation for the workpeople occupies as much ground, and must have cost as much money, as many a factory complete.'

As new sections of the Alexandria works were finished the corresponding department at Bridgeton was closed down, and thus a steady flow of production was maintained. On 26 June, 1906, to the accompaniment of special trains and the full fanfare of the Govan publicity machine at capacity, Alexandria was opened by my father, who struck an optimistic note by stating that four million pounds were still invested in the declining horse-and-carriage business, and that this should be an indicator of the potential of the motor industry. He was right, of course, but Argyll were not to be the beneficiaries.

What was wrong with Alexandria was not so much the Ruritanian palace atmosphere of the office suites, but the fact that it was created on a scale that could be financed only by mass-production, and a study of Govan's manufacturing methods reveals that he was no mass-producer. Engines were still hand-built and the oil grooves in the bearings were cut by hand. They were extensively bench-tested, the better ones being speeded up to 1,250 r.p.m., and assigned to 'de luxe' and 'sporting' cars. Every chassis was subjected to a hundred-mile road-test, and bodies received thirty to thirty-five coats of paint and varnish. W. A. Smith might trumpet joyfully that the 'labour-saving tools' in the new factory reduced the time required for machining a cylinder from thirty hours to forty-five minutes, but Alexandria was never more than half full, and the firm's press photographs of the works in action are a dreadful give-away, showing misty, echoing halls, with the odd chassis conveniently posed in the foreground.

The end of 1906 saw Argylls laden with fresh triumphs: Robertson Grant had performed with distinction in the Herkomer Trophy Trials, and McTaggart had broken the Irish 'end-to-end' record. A. E. George's second place in the T.T., had, it is true, been marred by disqualification, but a 10/12 had ground its way up Loch Striven Head with five people on board, and the enterprising Eustace Watson, the firm's London manager, had driven one of the new 14/16 cabs from Glasgow to London. This ingenious device seated the driver over the engine, and, Alexandria claimed, had been designed and built in a few weeks. It was quite popular. The 1907 range embraced the 10/12, three four-cylinder cars with Aster engines, the 12/14, 16/20 and 26/30, and the 14/16 with Argyll's own engine, which was an Aster in all but name. The firm also offered a range of cab-over-engine town carriages and trucks, while an incursion into bus manufacture was planned late in 1906, when Argyll and Stirling joined forces for the series production of twenty vehicles a week at Alexandria. Nothing came of this project.

In the eyes of the public, the sky was unclouded. In January 1907, the irrepressible Govan issued a challenge to the manufacturer of any six-cylinder car to match the smoothness of running and standing-start acceleration of his own 14/16, the only stipulation being that a standard gearbox was used for the test. A substantial correspondence ensued, in the course of which *The Autocar* chipped in with a suggestion that only cars that had passed a 4,000-mile test should be acceptable for display at the Shows—which idea did not, apparently, please Mr Govan. Nor did he enter an Argyll for the Crystal Palace Automobile Club's Flexibility Trials in March, though three makers of 'sixes'—Napier, Ford and Brooke—did. In the meantime, Grimwade and Tarrant successfully completed an 899-mile run in Australia on a 1904 10/12 h.p. car, while Argylls were entered in both the Herkomer and the Criterium de la France, albeit without notable success. In May, Govan achieved a 'non-stop' in the Irish Reliability Trial on a 12/14, furnishing yet more copy for his advertising department. A week later, he was dead of ptomaine poisoning. He was only thirty-eight.

With Govan gone, most of the dynamism departed from Alexandria, and though the competition successes continued and the London house continued to distribute solid oak canteens to their monthly prize-winners, the firm was slipping over the edge. Two new models, an 84 × 110 mm. Aster-engined 12/16 with a neat monobloc unit, and an 120 × 140 mm. Forty with paired cylinders were announced for 1908, both having side-valves in an L-head. This Forty had the first engine of entirely Argyll design, incidentally. A customer in Syria purchased an odd hybrid, consisting of a 40 h.p. engine installed in a 2-ton truck chassis, for desert work. This wore vast Shrewsbury Challiner solid tyres on sheet steel disc wheels, an Aster-made unit being installed to ease the spares situation in French colonial territory. Argylls cleaned up a class win in the Scottish Reliability Trials, but in August, the second company ran out of cash—and into liquidation, though Alexandria was kept expensively open, and cars continued to be made. Even then, the publicity department was quick to point out that the company's numerous provincial subsidiaries were unaffected: the Liverpool house might be selling Delaunay-Bellevilles on the side, but Southsea had recorded a profit of £1,532, and Southampton one of £21!

In November, a reconstruction scheme was worked out, the assets at Alexandria were written down from £710,000 to £322,000, and yet another company, Argylls Ltd., was started under the direction of Colonel J. S. Matthew, from the Scottish Dunlop Company. At first, all went well, the balance sheet in November 1909 showing a profit of £1,600 on the first year's working, and 'plenty of cash in hand'. With Alex Davidson of M.M.C. as works manager, and M. Perrot, late of Brasier, as chief designer, it was easy to forget that some 1,500 men had been laid off in the crisis a year earlier. The new 12 h.p. model was a success, and fifty cabs had even been exported to New York.

The 1910 range featured a 10 h.p. (90 × 140 mm.) monobloc 'twin' at £275, the 12/14 at £285, a 15 h.p. (80 × 120 mm.), at £350, the dear old 14/16 at £375, a new Perrot-designed Twenty (90 × 140 mm.) at £425, and a new six-cylinder Thirty (90 × 140 mm.) which was said to be good for 60 m.p.h. and cost £525. These cars had a 'simple, safe gate change of elegant design', the three new models having four forward speeds. The day of the Govan gearbox was over.

Colonel Matthew, in introducing the new cars for 1911, announced that 'every part used in the entire range of models is interchangeable'. The trouble was that there were too many models. The 10 h.p., 20 h.p. and 30 h.p. were continued unchanged, but a new 12 h.p. with 72 × 120 mm. monobloc engine and four-speed gearbox was offered at £325. More important still, it had four-wheel brakes, of the type all too often ascribed to Perrot. They were actually designed by J. M. Rubury, who sold his rights to Perrot for a paltry £200 in 1914, after the collapse of Argylls Ltd.; the pedal operated on the front wheels and the lever on the rear. The new management, incidentally, had pushed production up from 240 cars in 1909 to 452 in 1910, but as Alexandria had been designed for four-figure outputs, this was not as helpful as it might have been.

Meanwhile Argyll, like many others, had looked upon Charles Yale Knight's double sleeve-valves, and seen a lot of imaginary writing on the wall. A great deal of nonsense has been written about Argyll's incursion into sleeve-valvery, and it has been asserted that the Burt-McCollum engine was unsatisfactory. It was not: it was simple in operation and the measure of its success can be gauged by Scott and Hornsted's amazing performance at Brooklands in May 1913, when a tuned 15/30 took 26 Class D records, including fourteen hours at 76·43 m.p.h. Things simply did not go right for

Argylls, who landed themselves with £50,000 worth of litigation against the Knight patentees, which they could ill afford on top of a factory that was basically uneconomic and cost £12,000 a month to run. Quite a lot of play has been made of the odd fact that McCollum consulted his dead father by planchette during the negotiations with Argyll, the scoffers having conveniently forgotten that this primitive form of spiritualism was 'all the rage' in 1910.

From 1912 onwards, the Burt-McCollum single sleeve-valve engine obtruded itself into the Argyll range. In 1912, the 12 h.p., the 80 × 120 mm. 'Flying Fifteen' and the Twenty were continued, only the big 25 h.p. car utilizing the new valve gear. 1913 saw a single sleeve-valve 15/30 replace the Fifteen and Twenty, though the former was still available in taxicab form; and in the company's final season—1914—only the 12/18 remained of the poppet-valve range, this model being quietly dropped in May, a month or two before the cataclysm at Alexandria.

The single sleeve-valve Argylls were not only technically interest-ing, they were pretty cars, with attractively-styled bodywork well set off by detachable wire wheels. They were also fairly expensive, as in 1913 a 15/30 h.p. streamlined torpedo cost £575, fully equipped, and a similarly-bodied 25/50 h.p., £750. For these prices, incidentally, one got a 'double-deflecting metal windscreen, with patent attachment for hood, a patent one-hand hood, Kamac covered, Lucas side and tail lamps, Lucas horn, number plates, well in stepboard and special bracket, carpets to rear floor and rear of driver's seat, combined footrest and tool case, concealed wells for spare fuel and lubricants, patent leather valances'—and even a spare wheel; not a Stepney. Transmission was by overhead worm, and, most important of all, the cars had Argyll's new four-wheel braking system, diagonally compensated; in this both pedal and lever operated on all four wheels—in the opinion of many, the best and most efficient f.w.b. system available before the first World War. The first year of sleeve-valves only succeeded in boosting sales by some seventy cars, but there was no doubt about it— Argylls had something to sell, and customers included Dom Manoel d'Arriaga, the first President of the Portuguese Republic, and the ill-fated Captain C. W. Kelsey, who attempted to drive from the Cape to Cairo in a specially-prepared 25/50. Despite the fact that no less a person than E. J. Robertson Grant tested this car *in* Loch Lomond, the expedition failed. It is hardly fair, however, to blame the Argyll, which was dreadfully overloaded, while its unhappy captain died after being mauled by a leopard. I drove past the scene of this tragedy at Broken Hill in December 1959—the road is now excellent!

Catastrophe was round the corner. Knight and Kilbourne, who had apportioned the manufacturing licenses for their engine to a cross-section of highly reputable manufacturers, were hot on the trail of any possible infringements, and in March 1912 they suffered the indignity of losing an action brought against Rolland-Pilain, makers of a single-sleeve engine. Three months later they instituted proceedings against Argylls Ltd. The long-drawn-out litigation— Argylls won their case in July 1912 and saw the Knight appeal dismissed the following February—cost the Alexandria firm a reputed £50,000, for which not even Charles Yale Knight's sporting gesture of a congratulatory telegram after the 15/30's record run could compensate. As early as July 1912, *The Autocar* was claiming of the Argyll engine that 'manufacture has commenced in France, Switzerland and Canada', but only Piccard-Pictet seem to have built Argyll engines in series, through the aero-engine firm of Gnôme-et-Rhône showed a keen interest at one time.

The Argyll record attempt, with its classic pitwork, provided a further blaze of publicity, but the company had already plunged into another expensive project—the manufacture of aero-engines on Burt-McCollum principles. Alexandria, as we know, had the right ideas, but they had them some twenty years too soon. The 1914 Aero Show saw a six-cylinder 120 h.p. motor, with separate cylinders. These had sheet steel water-jackets, air-cooling ribs being machined on the lower portion of each 'pot'. The Royal Aircraft Factory was very favourably impressed, and Argylls were offered a production contract at a price which would have covered all their expenses, but the events of the summer of 1914 killed this project stone dead.

Matters were coming to a head. A 10s. Argyll share quoted at 4s. 3d. in January 1914 had dropped to 4s. in March, and to an abysmal 7½d in June. There was no working capital. Two hundred unsold 1913 models were lying at the works, and all attempts to come to an agreement with other companies had failed. Rumours of an impending merger between Argyll and Arrol-Johnston were in the air; serious negotiations were certainly made with Darracq for a take-over bid, which the Bank of Scotland vetoed, the traditional friendship between the Scots and the French notwithstanding. Under this deal Colonel Matthew would have kept Bridgeton, which had been retained as a service depot and body shop, and which would have sufficed to cope with the existing demand for Argyll cars. In addition, he would have had the sleeve-valve rights, which Darracq, fresh from the disastrous skirmish with M. Henriod and his 'valveless' engines, emphatically did not want. All to no avail. On 17 June 1914 a liquidation meeting took place, and strong words were exchanged.

The burden of the creditors' song was that Argylls, having built up a solid reputation for 'a good and reliable car of medium power at a reasonable price', had plunged into the exotic depths of Mr McCollum's engine, laying themselves open to expensive and unproductive litigation. They had tried to support an uneconomic factory on nothing better than a gargantuan overdraft, and they had added insult to injury by wasting vast sums of money on a highly tentative aero-engine. What few sales there were had fallen to nothing when rumours of an impending liquidation began to circulate. 'The management,' the creditors asserted, 'were not fit to run a hen-coop.'

They never had another chance to run anything. The meeting, justly or unjustly, went against Colonel Matthew. Alexandria passed into the hands of Their Lordships of the Admiralty for £153,000; the London end of the business was purchased by Mr A. H. Lindsay, who continued to run the Argyll Service Station at Hornsey, and with the outbreak of war a few weeks later Argylls lapsed into limbo.

This should have been the end. In the eyes of all Argyll's friends, and both poppet and sleeve-valve units had made many, it was. Few people paid much heed to a small paragraph which appeared in the motoring press in October 1915, announcing that John Brimlow had taken over the old Bridgeton Works, and proposed to resume production on a less flamboyant scale after the war.

Brimlow implemented his promise, and the Argyll survived in production until 1928, and on paper until 1932. But it was a pallid ghost of its former self. It is doubtful if more than three hundred cars were produced between 1920 and 1928, and these were largely assembled vehicles, engines and rear axles being made for Brimlow by Greenwood and Batley of Leeds, while Wallace (Glasgow) Ltd., who had purchased the manufacturing rights of the Burt-McCollum engine, also made some units. Greenwood and Batley, incidentally, also supplied similar single sleeve-valve engines for the Magnetic Car Co. Ltd. of Chelsea in the nineteen-twenties.

However, the revival looked quite impressive at the 1920 Show, where there were again two Argyll stands, one occupied by Bridgeton and the other by the resourceful Mr Lindsay, who was offering an intriguing light car with a three-cylinder air-cooled radial engine of 76 × 89 mm. (1,230 c.c.), with two overhead valves per cylinder.

Three forward speeds were obtained by an ingenious form of friction drive, quarter-elliptic springs were fitted all round, and a two-seater cost 300 guineas. The co-designer of this R.L.C. was none other than J. M. Rubury of four-wheel braking fame. Only one R.L.C. was made—it was sold to France, and may have formed the basis for the Lafitte design which so intrigued A. G. Grice at a later date.

Bridgeton confined themselves to reviving the 15/30, which had acquired an electric starter and now cost £900, thanks to post-war inflation. Styling was little changed from 1914, and, though Brimlow asserted that the cylinders and valves had only eighteen working parts against seventy-five for a conventional side-valve unit, nobody was particularly interested. Only eleven were made. The following season—1922—the 15/30 was joined by the 68 × 103 mm. Twelve, with a Solex carburetter and optional coil or magneto ignition. Thirty b.h.p. at 3,000 r.p.m. was claimed from the neat little engine, while decarbonization was deemed necessary only at 30,000-mile intervals. It was listed at £495, and two were entered in the 1924 R.A.C. Small Car Trials, in which they signally failed to distinguish themselves, Parker's car consuming fourteen pints of oil in 1,000 miles. Road test reports, however, emphasize a top-gear flexibility superior to contemporary poppet-valve machinery, and for 1926, Argylls introduced a sports-model 12/40 tourer with front-wheel brakes at £475, f.w.b. being an optional extra on the standard vehicles.

The clock was running down. The famous firm made their last appearance at Olympia in 1927, by which time the 12/40 had been bored out to 71 mm., and front-wheel brakes were standard throughout the range. Wallace (Glasgow) Ltd. were out of business, and Continental Motors Corporation had bought the Burt-McCollum rights in 1925. Brimlow had no source of engines, and the 12 h.p. at £295 was, in any case, no competition for Morris or Clyno. An 18/50 h.p. six-cylinder car was announced, but it never appeared, and after 1928 the Bridgeton Works were little more than a service station. The Argyll died quietly, unnoticed, and scarcely mourned.

I visited Alexandria three years ago, and saw the indelible frescoes on the outer walls which reveal its identity to those who would dismiss it merely as the Royal Naval Torpedo Factory. It never made a car again, yet the motor industry did not lose interest entirely. In 1924, the late Lord Invernairn approached my father through Mr G. H. Allsworth of Beardmores with a view to purchasing the works from the Disposals Board. The plan fell through, probably because the price asked for the works was too high.

Continental themselves never did much with the single sleeve-valve designs, but in 1934 it suddenly acquired a new lease of life, when A. H. R. (later Sir Roy) Fedden of the Bristol Aeroplane Co. Ltd. introduced the 'Perseus' radial engine, first of a series of units of Burt-McCollum type which were to dominate the company's production programme through the war, and right up to the days of the gas turbine. Thousands were made, and they powered such famous aircraft as the 'Beaufighter', 'Wellington' and 'Tempest'. It is amusing to note, however, that when Bristols opened a Car Division in 1946, they eschewed the single sleeve-valve in favour of the more conventional 2-litre German B.M.W. design.

I found the last trace of Argyll in, of all unlikely places, the London telephone directory. Following my nose, I drove out to Priory Road, Hornsey, where the famous name still adorns Mr Lindsay's garage and general engineering works. Photographs of Alexandria decorate his office, and he still displays the keenest interest in Argyll cars. But the hoodoo haunted the company to the bitter end. 'We'd still be servicing Argylls,' he told me, 'but a bomb destroyed all our stocks of parts. We were working on Argyll taxis for many years after the war, and as late as 1938 we had an old Argyll as a service van.'

Alexandria, admittedly, was an extravagance beyond the means of any British car manufacturer in 1906, yet I feel that Argylls were an unlucky firm. The death of Govan, the long drawn-out lawsuits, and the foreclosures on the eve of success with the aero-engine, were all misfortunes which turned the tide against them at the worst possible moments. I would like to have heard my father's views on the company, for he always had a soft spot in his heart for them, and I sometimes wonder if the Scottish motor industry might not have undergone a renaissance, had the Beardmore project materialized. As it is, it has taken a localized industrial depression to lure the car manufacturers back across the Border and add lustre to the still rising sun of Albions.

CHAPTER 4

Traveller to Scout:
A Birmingham Miscellany

'We make our carriage with two speeds—one for hills, the other for level ground. Downhill it runs free, and the engine rests.'
Alldays 'Traveller' catalogue, 1901

'. . . the Rhode was designed and built throughout by us in our own Works—note not assembled, using an axle made by one firm and an engine by another; for by following the latter course we could not have realized the ideals which we had set out to attain.'
From the Owner's Manual of 'The Remarkable Rhode', 1924

'The B.S.A. Scout is a car which lives up to and even surpasses the great expectations regarding comfort and performance which its graceful lines and pleasing appearance arouse.'
B.S.A. advertisement, 1936

BIRMINGHAM is the arsenal of the British Commonwealth, a booming city of well over a million people. It·is the home of the famous house of Austin, and also produced Wolseleys and Lanchesters in their golden years. From Birmingham still come many of the great names of motor cycling—Ariel, B.S.A., Enfield and James, for instance—so it is with a sense of anti-climax that we turn to its crop of Lost Causes. Calthorpe, Rhode, Enfield, Alldays and B.S.A. are not vehicles that would delight the eye of any fanatical V.S.C.C. member. Their story is the inevitable one of steady *crescendo*, followed by a dreary *diminuendo* in the face of straitened finance, cut-throat competition, and a buyer's market; but of these five, only Rhode and Calthorpe are dead. Alldays and Onions are still in business, as is the Enfield Cycle Co. Ltd., who sloughed off their car side as early as 1906. Even this never very successful car-making offshoot can claim a niche in history as the ancestor of the present-day Aston Martin, and it is libellous to stigmatize the B.S.A. as a Lost Cause, for the name now covers the biggest motor cycle manufacturing group in Great Britain, though their cars, which were no 'Golden Flashes' or 'Road Rockets', departed from the scene in the blitzkrieg of 1940–1, and were unmourned. The Birmingham cars also are of technical interest, for Rhode anticipated Singer in

41

marketing a cheap light car with an overhead camshaft engine, and the otherwise undistinguished B.S.A. featured front-wheel drive and i.f.s. in 1929, whereas André Citroën's famed *traction avant* was still a top-secret prototype as late as 1933. Calthorpe's brief moment of glory came in an entirely different field, for they entered a team of tuned touring cars in the *Coupe des Voiturettes* in 1909, two years before Louis Coatalen ventured his famous Sunbeams farther afield than Brooklands.

The story of Birmingham as an industrial city goes back to the reign of William III, when the town's gunsmiths entered into associa-tion for their mutual benefit. From this guild stemmed the vast ramifications of the Birmingham Small Arms Co. Ltd. By the turn of the century it was firmly established as a cycle manufacturer as well as in the armaments field, and in 1903 it was making sprung frames for motor cycles, though complete models were not marketed for another seven years.

It may surprise some readers to know that B.S.A. entered the car business some four years before they embarked upon their far more successful career with two-wheelers.

They went about the business efficiently. To manage their new motor car department, they hired Colonel Baguley, who had been in charge of the Ryknield Motor Co. of Burton-on-Trent, a concern founded to build lorries for the local breweries. Ryknield had also made a few private cars under the guidance of Baguley and the Salmon family. Working under Baguley was Leslie Wilson, later to become famous as Secretary and organizer of the Shelsley Walsh hill-climb from 1913 to 1958. B.S.A. were in no hurry to put their cars on the market—three prototypes of their first model, the 18/23, were on the road early in 1907, and small-scale production started that year, but no official press release was made till 1908, and the *marque*'s first public appearance was at Olympia the following winter.

The 18/23 was a conventional vehicle with side valves in an L-head, bore and stroke being 89 mm. and 120 mm. respectively. A three-speed gearbox was used in conjunction with a Hele-Shaw multi-plate clutch, ignition was by Bosch high-tension magneto, and cooling was by thermo-siphon. The price, in 1908, was £510. Alas, the prototype chassis was found to weigh a formidable twenty-six cwt., and some drastic paring had to be undertaken. It was sub-sequently replaced in 1910 by the improved A.1 type with leather cone clutch, which was extensively tested in France, Italy and Switzerland by Leslie Wilson. In those days the engineering of mountain passes left a great deal to be desired, and it speaks volumes for driver and car alike that no mechanical trouble was encountered. With commendable foresight, the Sparkbrook test department had fitted the prototype with Rudge-Whitworth detachable wire wheels, so that the changing of three sets of tyres *en route* was not so tedious a business as it might have been. The use of steel-studded tyres was less fortunate—intended for slippery pavements, they broke up all too easily on the dry, rough surfaces of the Alpine roads. Leslie Wilson remembers taking a tip from an old French chauffeur, and straining all his petrol through a chamois leather, thus averting blockages resultant from foreign bodies in the fuel. About 150 18/23s of both types were made.

For 1909, B.S.A. also produced a rather similar 14/18 (Type C.1) of 90 × 100 mm. bore and stroke. This followed the design of the bigger car, but in its original form it, too, was overweight and underpowered: consequently the stroke was lengthened to 115 mm. giving a capacity of 2·9 litres, and a four-speed gearbox substituted for the earlier model's three-speed type. This 15/20 (Type C.2) attracted some very pretty coachwork by specialist coachbuilders, and was more or less the 'stock' B.S.A. type in 1911, the car division's last full year of independent manufacture. It even featured in contemporary competitions, S. T. Birkin winning three handicap events at the M.C.C. meeting at Brooklands in July 1911, while in July 1913, one J. Allday used one to take second place in the Novices' Class of the Sutton Coldfield Automobile Club's Cropredy hill-climb. This Mr Allday was not only one of the Alldays of Alldays and Onions Ltd., but the future Life Patron of the Veteran Car Club of Great Britain.

Meanwhile Colonel Baguley hankered after a big car to round off the range. The press was full of the exploits of the famous 40 h.p. 'Pekin-Paris' Itala, and one of these chassis was secretly purchased and brought to the B.S.A. experimental workshops, where it was stripped down to the last nut and bolt. Draughtsmen swarmed over the pile of parts, making exact drawings of every component, and at the end of 1908 there emerged the B.S.A.-Itala, as it was known to the works, or the 25/33, as it featured in the catalogue. Its 115 × 130 mm. T-head engine, four-speed gearbox, Hele-Shaw clutch, shaft drive and vast transmission brake were all authentic Itala, and Leslie Wilson recalls its ability to idle at incredibly low speeds. Having driven the 1907 120 h.p. Itala, all fourteen and a half litres of it, I can testify to this fascinating characteristic at first-hand. The only change made was the substitution of the 'unreliable' low-tension ignition by a Bosch H.T. magneto, and all production cars had limousine or landaulet bodies, which taxed to the full the engine's slogging abilities. The price in 1909 was £670.

B.S.A. also built the Drewry railcars with two and four-cylinder engines, controllable from either end in the manner of the G.W.R.'s later aerodynamic A.E.C.s: they were tested on a special length of track in the works, and most of them went to South America, where they were used for permanent way inspection. Altogether, a promising, if unspectacular business was building up, but the blow was to fall. In December 1910, Leslie Wilson recalls, the staff were given provisional notice, as 'anything might happen'. Wilson himself set up in business in Birmingham, selling the American Hupmobile light car, while Baguley went back to Burton-on-Trent, where he made cars of 15/20 B.S.A. type under his own name, and also took under his wing the Ryknield truck and the four-cylinder light car which Mr Salmon was developing. For the time being, however, B.S.A. carried on, and the 1911 range consisted of the 15/20 at £435, the 25/33 at £640, and a 105 × 120 mm. 20/25 at £556. Zenith carburettors replaced the B.S.A. type hitherto used, and dual ignition was adopted. But the step had been taken that was to rob the *marque* of its individuality: the company had amalgamated with Daimler.

In actual practice, the B.S.A. company had purchased the Daimler Motor Co. (1904) Ltd., and not vice versa, but from the private-car viewpoint, B.S.A. had got the worst of the bargain. Henceforward Daimlers were to dominate the situation.

For 1912, the staple model was a 13·9 h.p. (75 × 114 mm.) four-cylinder, with a three-speed gearbox mounted in unit with the back axle, and Daimler final drive by overhead worm. The engine was a Knight sleeve-valve of Daimler manufacture, and the price of the tourer was £325. A pressed-steel body made at the Sparkbrook works was a pioneer feature of the 1913 models, and 1914 cars differed in having a petrol gauge on the rear-mounted fuel tank, a pull-on handbrake and modified styling, the price being unchanged; though the provision of electric lighting raised the price to £350, and a starter could be had for £15 more. An identical car with a different radiator was made for Siddeley-Deasy, who sold it as the Stoneleigh!

B.S.A. took a long time to reappear after the war, but eventually came up in October 1921 with something that owed little or nothing to Daimler influence, in the shape of a 10 h.p. light car. True, it had underslung worm drive, but its engine was a hearty little

1,100 c.c. (89·75 × 85 mm.) o.h.v. push-rod, air-cooled vee-twin, designed and made by Hotchkiss of Coventry. Output was 18 b.h.p. at 2,600 r.p.m., quarter-elliptic suspension was used all round, and it retailed at £340, complete with electric lighting and starting. This was quite a lively little car, even if the noise level rose beyond Daimler standards, and it was turned out at a rate of 1,000-odd a year between 1922 and 1924. A pre-production road test gave the maximum speed as 52 m.p.h., the fuel consumption as over 38 m.p.g., and oil consumption as 1,000 m.p.g., while the car was said to have covered seventy-seven miles on North-Country roads in two hours. One of the first examples was sold to the Bishop of Auckland, New Zealand, and the cars did well in trials, notably in the hands of A. W. Brittain.

B.S.A. also offered other models from 1923 to 1926, but these were four and six-cylinder Knight-engined variations on a theme by Daimler. It may be mentioned in passing that in 1923 a 59 × 94 mm. (1,542 c.c.) 'six' was shown at Olympia—the spiritual ancestor of such machinery as the Wolseley 'Hornet' and the Morris Ten-Six. A 16 h.p. six-cylinder B.S.A.—alias 16/55 Daimler—cost £465 in 1926, but very few were made.

In the meanwhile Hotchkiss had been absorbed by Morris, and the motor cycle division of B.S.A. had bought the rights of the vee-twin, which they proceeded to develop and install in a most ingenious three-wheeler, designed by F. W. Hulse, which was unveiled at the 1929 Motor Cycle Show. The 1,021 c.c. engine drove the front wheels through a spur-type differential and three-speed and reverse gearbox with a 5·25 : 1 top gear. Further, it had no front axle, the wheels being independently sprung by eight transverse springs, four on each side. There was an eight-inch internal expanding brake on each wheel, ignition was by coil, and an electric starter was standard equipment. The list price was £120, and its comfort, mechanical quietness, and 'sports-car' looks drew many admirers even from the tough ranks of the motor-cycling fraternity.

With its light fabric bodywork the B.S.A. was quite rapid, but unfortunately it never had the performance of the Morgan, and the spectre of its Malvern-built rival dogged it right up to 1940. The 'Beeza' was undoubtedly more comfortable and less tricky to drive, but from a maintenance angle a single chain-driven rear wheel was less complex than two shaft-driven front wheels. When B.S.A. 'scooped' the luxury three-wheeler market in 1933 with a 60 × 95 mm. (1,075 c.c.) four-cylinder side-valve car (Type TW-33-10) at

£125, Morgan followed suit by installing the much cheaper and simpler 8 h.p. Ford engine in their 'Family' chassis. The B.S.A. might accelerate without snatch from 10 to 65 m.p.h. on top gear, but the majority of the three-wheeler public did not want this. Even when the B.S.A. engineers tried four wheels, Morgan's reply was more effective, and there is no comparing the Morgan 4/4 with the B.S.A. 'Scout' by any standards other than price.

Incidentally, B.S.A. had augmented their three-wheeler range with a four-wheeled car at £130 in 1932: very few of these were made, and were in fact standard three-wheelers with a dead axle added at the rear. They did, however, offer something more inspired the following year in the shape of a 1,075 c.c. Nine with front-wheel drive, available as a sports tourer, sports coupé or five-cwt. van. This T.9 model cost only £160 as a tourer. All these vehicles were made in the motor cycle works at Small Heath and sold through the B.S.A. chain of dealers, but from 1933 to 1936 the firm supplemented these with yet another line of small, cheap Daimlers, fluid flywheel and all. These consisted of a 1,185 c.c. Ten with saloon bodywork by the Pressed Steel Co., very similar in general layout to Lanchester's 10 h.p. model but with a side-valve engine. The price was £230, and it brought the fluid flywheel within the reach of a still wider section of the car-buying public. There was also an o.h.v. 1,378 c.c. 'Light Six', which was no more than the corresponding 1935 Lanchester model with a B.S.A. radiator.

In 1934 the f.w.d. four-wheelers were dropped, and B.S.A. made only these sub-Daimlers, but in the following year they came up with a rehashed 1,075 c.c. f.w.d. model with two-seater sports body. The 'Scout', at £149, was a pretty little machine of no particular distinction. Nineteen thirty-six saw the height of meaningless complexity, for the B.S.A. group, not content with five Daimler models and the Lanchester Eighteen in the big-car class, were putting out o.h.v. 'Light Sixes' under Lanchester and B.S.A. imprints; three rear-wheel-drive four-cylinder Tens—the original 1,185 c.c. B.S.A., a larger and more expensive 1,330 c.c. variant, and the o.h.v. Lanchester; two f.w.d. four-wheeled 'Scouts', the 1935-type Nine and a 1,203 c.c. Ten; and the three-wheeler in two and four-cylinder forms! The public could not comprehend, let alone absorb such a diversity of models, and for 1937 the B.S.A. side was firmly pruned, leaving only the 10 h.p. 'Scout' in improved Series 4 form. This survived until the outbreak of the war as the sole representative of British f.w.d. design, and one of the very few independently-suspended British cars in the lower price bracket. The two-bearing crankshaft was not a strong point, and its competition appearances were confined to *concours d'élégance*, though an adaptation of the basic design, the Palmer-Reville Special, was evolved for dirt-track work. The 1937 'Scout' had Bendix brakes and a dashboard gearchange reminiscent of the Citroën, and cost £159 10s. for a two-seater. A twin-carburettor engine was available to order. By 1939 it had acquired a three-bearing crankshaft, a few more much-needed brake horses and easy-clean wheels, and would touch 70 m.p.h. in favourable circumstances. A neat four-seater saloon listed at £196, while for 1940 a drophead coupé was added to the range. It did not reappear after the second World War.

B.S.A.'s biggest impact on the car-buying public had been in the nineteen-thirties, when they were turning out some two thousand cars a year, but Alldays and Onions and their associate company, Enfield, had faded out in the nineteen-twenties. Both concerns had long and distinguished histories before they took their first steps towards car manufacture in 1898–9. Neither firm set their sights higher than the quadricycle: the Enfield was a De Dion-type article offered with a choice of a 3½ h.p. fully water-cooled engine or a 2¾ h.p. unit with air-cooled barrel and water-cooled head. The works prototype, incidentally, came to Beaulieu after many years in storage in 1958, and took part successfully in the 1959 London–Brighton Run. Alldays were slightly more ambitious with their 'Traveller' *voiturette*, advertised as an ideal mode of transportation for the commercial traveller. Built under the management of Mr Gascoigne, formerly of the Anglo-French Motor Co., an abortive Birmingham firm which had assembled or imported carriages, it was, in fact, a 'grown-up' quadricycle with wheel steering, a fore-carriage for the passenger, footboards and hand-starting, and the De Dion-type engine, rated at 4 h.p., had a water-cooled head. It remained in production until 1904, by which time it had been supplemented by the first of a long series of successful, if uninterest-ing, light cars in the shape of the 6½ h.p. 'single' at £175. The 1-litre engine had trembler coil ignition, and a two-speed gearbox with direct top was deemed sufficient, but shaft drive, mechanically-operated inlet valves and a channel steel frame were advanced practice for a light car of the period, while the front passenger seat could be swung to give access to the tonneau at the rear, an anticipa-tion of two-door saloon practice in a later era. In 1904 the rear-entrance style of body, a legacy of the horse-drawn vehicles, was still the vogue. A car of this type won a Silver Medal in the Small Car Trials of 1904, apropos of which a contemporary journalist commented: 'This car is not fast, but is sensibly built to run close to the legal limit.'

The legal limit was, of course, 20 m.p.h., and right up to 1914 Alldays concentrated on simple, straightforward, inexpensive light cars calculated to appeal to the Midland businessman. Their hill-climbing powers were proverbial, and in the 95 × 114 mm. Ten (later 10/12) introduced in 1906 they had a winner. This had side valves, a three-speed gearbox and shaft drive, and featured in the firm's range right up to 1912, at which time it cost £262, and must have run into some heavy competition from four-cylinder cars such as FIAT and Delage. In 1906, these cars took the first three places on formula at Shelsley Walsh, won on formula at Aston Clinton, and won their class in the Longleat Speed Trials, while a works-sponsored test run from Coventry to Daventry on top gear also hit the headlines. In July 1909, a 10 h.p. Alldays and Onions was victorious in the Grahamstown hill-climb in South Africa, beating a Star. Many of these little vehicles were sold as light vans, one of them serving as a travelling bank in the wilds of Sussex, while Lever Brothers were offering another in 1908 as a prize in a soap-selling competition open to their representatives.

Over at Redditch, Enfields had graduated beyond the quadri-cycle stage, entering a 6 h.p. two-cylinder car in the 1901 Glasgow Trials. Its vee engine was certainly of Ader manufacture, and the chassis was probably also imported or 'bought out': rumour has it that their first cars were Vinots bearing the Enfield emblem, but I have been unable to confirm this. By November 1903, however, it was announced that an entirely separate factory had been estab-lished at Hunt End, Redditch, for car and motor cycle production, and *The Motor* reported that they were turning out two models, a 6 h.p. single-cylinder *voiturette* with De Dion engine, and a 10 h.p. 'twin' with a side-valve Enfield engine, a three-speed gearbox and a four-seater tonneau body.

In 1906, the car and motor cycle sides were finally divorced and the Enfield Autocar Co. Ltd. was set up under the management of Mr Jenkins, an American, to handle car production. The new cars were designed by M. Guillon, formerly of the Belgian F.N. Com-pany. They were said to be made entirely at Redditch, and were conventional four-cylinder vehicles with cylinders cast in pairs, pressed-steel frames, thermo-syphon cooling and shaft drive. The 15 h.p. (100 × 130 mm.) sold at £420, and the 24 h.p. (120 × 130 mm.) at £525. A round radiator characterized the Enfield of this period. It was also announced that E. H. Lancaster, the 'expert to the Automobile Club', was acting as consultant to the firm. As Lancaster had worked with Panhard et Levassor, had brought Alfred Harmsworth's 40 h.p. Mercédès (the very first car of this breed to cross the Channel) to England in 1901, and had been responsible for Clément distribution in London, this augured well for the firm.

Unfortunately, Enfield Autocar were running into financial difficulties. In October 1906, Lancaster and Guillon produced a 15 h.p. four-cylinder at £375, with coil ignition. 'Simplicity,' they assured the public, 'is the keynote', but they promptly met with trouble when they attempted to drum up export sales by displaying the car at the Paris Salon, for it was impounded by the police, and its gate-change lever forcibly removed, on the pretext of a patent infringement—presumably at the behest of Louis Renault. With great difficulty, the Enfield was prised loose and discreetly shipped to Dublin for the Irish Automobile Club's Show. The Irish were probably more sympathetic, but hardly offered a comparable market. Even the adoption of a one-model policy for the 1908 season could not save the ship, though the 95 × 115 mm. Eighteen at £367 seemed an attractive enough proposition. Like previous Enfields it featured coil ignition with a magneto as an optional extra, and an attempt was made to attract novice purchasers by marking the flywheel to aid timing and supplying a complete set of charts with the car. All to no avail, for in February of that year a petition for the winding-up of the company was presented.

For the next two months, chaos reigned. Lancaster resigned after an attempt to find new capital and re-form the company had failed. At this juncture the Receiver put the firm up for auction, but the shareholders were apathetic, and no bid above £10,000 was recorded. Finally, in April, Mr W. Allday of Alldays and Onions purchased the concern, and it was announced that production would continue at Redditch.

Between 1908 and 1914, the products of the two firms were steadily rationalized. Alldays had added a 'four' in the shape of a 95 × 120 mm. Sixteen at £375 in 1906, while this had given way to a Twenty, using the cylinders of the staple Ten, the following season. By 1910 both *marques* offered the two-cylinder 10/12; the 86 × 108 mm. four-cylinder car of Enfield design, which Alldays called a Fourteen and Enfield a Sixteen; and a 95 × 114 mm. Alldays-designed car which could be purchased as the 20 h.p. Alldays or the 18/22 h.p. Enfield. The Alldays versions were slightly less expensive, and there was also a big 120 × 135 mm.

Enfield 30/35 available at £441. Enfields offered detachable wheels as an option in 1911, and provision was made on Enfields and Alldays alike in 1912 for the fitment of compressed-air self-starters. It was reported that year that the service department of Birmingham Tramways were still getting good service from a 10 h.p. Alldays delivered in 1904.

More interesting still, 1912 saw the introduction of an odd little three-wheeler with a single-cylinder water-cooled engine at the rear, chain drive, and a two-speed epicyclic gearbox with reverse. It looked not unlike an A.C. 'Sociable', and was marketed by Enfields as the 'Autorette'. There was no Alldays counterpart, but in 1913 the latter firm made its contribution to the cyclecar craze with a single-cylinder water-cooled four-wheeler, which had shaft drive and was known as the 'Midget'. At Olympia in November, 1912, it appeared in its original form, but a month later Alldays had second thoughts, and showed another variant with an 85 × 88 mm. air-cooled vee-twin engine, but still with the flat radiator. Both brakes operated on the rear wheels, and 'complete, and ready for the road' the price was £138 10s. Enfields offered the same device—shades of B.M.C. and the ADO.15—under the name of 'Autolette', and claimed that it was 'the hottest thing on wheels'!

Both the twin-cylinder cyclecars, now fitted with an 86 × 92 mm. (1,069 c.c.) engine, were continued for 1914, at £130 and £138 for the Alldays and Enfield versions respectively, the main change being the adoption of a bullnose radiator. There was also a new four-cylinder (59 × 100 mm., 1,094 c.c.) variant, available at £158 for either make: Enfield's 'Nimble Nine' was also made in a long-chassis form at £168, for the benefit of long-legged customers. The range included four-cylinder models of 2·2 litres, 3 litres and 4·1 litres, the most expensive machine being the 24·9 h.p. Enfield at £400.

This complex programme of solid, reliable, uninspiring cars could comfortably be maintained in the economic atmosphere of Edwardian times, but the post-war world demanded something quite different, and rationalization was carried a stage further when, in December 1918, the two companies announced their fusion as Enfield-Allday Motors Ltd. Cars were to be made in the former Alldays and Onions works at Small Heath, and a formidable team was built up. A. W. Reeves, who had been responsible for the very successful 'Shelsley' and R.F.C.-type Crossleys, was in charge of design, and with him were A. C. Bertelli, of Aston Martin fame, and W. S. Renwick, who was later to be associated with Bertelli. Alas for the future, the company elected to launch a programme which was revolutionary by any standards.

The mainstay of the post-war programme was to be the extra-ordinary 'Bullet', which utilized a vertically mounted five-cylinder air-cooled radial engine. The valve gear consisted of two concentric sleeves, alloy pistons were used, and this odd unit, which had dimensions of 63 mm. by 80 mm. (1,247 c.c.) was claimed to develop 20·5 b.h.p. at 2,500 r.p.m. The transmission was, by contrast, fairly straightforward, the drive being taken through a single-plate clutch and a separate three-speed gearbox with direct-mounted central lever to a helical bevel rear axle. A tubular back-bone-type frame was used, suspension was by transverse cantilever springs front and rear, and the body and running-boards were mounted on outriggers. A 'cloverleaf' three-seater body cloaked this intriguing chassis, the engine nestled behind a wire-mesh grille, and the 'wave-spoked' wheels gave the car a traction-engine look, though normally they were concealed by metal discs. As a second string, the firm offered a 2½-litre 15 h.p. 'six' said to develop 52 b.h.p.: this featured the same valve gear and separately cast cylinders, but was otherwise conventional in layout. The initial specifications, as published, were sketchy, and readers of *The Autocar* complained that no indication was given of price, let alone braking arrangements!

In February 1919, prices were fixed at £275 for the 10 h.p. 'Bullet' and £475 for the 'six', but a week later these purely hypothetical figures were raised by £20. In June, *The Autocar* was allowed to inspect a 'Bullet' chassis at the works and confirmed that the car had internal-expanding brakes on the rear wheels, though their reporter could find no evidence that it had been out on road test, and there was no sign at all of the six-cylinder machine.

At the 1919 Show, the decision was made to drop the 15 h.p. car in favour of the smaller machine, which appeared as a *fait accompli* on the Enfield-Allday stand, competing, incidentally, with two other radial-engined cars in the shape of the R.L.C. and Roy Fedden's Cosmos-engined C.A.R. at £350. About five 'Bullets' went on the road, and orders started to come in. But no cars were delivered, and in August 1920, the makers explained why. Production costs, they said, had risen out of all proportion due to the moulders' strike, and there was no possible chance of selling the 'Bullet' economically for less than £550. Worse still, the new system of taxation had resulted in the car's annual rate of duty being assessed at £15 instead of £10. In the circumstances, they had decided to refund all deposits, though they promised to reinstate orders when the time came to put the 'Bullet' into production. It was an unpromising situation. The cost of the experimental programme had been high, and the remaining funds had been dissipated on returned deposits. After nearly two years of peace Enfield-Allday, like Arrol-Johnston the previous year, had nothing to sell. It was Bertelli who rushed into the breach with a 63·5 × 117·5 mm. (1,481 c.c.) Ten with inclined side valves, a three-speed gearbox with central change and cantilever rear suspension. This was actually ready in time for the 1920 Show, with a £575 price tag. It was a pleasing little car, but it must have been a disappointment to the customers, who were being offered just another Ten, in lieu of the exciting 'Bullet'. A smart and very Aston Martin-like saloon, with vee windscreen, was made on this chassis, but at £850 it was priced almost as unrealistically as the Squire of a decade later. The design was developed, and by 1922 the sports model was combining a 60 m.p.h. top speed with commendable flexibility in the hands of *The Autocar*. It was joined in 1923 by a 12/30 of similar design, but with a four-speed gearbox and the bore increased to 69 mm. The company was reorganized that year, and struggled on till 1926, only the 10/20 being listed in the last two years of manufacture. About a hundred production cars were turned out between 1919 and 1926. Alldays and Onions, meanwhile, had carried on the manufacture of the Allon two-stroke motor cycle as an entirely separate concern up to the middle 'twenties, after which they switched to the manufacture of fans and blowers. In this capacity they are still very active.

But unlike most of the Lost Causes, Enfield-Allday in its declining years fathered an illustrious line. Bertelli had raced his cars enthusiastically, entering a revised 10/20 in both the J.C.C.'s 1921 200-Mile Race and the international 1½-litre Isle of Man T.T. in 1922. These machines had two overhead inlet valves per cylinder, side exhaust valves being retained, and 40 b.h.p. was claimed, together with a sustained speed of over 80 m.p.h. The T.T. car was specially fitted with cable-operated front-wheel brakes, but its high weight went against it; none the less, it was the first British car to finish. In 1922, three cars were entered for the 200-Mile Race, two of them, driven by the designer and Captain Woolf Barnato, having the i.o.e. engine and the third car, driven by J. T. Chance, retaining the touring s.v. unit. Only Chance finished the course.

Bertelli left Enfield-Allday after this, and his entries for the 1923 event bore his own name. He used $1\frac{1}{2}$-litre Argyll-type Burt-McCollum single sleeve-valve engines in Enfield-Allday chassis, and the machines were prepared in association with Barnato at Lingfield. They met with no success and never reappeared, but in 1924 he and his former colleague, Renwick, formed the firm of Renwick and Bertelli Ltd. This little company built only one car, 'The Buzzbox' (ON 6638), which consisted of the bottom end of a 10/20 Enfield-Allday engine with push-rod o.h.v. head of Bertelli design, mounted in an Enfield-Allday chassis, but from this was to stem the revival of the Aston Martin car. With the winding-up of Bamford and Martin Ltd. at the end of 1925, Lionel Martin's old team, which included Captain J. T. Wood of G.W.K. fame, departed from the scene, but in October 1926, Aston Martin Motors Ltd. was formed, with works at Feltham. For the next thirty-four years, under successive managements, the descendants of the Enfield-Allday were to wear the green proudly, and eventually, in 1959, to bring the Sports Car Championship home to Britain.

While Enfield, Alldays and B.S.A. were well-known in the car world in 1914, it is unlikely that the average car enthusiast was aware of the activities of Messrs. Mead and Deakin at Tyseley, Birmingham—that is, unless he had recently graduated from motor cycles. For the partners had made their name with the 'Canoelet' coachbuilt sidecar, which appeared in 1911. At that time, the sidecar was not in general use, and those that did exist were made of wicker. For the motor cyclist on courtship bent, there were only two alternatives—the forecarriage, an obsolescent device typified by the earliest Enfields, Lagondas, and Rileys, in which the passenger was provided with a fair degree of suspension but sat right on top of the accident, and the trailer, which combined the flimsiest of wicker *carrosserie* with a disconcerting tendency to detach itself on corners and pitchfork the beloved into a ditch. The sidecar combined the virtues of safety and sociability, though the noise-level of the average Edwardian motor cycle did much to offset the latter asset.

As early as 1904, however, F. W. Mead and Thomas Deakin had explored the possibility of car-making, and had built a prototype, which they called 'Medea'. This was completed in 1907, and sold about two years later to a doctor, who proceeded to charge a lamp-post with it. It had shaft drive, and was powered by a 6 h.p. single-cylinder Fafnir engine purchased as 'surplus' from Swift of Coventry. Between 1912 and 1916 several more experimental Medeas were built, culminating in a conventional 8/10 h.p. machine with shaft drive, which was tried with the 750 c.c. four-cylinder monobloc

53

Salmon, and later with a 60 × 110 mm. s.v. Chapuis-Dornier. The tubular radiator was framed by a shell reminiscent of an early Vintage Standard, and the electric sidelamps were built into the wings. Although experiments continued until 1916, the car never went into production.

After the war F. W. Mead, encouraged by the success of the 'Canoelet' venture, which had enabled them to market a coachbuilt sidecar for only twelve guineas pre-war—not much, when one considers that the wicker 'dog-baskets' retailed for about £7— decided to build a cheap light car with a respectable performance. The name Medea was dropped because, as he says, a friend of his had reminded him that that lady had been 'a very bad girl'. Evidently the press thought so too, for they usually spelt it 'Media'. Mead had no intention of assembling a composite car from parts bought piecemeal from sundry suppliers, and the Rhode company made great play of this in their publicity. Apart from the gearbox and electrical equipment, everything was made in the Tyseley works.

The original Rhode was rated at 9·5 h.p., and had a 1,087 c.c. single o.h.c. engine developing 19 b.h.p., in unit with a single-plate clutch and a three-speed Wrigley gearbox. There was no differential, and no electric starter, while the lubrication system was peculiar to the *marque*, and most ingenious. The oil lived in a pit surrounding the flywheel; it was scooped up, and flung into a reservoir, whence it flooded through large diameter pipes to the main bearings, which had trough-and-dipper feed. It also flooded to the valve case, and returned via the vertical shaft tunnel to the sump. Rhodes proclaimed the virtues of a system in which there were no small diameter pipes to clog, and no pump to give trouble.

The bodywork was a curious mixture of ingenuity and crudity. On the original 1921 'Chummy' model, which listed at £275, the spare wheel was recessed in a horizontal locker in the tail, but in the interests of economy the bodywork had no curved metal sections, the only curves being the wooden rear quarters. The car was ugly, and it was noisy. But it went exceedingly fast for its day, the makers' claim of 52 m.p.h. being distinctly conservative. It was also reliable, two Rhodes used as staff cars by *The Autocar* in 1922 going through a month's hard driving with four minor adjustments and one puncture.

Up to 1925, when the S.M.M.T. ruled that members could not participate in any competition other than those approved by the Society, works-entered Rhodes were prominent in reliability trials, the principal driver being B. Alan Hill, later in charge of public relations at Standard-Triumph. He won some fifty awards in four years, including three Silver Cups in the Scottish Six Days' Trials, the Premier Award in the Light Car Trials sponsored by the R.A.C. in 1924, and Gold Medals in the J.C.C.'s Brooklands High Speed Trials of 1925 and 1926, which must have been quite a test for the Rhode's odd lubrication.

For the next five years, Rhode continued to evolve their o.h.c. model, the basic features being retained, though agents protested that the plate clutch was so easy in operation that it bred bad drivers! In 1922, a *de luxe* model, with speedometer and electric starter, was added to the range at £307, later reduced to £265, while in 1923 there was made available a distinctly stylish sports two-seater, with racing cams and high-compression pistons, at £295.

For 1924, the range was augmented by a 66 × 90 mm. (1,232 c.c.) 10·8 on similar lines to the original 9·5, which was continued in 'Occasional Four' and sports forms at £180 and £270 respectively. The Sports, incidentally, was put out in 'house colours' of black and white, with wire wheels, even the spare petrol can on the running board being painted to match. A four-speed gearbox was an option this year; electric starters were standard, and a differential was provided on all models save the touring 9·5 h.p. cars.

Only the bigger engine was available in 1925, Rhode making their contribution to the price war by putting out an 'Occasional Four' at only £198, though side curtains (at £3 16s per set) and a starter (£15) had to join the extras list in order to attain this target. The sports model, complete with f.w.b. and ten-inch rear drums, Hartford shock-absorbers and a vast polished copper exhaust pipe, offered enthusiasts a rousing and noisy 70 m.p.h. for £345.

This was, unfortunately, the end of the upward trend. It is unlikely that the trials ban hurt: indeed, F. W. Mead ascribes the car's failure, ironically enough, to its being 'too successful'—but this year the firm made two expensive mistakes. First of all, they tried to enter the commercial vehicle market. Hitherto only a few five-cwt. vans had been made on the private-car chassis, against the wishes of the designer, who maintained that this adaptation would lower the Rhode's prestige. Now they launched out with a '20/25-cwt.' truck, sponsored by Mead and Deakin, the parent company, and known as the M. and D. For its day it was advanced, since it featured a 2½-litre o.h.c. four-cylinder engine on Rhode lines, electric lighting and starting, and Alford and Alder f.w.b. Only about six were made, and it got no further than certain other

55

experiments which Mr Hill recalls, including an ingenious three-speed epicyclic gearbox and even a folding caravan.

Far more disastrous was the 1926 11/30 and its sporting counter-part, the 11/38. The agents had asked for a quieter, smoother car, so Mead brought out an o.h.v. push-rod engine of similar capacity to the 10·8 and put it in the existing chassis. The result was an altogether heavier machine which, though it proved capable of climbing a 1-in-5½ gradient at 11 m.p.h. in second gear, thanks to its four-speed box, had won docility at the expense of performance. Its compensated four-wheel brakes had twelve-inch drums, and worked very well, 'each brake installation being interchangeable', a hand-wheel by the driver's side enabling adjustment to be carried out while the car was in motion. The quieter engine, unfortunately, revealed the acoustic shortcomings of the gearbox, and a trivial fault in the induction system was rectified only after customers had complained of an ominous thump in the engine. A two-seater cost £210 in 1927, but it was not light at sixteen cwt., and the 45 m.p.g. claimed for the 1924 models was no longer possible. After two discouraging seasons, Rhode discarded the push-rod engine, and went back to the well-tried o.h.c. unit for 1928, installing it in a new long (10 ft. 4 in.) chassis. Wire wheels and Rhode compensated f.w.b. were standard, while the staple body style was an unusual fabric saloon with oval quarter-lights and a rear trunk, known as the 'Hawk'. Late in 1928, the firm went into liquidation, though a few 'Hawks' were still made, a metal-panelled version figuring in the 1929 programme. In August of that year, it was announced that McKenzie and Denley Ltd. had purchased the firm from the Official Receiver, and would continue production. About 5,000 cars had left the works between 1921 and 1928.

H. B. Denley had driven Rhodes in trials in past years, and a few 'Hawks' were in fact turned out between 1929 and 1931. These had the twin-carburettor o.h.v. push-rod 4ED Meadows engine in place of the old Mead-designed o.h.c. unit, a four-speed gearbox and a simplified form of cable-operated braking. In 1931 form, with grouped chassis lubrication, it sold at £375, and the makers claimed a maximum speed of 70 m.p.h., with 55 m.p.h. possible on third. As tested in March 1930 by *The Autocar*, it recorded only 62 m.p.h., however. The 'Hawk' continued to make its annual appearance in the *Buyers' Guide* until 1935, but I have never seen a Rhode which claimed to be post-Vintage—in fact, my own 10·8 tourer aside, I have never seen one at all. F. W. Mead did not re-enter the motor industry, though his son Richard later built bodies for one of the more promising Lost Causes of the nineteen-fifties—the Rover-based 2·1-litre Marauder, which faded away in 1953 after only a handful of cars had been built.

The Rhode aside, Birmingham's Lost Causes have left their mark behind. Both Royal Enfield and B.S.A., their cars forgotten, are still world-famous as manufacturers of motor cycles, while the fans and blowers of Alldays and Onions and the Aston Martin car stand as the living heirs of the Enfield and Alldays car ventures. But what of the others—the Calthorpe, for instance? I do not think I could ever enthuse over this company's stodgy touring productions, any more than did *The Autocar* in 1905, on the occasion of the make's debut at the Agricultural Hall Show. While *The Motor* praised the 'easy access to the engine', they wrote:

'It is by no means a model of accessibility, the electric ignition arrangements being the chief offenders in this respect. We have no doubt a little experience on the road will enable the makers to remedy this defect.'

Yet Calthorpe entered cars four years running in the *Coupe des Voiturettes* and its successors; they built a most attractive miniature car in the shape of the 1914 1,100 c.c. 'Minor'; and were only brought down by a series of complicated share deals in the early nineteen-twenties, after a brief period of success in which they were turning out their attractive 10 h.p. 'Sporting Four' at the rate of fifty to seventy a week. In 1924, when Calthorpe entered upon their death throes, Birmingham was also making the Ariel, the Ashton-Evans, the Bayliss-Thomas (an offshoot of Excelsior Motor Cycles), the Hands (made by one of the founders of Calthorpe) and the McKenzie, not to mention the mechanical components of the Sizaire-Berwick, by this time a glorified Austin. None of these cars was of particular interest.

What killed the Lost Causes of Birmingham? The cheaper assembled vehicles could not compete with Morris, any more than could the Clyno or the G.W.K. A change of policy killed the Rhode by destroying its individual merit; Enfield-Allday succumbed to one of those extraordinary outbursts of exuberance that seize hold of designers, and which result in insurmountable financial deficits.

With B.S.A., it is a different story. It has been unkindly said that no firm ever made both a good motor cycle and a good car, and there is some truth in this. The Colliers of Matchless, Raleigh, A.J.S., Brough, Henderson—how many of them left any mark in the car world? There are, of course, exceptions—B.M.W., for instance, have been turning out consistently successful vehicles for years, and their flat-twin motor cycles occupy much the same relative niche as did the immortal '328' sports car of 1936, while Peugeot have contrived to make everything from scooters to medium-sized lorries without embarrassing failures. But the B.S.A. car never made the grade: the Daimler amalgamation stifled the original Baguley designs, the rear-wheel-drive cars made intermittently between the wars were devoid of any individuality whatsoever, and the f.w.d. vehicles, though they displayed great technical ingenuity and were blessed with pretty lines, were never more than 'sporty runabouts', and they lost out to M.G., Singer, Morgan, FIAT and their other rivals. The three-wheeler market, of course, suffered a serious blow when the tax rate on conventional cars was cut to 15s per unit of horsepower in 1934, causing the death of the Coventry-Victor, Raleigh and J.M.B. in one fell swoop. But it did not kill the Morgan, which lasted on into the nineteen-fifties before the firm finally went over to four-wheelers for good.

Not that the B.S.A. is a complete Lost Cause: the design staff can comfort themselves with the knowledge that many people, myself included, now motor in small four-cylinder cars with independent suspension and front-wheel drive—and we like it!

CHAPTER 5

Bus Ride to Oblivion:
The Sad Tale of the Crossley

'Crossley Motors, having reached a position of pre-eminence in the building of fine quality cars in a world which, up to that date [1933] still appreciated superb workmanship, could not and would not compromise the company's reputation. A change to mass production methods, with all it implied, was absolutely alien to their life-long policy. So with that cold, iron courage that is ever more rare than any hot-blooded bravery, the Directors decided to maintain the criterion they had hitherto set, but to confine their energies to the commercial vehicle market.'

A History of Crossley Motors, 1951

'The Crossley Ten has quickly established its supremacy among light cars.'
Crossley advertisement, August 1932

On a dark morning just after Christmas, 1958, two men in a Land Rover drove northwards across the New Forest. Their destination was Errwood Park, Stockport, and the purpose of their journey to collect the last remnant of Crossley Motors Ltd.—a 1924 19·6 which had served for nearly thirty years as the firm's fire-tender. They must have been among the final visitors to the plant, which was deserted, apart from a few faithful members of the staff engaged in clearing up. They brought the old Crossley back with them to the Montagu Motor Museum at Beaulieu—a last generous gesture by a dying firm.

Yet when the old car first served the Company's fire brigade, in 1929, Crossley were still very much alive: not only that, but they had but recently supplied cars to the Reigning Monarch and the Heir to the Throne. The name was a household word, and though mass production was not a phrase to be used within earshot of the Gorton works in Manchester, the green cross was frequently encountered on the roads of Britain. More than that, the name was known to every man who had served with the British and Empire forces in the late war, while in the Republic of Ireland it had a far more sinister significance, for had not the 25/30 tender been the regular transport of the detested Black-and-Tans? How often, by contrast, does one now encounter a Crossley, apart from post-war double-decker buses? A big V.S.C.C. event will attract perhaps the odd 2-litre 'six', and on Bank Holidays one may pass a tired-looking example of the post-Vintage Ten making its weary way down the bypass to the sea—but that is all. Only Arrol-Johnston, of all the Lost Causes, is deader.

Much of Crossley's advertising up to 1914 bore the by-line 'Of Gas Engine Fame', despite the fact that after the formation of Crossley Motors Ltd. In 1910, there was no official connexion with Crossley Brothers, the parent firm. F. W. and W. J. Crossley embarked upon the manufacture of stationary gas engines in 1866, and their business became a public company in 1897. The brothers were intensely religious, refusing to make their engines available to breweries for conscientious reasons, while Frank Crossley built himself a house in the slum area of Ancoats, so as to be near his workmen. Among their employees was Dr Hewlett Johnson, later Dean of Canterbury, who was trained as an engineer: it is significant that upon his appointment as Dean of Manchester in 1925, his ex-parishioners at Altrincham presented him with a Crossley Fourteen.

The Crossley gas engine business was firmly established when, in 1903, Charles Jarrott and William Malesbury Letts entered into partnership in London to sell cars. Jarrott was already a famous racing motorist, while Letts had been a pioneer in establishing contact with the young American motor industry. They were not, however, content to sell De Dietrichs and Oldsmobiles, and cast around for something British worthy of gracing their showrooms. Apart from the Napier, already firmly under the aegis of Jarrott's friend and rival S. F. Edge, there was nothing—so the partners commissioned J. S. Critchley, former works manager at Daimlers, to design them a big high-performance car, and persuaded the progressive Sir William Crossley to make it for them.

What emerged at the 1904 Crystal Palace Show was not so much revolutionary as thoroughly sound, solid design, with more than a suggestion of Mercédès about it. The engine was of four-cylinder T-head type, with cylinders of 108 mm. bore and 130 mm. stroke, cast separately, giving a capacity of around 4·6 litres. The buyer had a choice of low-tension magneto or coil ignition, a 'special Crossley carburettor' was fitted, and the transmission and braking arrangements were typical of a high-powered car of the period: a cone clutch, four-speed gearbox, and final drive by side chains. With some 25 b.h.p. available at 900 r.p.m., the Crossley was said to be capable of 48 m.p.h., and the manufacturers claimed that long engine life was assured by 'scientific testing and analysis of all metals used'. It was said that it would tick over smoothly at 80 r.p.m., and *The Autocar*, which had a trial run early on, commented on its smoothness, flexibility and hill-climbing power. *The Car Illustrated* was even more lyrical: in his report on the Crystal Palace Show in February 1904, its correspondent wrote: 'I saw nothing that was really good at the Paris Show which does not seem to have been embodied in this new Crossley vehicle', though he rather gave the game away by referring to Crossley's wonderful new carburettor as a 'Krebs type', and correspondents in the same paper were even more scathing, venturing to suggest that the so-flexible power unit was imported.

This was not true. Henry Sturmey of *The Autocar* was nearer the facts when he asserted, in a survey of allegedly British exhibits at the Show, that the Crossley used English machinery in a French chassis, since the frames used on all cars up to the end of 1906 were made to the firm's order in Belgium.

Having completed his design work for Crossley Brothers, Critchley set up as an engineering consultant in Chelsea, and for the next few years the chief engineer at the Openshaw Works was Walter Iden, who had come from the Coronet Motor Co. of Coventry. It is interesting to note that in 1917 Iden returned to Crossley, whom he left after the divorce of the car and gas engine interests, having worked in the interim for the Associated Equipment Co. Ltd., the firm which was to absorb the remains of Crossley's motor vehicle side in 1951.

The 22 h.p. Crossley sold at £900 complete in 1905, and was already acquiring a sound reputation. In June, a car, still referred to as a 'Crossley-Critchley', won the Appearance Competition—what we should now call a *concours d'élégance*—at the Ladies' Automobile Club's Ranelagh Gymkhana. During the period of the last of the Gordon Bennett races, Jarrott occupied himself with extensive Continental testing of the cars, thus anticipating Henry Royce by some years. There was even a brief liaison with the firm's fellow-Lancastrians and subsequent rivals in omnibus manufacture, when the London and Suburban Omnibus Co. Ltd. put a 30 h.p. Leyland omnibus with Crossley engine into service between Surbiton and Kew Bridge—one suspects, though, that this was merely an interim measure while Leylands, who so far had interested themselves solely in steam, evolved an efficient petrol engine of their own. For 1906 Crossley announced a new model, a 40 h.p. (120·7 × 152·4 mm.) on very similar lines to the 22 h.p., though it used a water-cooled transmission footbrake of the type favoured by FIAT and Itala. The contemporary illustrated description goes on to tell us that 'a finger-plate is required for reverse', a formidable description for a little catch on the gear-lever. While other manufacturers, Rolls-Royce and Lanchester included, were going to town on the new-fangled six-cylinder engine, Crossley would have none of it. Down the road at Clayton, Robert Crossley was proclaiming the virtues of the multi-cylinder engine and prophesying the imminent advent of the six-cylinder *voiturette*. This Mr Crossley was no relation of Sir William's, nor had he, at this stage, anything to do with his namesake's cars, being a director of Belsize Motors. He subsequently worked at Gorton both before and after the first World War, though he did not live to see the firm make a 'six', as he died in 1925. The complexities of the family were such that once a malicious shareholder is said to have caused alarm and despondency by inquiring at a Crossley Annual Board Meeting whether Amy Crossley would benefit under a new share issue. Nobody had remembered that this Miss Crossley was a second-hand clothes and furniture dealer in Salford whose advertisements were plastered all over the Corporation buses!

Jarrott, meanwhile, had gone to considerable pains to publicize his cars, and in January 1906, his Crossley became the first car to climb Arthur's Seat at Edinburgh. His thunder was stolen by the irrepressible F. S. Bennett, who proceeded to duplicate the feat in his famous 9 h.p. single-cylinder Cadillac, now in the Montagu Motor Museum. In April, Jarrott redressed the balance by driving from London to Monte Carlo in $37\frac{1}{2}$ hours on a 40 h.p. Crossley tourer. This record, likewise, was short-lived, the Hon. C. S. Rolls making a faster run in May with a 1906 T.T.-type 20 h.p. Rolls-Royce; but Jarrott was back again the following March and slashed the record to 35 hours 20 minutes, in spite of three punctures and a broken oil pipe. Crossleys were unlucky again, however, for within a fortnight E. A. Paul's 60 h.p. six-cylinder Napier had beaten Jarrott's new record.

In the meantime Iden had been playing with shaft drive. A 20 h.p. 'chainless' car had been seen at the 1906 Agricultural Hall Show, and for 1907 the first 'all-British' Crossley car was announced, in the shape of a revised 30/40, likewise with live-axle transmission. A four-speed gearbox with direct top was used, and this car bore the first true Crossley radiator, complete with green cross emblem, in place of the mock-Mercédès variety used on the 22/28 and the old Forty. The price of a complete car was £800. Chain drive was made optional on this model from May 1907, but by 1909 it had been dropped for good, and types listed were the Forty at £700, and a companion 101·6 × 127 mm. 20/25 at £550—this, be it said, was the progenitor of the famous R.F.C.-pattern 25/30, which was in continuous production until 1925, the war years included.

In June 1909, it was announced that the company had recognized 'the need for smaller cars' and was coming out with a 12/14 (80 × 120 mm.) at £385 and an 18/20 (101·6 × 127 mm.) at £495. These were the work of G. Hubert Woods and A. W. Reeves, and the smaller car had a conventional monobloc engine with enclosed side valves, thermo-syphon cooling and 'double lever expanding clutch'. The vertical gate change was hardly a commendable feature, but the wood or wire wheels were detachable, and, most important of all, four-wheel brakes of Allen-Liversidge design were standard equipment. *The Autocar* was enthusiastic. 'The steering,' their tester said, was 'delightful; the car can almost be steered with one finger'; while the new braking, which was tried out on greasy roads, provided 'not the slightest sensation of skidding'. Early in 1912, however, the front-wheel brakes were quietly abandoned. Their development cost a lot of money, and both durability and handling were affected. Cecil Bianchi, who was responsible for all Crossley's test work as works manager (and later chief engineer) till 1927, comments:

'This was to my mind one of the Crossley tragedies. If only we had thought to couple all four brakes to the foot pedal, our troubles would have been over: instead, the footbrake pedal was coupled to the front axle only, the rear axle brakes being coupled to the side lever. Result, locking of front wheels and loss of steering, the whole load of braking being taken on the front axle and springs, which gave endless bother in broken springs, twisted axle beams, and stub-axle failures, even with radius rods fitted.'

Crossley, like those other pioneers, Argyll and Arrol-Johnston, were not, therefore, among the first in the field with f.w.b. after the first World War. Nor did they do anything with the pneumatic suspension of Cowey design which was seen on a 40 h.p. Crossley chassis at Olympia in 1909, though Coweys themselves subsequently made a few similarly sprung light cars with De Dion engines.

These frustrations were but pinpricks, however. In December 1910, Crossley Bros. Ltd. transferred the motor-car side of their business to Crossley Motors Ltd., who clinched the deal by acquiring their other parent, Charles Jarrott and Letts Ltd. The directors of the new concern, now established in the Gorton works which were to be the home of Crossley pleasure cars to the end in 1937, were Sir W. J. Crossley, Kenneth Crossley, W. M. Letts, G. Hubert Woods and A. W. Reeves. Dual ignition was adopted on 1911 models, when the old Critchley-type Forty was finally discontinued, while the Fifteen and Twenty, as the two Reeves designs had been rechristened, continued without further change into 1912. In 1913, front-wheel brakes were officially dropped, but Crossley-made electric lighting and starting were adopted, and these two models represented the staple output until the abandonment of private car manufacture as such in August 1914. For the 1915 models, incidentally, the 'bullnose' radiator was adopted for the 'Shelsley' sporting models, though flat radiators were regulation wear on both touring and Service machinery.

The last four years of peace saw the name of Crossley writ large in competition circles. Both the new four-cylinder cars, especially the 2·6 litre Fifteen in 'Shelsley' form with sporting two-seater or torpedo body, were quite impressive performers, the latter combining a genuine 60 m.p.h. with the ability, in 1914 form, to average 30 m.p.g. at 30 m.p.h.

In this context, it is amusing to note that thanks to improved aerodynamics the 1953 4·6-litre Bentley 'Continental' could better this latter figure, though it is hard to imagine anyone trying! Hubert Woods was an energetic driver of his own machinery, and as early as July 1910, he was recording fastest time of the day at Kettleby hill-climb on a 20 h.p. car, which was said to develop a respectable 62 b.h.p. at 2,000 r.p.m. The Crossleys were present at practically every speed meeting, generally with pretty four-seater bodies that would not have looked out of place in 1925 (they didn't, for there was little difference between the shape of a 1914 Crossley and its counterpart of ten years later). At Coalport in 1911, Woods was beaten only by C. A. Bird's vast 65 h.p. Napier, while he took second place on formula at Shelsley Walsh.

In 1912 successes included class wins at Rivington Pike, Pateley Bridge and Aston Clinton. At Brooklands, Cecil Bianchi collected a number of class records, and Woods made the first official record climb of the Test Hill at 23·52 m.p.h., an interesting contrast with the 20·27 m.p.h. recorded by a 60 h.p. Napier in 1910 and the 29·29 m.p.h. made by the Light Sports Railton in 1935. The July meeting at Saltburn Sands was a Crossley benefit, Letts on a Fifteen and Woods on a Twenty collecting no fewer than eight first places between them. True, there were the failures: in one of the standard car races at Brooklands in 1912, the cars non-started, and in the second, Bianchi retired after his magneto fell off. The modified 3·3-litre 'Shelsley'-type car entered for the 1914 T.T. failed to last into the second day's racing. The firm's only other T.T. entries were

Ersatz Burney: the tail end of that plumber's paradise, the Crossley-Burney of 1934

A Silver Hawk two-seater of 1921

The 1938 Railton 'Cobham' saloon

Thirty thousand miles in thirty thousand minutes: the Cordery sisters and their Invicta about to bring the Dewar Trophy back to Cobham, Brooklands, 1929

White elephant *par excellence*: the 1948 Invicta 'Black Prince' 'Byfleet' drophead coupé

likewise unsuccessful, the 1905 car being withdrawn before the race and the i.o.e. Vernon-Crossleys of 1932 proving a disappointment, to put it mildly. Jarrott and Letts went as far as to enter a 'Shelsley' driven by W. L. Sorel, who was later to look after Ettore Bugatti's British interests, in the 1914 Swedish Winter Trials.

Crossleys were still fascinated by the idea of a small car, even the Shelsley being considered too big, so three 10 h.p. prototypes were made in 1913. These were miniature replicas of the Fifteen, and could have made, one suspects, quite a big hole in the market in which Morris, Singer and Calthorpe were jockeying for leadership. There are also rumours of a further batch of small prototypes round about 1923, based on the Fourteen of the period, but I have been unable to discover anything of their history.

More important than this, Crossley were laying the foundations of a connexion that was to do more than anything to make their name a household word. In March 1913, six 20 h.p. tourers were delivered to the infant Royal Flying Corps, another eighty-three being in service by January 1914, including a landaulet for the Commanding Officer at Farnborough, home of the Royal Aircraft Factory. Cars were also delivered to the Royal Naval Air Service, and the Commander-in-Chief, Aldershot, rode in a Crossley. Officially, all output after August 1914, was earmarked for the War Office, but Jarrott and Letts still sold the vehicles to Allied governments in the same way as they supplied civilian customers pre-War. The Crossley was ubiquitous as a tender, a light lorry, a staff car or an ambulance. In 1917, extensive cross-country tests were carried out by a Russian purchasing commission at Oxshott, various British firms submitting entries, among them A.E.C., Austin, British Berna and Dennis.

As Crossley's official history puts it:

'When the majority were either wrecked or hopelessly bogged in the mire, the Russians bowed their thanks and quietly withdrew. Later on, instead of placing an order, *they set up an entire factory* at Lebedev, and built Crossleys to drawings supplied by the Company.'

Crossley also built Beardmore in-line and Bentley BR.2 aeroengines, but they emerged from the war with one incomparable asset, shared by no one else save perhaps Vauxhall: they had been in continuous production with what was virtually their standard private car chassis from 1914 to the Armistice, and reconversion was no great problem. When the Managing Director, A. W. Hubble, stood on a crate in the Gorton works on 11 November 1918, and announced the end of hostilities to his employees, he had good reason for jubilation.

True, some of the managerial staff had dispersed: just before the war, Woods had joined Westinghouse and Robert Crossley had departed to Darracq's London depot, while A. W. Reeves was conducting a diversity of curious experiments for the combined firms of Enfield and Alldays at Birmingham, but Bianchi was still at Gorton, and the firm now had the services of T. Wishart as designer. Wishart was to be responsible for all the remaining private cars to leave Gorton.

In February 1919, deliveries of the R.F.C.-type 25/30 in post-war guise commenced. It was substantially the same car as had been listed in 1914, apart from the adoption of aluminium pistons and the rounded radiator, but the manufacturers now claimed not only 60 m.p.h. but also the ability to surmount a 1-in-4 gradient with a load of 30 cwt. A tourer could be had for £995, but the cheapest closed cars listed at a formidable £1,300.

The immediate reactions of the public were gratifying to the Gorton firm, who had expended quite a lot of cash during the war publishing leaflets listing 'Ten reasons why your car should be a Crossley'. As yet no use had been found for the wartime aero-engine works at Stockport, but Gorton was working full-time, and in the immediate post-war car shortage the 25/30 was attracting the attentions of the specialist coachbuilders, Mulliner and Regent especially turning out some very pleasing bodies, while Plaxtons of Scarborough and Smiths of Stockport made a speciality of the Crossley. *The Autocar*'s representative, who was taken for a run in a new tourer by Lieutenant-Colonel Jarrott in September 1919, registered mild disappointment that this particular machine would not do much more than 50 m.p.h., but the Prince of Wales chose a fleet of them for his Australian tour that winter—the first of many occasions on which Royalty was to favour the green cross.

It is perhaps surprising that the R.F.C.-type Crossley sold so well, in spite of its known merit, for vast numbers of ex-Service examples were coming on the market. In May 1919, it was reported that several hundred brand-new chassis were lining the verges of suburban roads in London, while whole fields on the site of the present Slough Trading Estate were crammed with war-surplus vehicles. The 25/30 was probably as common as was the Humber 'Super Snipe' in 1946. Numbers of ex-Servicemen used them to set up taxi services, while not a few bright spirits lengthened their frames by the crudest possible methods, and crowned them with fourteen-seater charabanc bodies. The old Crossley withstood all this abuse, and the engine survived in the firm's commercial vehicles for years after the 25/30 had been retired from the private-car programme. Towards the end of its days, its antiquity became obvious, and an old hire-car driver, writing nostalgically in praise of his 25/30 in 1956, recalled that he envied the Austin Twenty drivers their footbrakes on the rear wheels, for the Crossley's worked on the transmission, and was apt to be destructive of axle shafts.

Royalty 'discovered' the Crossley after the first World War. King Alfonso of Spain, a knowledgeable car enthusiast, always used this make on his visits to London, as did the then Crown Prince Hirohito of Japan, while the King of Siam owned no fewer than four 25/30 saloons. Crossley cars featured on the Prince of Wales' ambassadorial tours of Australia, India, South America and South Africa, and as a consequence of these successful excursions he became a regular customer, buying first a 25/30 which was displayed on the makers' stand at Olympia in 1922, then another 25/30 limousine with an instrument panel in the rear compartment in 1924, and finally an 18/50 six-cylinder in April, 1927. His brother, the Duke of York and future King George VI, rode in a fleet of 18/50 tourers on his tour of Australia in 1927, while King George V had two Crossleys—an 18/50 limousine with factory-built body and a special six-wheeler shooting car purchased in 1929 for use at Sandringham. It had the 3·8-litre 19.6 engine, front-wheel brakes, and a lavish Hooper touring body complete with clock and electric cigar lighters, in spite of which it was said to have exceeded 60 m.p.h. on test. The Crossley was also correct proconsular wear in the nineteen-twenties, both the Earl of Athlone, when Governor-General of South Africa, and Lord Irwin, the Viceroy of India, using 18/50s.

With Royal patronage and a solid, hard-headed North-Country background, one would have thought that the Gorton firm was secure. Unfortunately, one of the characteristics of all the Lost Causes is their tendency to fly off at tangents. Crossley's nearest approach to the fatal straight-eight was the Willys 88D, a few of which they imported in 1931, but they tried most other things. The first of these was the Avro amalgamation.

In 1919 the aircraft industry was in low water, and even Avro could not make much headway, since such aircraft as the market would absorb could be purchased cheaply from the Disposals Board. They had contemplated an entry into the motor industry, and in 1920 had three irons in the fire: the construction of 'Avrolite' bodies on aircraft lines for chassis such as the 'Model T' Ford, the manufacture of R. O. Harper's curious but effective three-wheeled 'Runabout', and the evolution of the Avro light car. This machine used the firm's system of body construction—sheet aluminium panels over a light timber framework—and the engine was a straight-forward 67 × 95 mm. four-cylinder 10 h.p., but a three-speed epicyclic gearbox with foot change, in the Ford manner, was featured. In May 1920, a fusion of interests with Crossley was announced, with a joint board of directors for the combined companies, but little happened except on paper, though Avros did take on the work of collecting ex-W.D. Crossleys from the dumps at Slough and reconditioning them. Their own car was allowed to fade away, though it is doubtful if this was due so much to Crossley influence as to the reconstruction of the R.A.F. by Sir Samuel Hoare and Lord Trenchard in 1923; for with the factory back at work on its famous 504 trainers, the need for other ventures ceased. An amusing footnote to this was provided by the Crossley Annual General Meeting in 1925, when the shareholders suggested that it might be a good idea for Crossleys to take up aero-engine manufacture. The Board did not take the hint, and three years later Avro threw in their lot with Armstrong-Siddeley, whose active aero-motor business was to help tide them over the dark years to come.

Not content with exploring the aircraft industry, Crossley were still hankering after a popular line, and Sir William Letts, who was inclined to look westwards, found an outlet both for their ambitions and for the empty Heaton Chapel works in the importation and assembly of Willys-Overland products. Willys-Overland Crossley Ltd. was formed in 1920, and at a dealers' conference that autumn John N. Willys, the guest of honour, talked glibly of a possible sale of 25,000 cars in the ensuing two years. This venture never paid off. Parts were imported initially from the U.S.A., and later from Canada, but the firm did not progress beyond mere assembly, though prototype car and truck engines were made for them by Coventry-Climax. At one point they even tried to beat the horse-power tax by installing the 14/28 Morris-Oxford engine in the Overland 'Light Four' chassis. The range of models offered included the Manchester truck and the various Overland, Whippet, Willys and Willys-Knight cars, the last mentioned having sleeve-valve engines. There were also the Falcon and the Stearns, made by firms acquired by Willys-Overland Motors Corporation in the later nineteen-twenties, but only a handful of these came to Britain. This little venture accounted for a good part of the £285,000 loss incurred by Crossleys in 1926, since the buildings alone at Heaton Chapel had depreciated by £200,000 in six years, it was said. It also landed the firm in hot water in October 1928, when an order for 2,000 Lycoming engines 'by a British firm' (Willys-Overland Crossley Ltd.) was announced, leading gossip mongers in the industry to allege that Crossleys, like Vauxhall, were 'going American'. None of its products was in the least interesting, and after a brief stab at a really cheap 'six' of reasonable h.p. rating (the 1931 15·7 h.p. Willys 'Palatine' at £259) and a skirmish with the light-car market, when they bought the car side of the bankrupt A.J.S. firm in 1931, they called it quits at the end of 1933 and wound up the unwanted subsidiary.

More interesting, if less significant in its impact, was the attempt to build Bugattis at Gorton. The details of this engaging little side-issue are still shrouded in mystery, since Automobiles Bugatti assured me, in a most charming letter, that to the best of their knowledge *no* cars were ever made in England, and production estimates quoted by various British sources range between nil and 1,000. The facts seem to be these. In November 1921, Sir William Letts announced that Bugattis were to be made under licence in England, the connexion between the two companies being Charles Jarrott and Letts Ltd., who handled the Bugatti in England and the Crossley in London. After this, we hear no more from published sources, though up to the early nineteen-thirties the name 'Crossley-Bugatti' features in lists of competition entries, while one of the founder-members of the Bugatti Owners' Club undoubtedly once owned one. Sanction was given for a batch of five hundred to be made, all of them the standard 'Type 22', and *not* the later and more potent 'Brescia'. These cars were made of British materials, B.S.F. threads and British measurements being used throughout. Only about twenty-five were completed; Bugattis could be made, as Crossleys found out to their cost, only by Bugatti craftsmen using Bugatti materials. Engine numbers ran from 1600 to 1625, in case any of my readers thinks he may own one!

More successful was the adoption of Kégresse track-laying principle, so effectively applied on the trans-Sahara Citroëns, to the 25/30 tender chassis, though as these vehicles were almost exclusively of 'commercial' type, they are really outside the scope of this book.

For 1921 the firm came out with a new model, not as a replacement for the 25/30, but as a smaller and more moderately-priced touring vehicle. This was the famous 19·6 of 89 × 150 mm. (3·8 litres). The s.v. monobloc power unit had, of course, four cylinders, the head being detachable. Fuel feed was by Autovac, and the four-speed gearbox had right-hand control. The rest of the specification was Edwardian, including the cone clutch and foot transmission brake. Despite a long (10 ft. 4 in.) wheelbase, high weight, a tricky gearbox and a fierce clutch, the Crossley was an excellent touring car, and lent itself to top-gear driving. This is my own view: *The Autocar* considered the gears 'extremely easy to change' even if top was too near the driver's leg. An interesting feature was the use of oil cups with semicircular covers, which were raised with the point of the oiler. These survived up to 1928. A tourer cost £1,085, and a sports two-seater £1,100. It acquired fabric universals in 1922, front-wheel brakes (at £35 extra) in 1925 (at which time the tourer was priced at £750), and disappeared from the range at the end of the 1926 season. A 19·6 tourer was subjected to a 25,000-mile R.A.C. trial in 1925, using Benzole fuel, Castrol oil and Rapson tyres. It recorded 59·07 m.p.h. over a flying mile and a half at Brooklands, but more illuminating are the running statistics, 20,000 miles of road work (on which coasting was strictly forbidden) producing a staggering 26·12 m.p.g., and 6,154 m.p.g. of oil. The tyres lasted for the whole distance, no major repairs were carried out, and all this on a frankly ponderous tourer weighing thirty-six cwt!

From 1923 to 1926, a sports variant of the 19·6 was offered. Known as the 20/70, this was a very choice specimen of the early Vintage sports-touring car: apart from the adoption of slipper-type pistons, knock-off wire wheels and lightweight polished-aluminium coachwork with flared wings, it differed very little from the stock article. The price in 1923 was £975, the makers guaranteed 75 m.p.h., and an owner, reporting on his machine in *The Autocar* in June 1923, said that it would idle along in top gear at 5 m.p.h., was capable of roll-free cornering at 40 m.p.h. (which, be it said, the 19·6 was not), and would reach 80 m.p.h. An official road test conducted two years later revealed a timed 75 m.p.h. on top, and a useful 57 m.p.h. on third. Old Dashwood Hill was surmounted at 24 m.p.h. on the highest ratio, but a frightening eighty-eight feet was required—with four-wheel brakes, too—to come to a halt from 30 m.p.h. It was remarked at the time that the 20/70 was one of the last surviving sports car designs with side valves, and its quietness was ascribed thereto, though it 'does not compare in smoothness with a "six" of good make'. Two cars of this type were raced successfully at Brooklands by Leon Cushman, lapping at 95–100 m.p.h. on occasion, while Frau Liliane Roehrs, a novice driver, drove one into third place in the 1926 Hainberg hill-climb in Germany. Four-wheel Perrot servo brakes were optional from 1924 onwards.

In 1923, the Crossley yearning for a smaller car was reflected in the introduction of the 12/14, later marketed as the Fourteen. This was an entirely conventional and uninteresting side-valve four-cylinder vehicle, which *The Autocar* summed up as 'a sensible car'. The 2,388 c.c. engine was mounted in unit with a three-speed gearbox, central ball change being used. As a consequence of the firm's practice of testing its cars in the Peak District, hill-climbing was good, but performance was typical of the period, no more than 55 m.p.h. being recorded. A tourer cost £475: by 1925, it was £100 cheaper, f.w.b. were an optional extra, and another 'improvement' (we wonder!) was a roller-type accelerator pedal. It lasted until 1928 in the catalogue, production ceasing some little time earlier. A car of this type won the Royal East African Automobile Association's Delamere Cup for fuel consumption in 1924: I came across one of these in Kenya early in 1960, so perhaps the breed was durable as well as frugal.

In 1924, the 25/30 provided most of the news, Major Court-Treatt using two of these, fitted with truck bodies, for his Cape–Cairo expedition. The journey took sixteen months (September 1924 to January 1926), and no mechanical renewals were found necessary. The manufacturers' publicity stressed the fact that on the final leg of the run—from the South Coast to London—the cars touched 45 m.p.h., but to me the most engaging facet of this exploit was that the metal roofs of the bodies could be removed, locked end to end and used as river craft, a function often suggested for the enormous detachable 'hard tops' supplied by Lancia with their contemporary 'Lambda'. It is hardly surprising after this that T. A. Grover chose Crossleys for his expedition to Nigeria and the Cameroons in 1926. It would be interesting to compare their story with that of the expedition which left England for Africa late in 1932 with a low-built sports Marendaz!

The introduction of the six-cylinder cars for the 1926 season really marks the end of the Golden Age of Crossley. The firm still had several years of apparent prosperity ahead of them, despite the persistence of the Willys-Overland dead wood, and it is not altogether fair to regard the Crossley 'Sixes' as degenerate. The makers might trumpet that four of their cylinders were as good as six of anyone else's, but the new 69 × 120 mm. (2,244 c.c.) 18/50 that appeared at the 1926 Show met with general favour; even S. C. H. Davis, who used one for a winter tour of Wales, talked of the 'silky

71

quality of a really good six'. Push-rod operated o.h.v. were used for
the first time on a Crossley, Perrot four-wheel brakes were fitted,
and right-hand change retained for the four-speed gearbox. A plate
clutch replaced the cone of four-cylinder days, this feature having
already appeared on the Fourteen, and two wheelbase lengths were
offered, the shorter one approximating to that of the superseded 19·6,
and the longer lending itself to limousine coachwork. Overall ratios
were lower, a 4·5 : 1 top being considered desirable even on the
tourer, which was listed at £676. Maximum speed was the same as
for the 'four' and braking vastly superior, while an example ran for
twenty-four hours over the Sitges circuit in Spain, averaging 48·5
m.p.h. A correspondent in *The Autocar* wrote to say that it had
caused him to forsake American cars: 'If there is anything better in
the motoring world at the price,' he went on, 'I have yet to meet it.'
A Dr Gorzo Nandor drove one into second place in the 3-litre class
of the Royal Hungarian Automobile Club's hill-climb in 1927.

The 18/50 was, however, underpowered, and for 1928 the bore
was enlarged to 75 mm., the result being the 3·2 litre 20·9 model,
which continued in the range in one form and another up to 1937.
In the middle of the 1928 season, this was joined by a new 65 × 100
mm. (1991 c.c.) 2-litre 'six' on very similar lines: characteristically,
it had a longish wheelbase of 10 ft. 3 in. and was listed at £495.

No major changes were made for 1929, the 2-litre and 20·9 h.p.
'Super Six' being the standard offerings. While right-hand change
and magneto ignition were still to be found on Crossleys, chromium
plate and spring-spoke steering wheels had been adopted, and for
£12 10s extra one could have one-shot chassis lubrication and safety
glass all round on one's car. That year, a 2-litre 'Shelsley' sports
tourer, listed at £625, was tried by *The Autocar*, revealing a surprisingly high maximum speed of 77 m.p.h., not to mention an overall
fuel consumption of 21 m.p.g. and a stopping distance of twenty-five
feet from 25 m.p.h. Less encouraging was the engine vibration, stem-
ming from the absence of a crankshaft damper, while no purist could
enthuse over the possible consequences of a 5 : 1 top gear on engine
life. It speaks volumes for the 2-litre that so many have survived.

There were no major changes in 1930, though in the Mont des
Mules hill-climb run in connexion with that year's Monte Carlo
Rally, Crossleys won first and second places in their class: the best
that the make could do in the Rally itself was thirty-eighth in
General Classification. Brainsby Woollard made a very pretty coachbuilt sportsman's coupé on this chassis, and a really hideous
armoured six-wheeler shooting-brake, sprayed in mottled khaki to

confuse the tigers, was completed by Barkers and shipped to a client in India. Henlys and Shrimptons, the joint Crossley distributors, held a Crossley week in May to drum up sales.

Round about this time, the late Maurice Sampson and F. Gordon-Crosby were touring British motor-car factories on behalf on *The Autocar*, and their comments on Crossley are illuminating. Despite the slump, Gorton does not seem to have been faring too badly, weekly production figures in May 1930 being estimated at thirty-five to fifty cars, by contrast with forty-five-odd in 1920 and rather less in 1925. Most of the cars seen at the works were 2-litres. It was noted that everything was made in the works, except castings other than in aluminium and brass. It was claimed that spares were available even for 1903 models—a remarkable feat, this, as I cannot find evidence that any cars had taken to the road in that year! Bodies were still made in the firm's own shops. The absence of conveyors was noted, chassis being built up on the floor of the assembly building, and bearings were still scraped by hand. Bus manufacture was, however, already looming large.

For 1931 the 15·7 and 20·9 appeared with twin-top four-speed gearboxes, under the attractive epithets of 'Silver' and 'Golden' Crossleys, while the 'Super Six' was continued as the 'Canberra' long-wheelbase limousine. These cars were still beautifully made, but had acquired central change, and the high waistline of the standard coachbuilt saloon bodies gave them a bulky look. Also in the range was a larger 78 × 120 mm. 'Six' installed in a six-wheeler chassis: an auxiliary gearbox gave an extra four speeds with a 15 : 1 top gear, but the car shown at Olympia in 1930 was strictly a luxury vehicle, with a Weymann-type fabric saloon body. Equipment included cigar lighters and a dictaphone, but no price was quoted.

This really marked the limit of the development of the big six-cylinder Crossleys. The 2-litre continued until 1934 and the 3-litre for another three years, but production dropped off sharply after 1932. Preselector gearboxes were added to the specification in 1934, when the 2-litre appeared with a very pretty Ranalah four-door sports saloon body, and a redesigned induction system which gave it 61 b.h.p. at 4,000 r.p.m. Though it was good for nearly 80 m.p.h. in this form, there were few takers at £695. The same sports engine was also offered in the standard 'Silver' Crossley, while in 1935 the 3-litre came out with a similar style of Ranalah body at £795. Restyled by Beauvais on the lines of the smaller 'Regis' models, it featured in the catalogue again in 1936 and 1937, but rumour had it that it was supplied only to V.I.P.s at Gorton.

73

Meanwhile, with what Crossley publicity described subsequently as 'cold courage', the decision had been taken to abandon private-car manufacture in favour of heavy goods and passenger vehicles. Whether this is the whole truth or not, their next step rendered it imperative. For 1932 saw a disaster, in the shape of the Crossley Ten.

With the introduction of this new low-priced model, the firm forsook their own power units in favour of the i.o.e. 63 × 90 mm. (1,122 c.c.) Coventry-Climax. This little engine was by no means impotent, developing 38 b.h.p. at 4,250 r.p.m., but I can find nothing else to commend the 10 h.p. cars. The styling of the "Torquay" and "Buxton" saloons of 1933/4 was not unpleasing, but the combination of too much weight, a 5.5 : 1 top gear, a preselector gearbox (adopted for the 1933 season) and Bendix brakes produced one of the most depressing pieces of machinery that has ever left a British factory. True, C. J. Joyce won an award for the best small-car performance in the 1932 R.A.C. Torquay Rally, and a Crossley Ten pulled off the Light Car Club of Australia's Rally Championship, but these were but straws in a wind that was not blowing in Gorton's favour.

In January 1932, it was announced that Vernon Balls, noted for his competition successes with Amilcars, had purchased three of these 10 h.p. cars and was modifying them for racing during the coming season. They duly appeared with cylinders linered down to 62·7 mm. bore to bring them into the 1,100 c.c. class, special valve gear incorporating two inlet valves per cylinder, aluminium pistons and a single down-draught S.U. carburetter, the standard coil ignition being retained. The frames were underslung, and a very attractive radiator was matched by a pleasing and functional two-seater body. They did not distinguish themselves. In the British Empire Trophy Race at Brooklands, one car non-started, and the other two were eliminated in the heats; and in the T.T. all retired, the least unsuccessful, Crowther's, lasting only 123 miles. More publicity was understandably given to the exploits of 'Connie', the 1912 15 h.p. saloon with which E. Hasel of Crossleys was competing in the big rallies. He came through the road section of the 1933 Scottish event without loss of marks!

Crossleys however, persevered with the 'Super Sports', and two cars—a two-seater and a very close-coupled four-door sports saloon—were at the 1932 Show. Fortunately they had second thoughts about putting it into production, though the two-seater prototype recently came to light in Cambridge.

In 1934, they acquired the manufacturing rights of Sir Dennis Burney's rear-engined design, production of which had just ceased at the Jam Factory. This was hardly a wise idea, and they received a share of the Maidenhead hoodoo for their pains. Using the Burney structure, with all-round independent suspension, Crossley added to this the mechanical components of the contemporary 2-litre, complete with Wilson preselector box, and put it on the market at £795. The aesthetic effect was ruined by the mounting of the proud old Crossley radiator on the nose. The ensuing complications involved the use of two separate tanks, front and rear, and as a consequence the cars suffered from overheating. They were said to be tricky to handle, while the practice of mounting the spare wheels in the doors made the opening and shutting of these very hard work. The battery lived under the vestigial front bonnet, and could only be removed, on its side, after several coach screws had been undone; yet this curious machine was quite fast, one former owner claiming a genuine 80 m.p.h. Just before the late war, Sir Dennis Burney bought one of these and started to experiment with it, with a view to bringing his design up to date, but the war killed this project, and the car in question ended up with a Vauxhall Twelve engine, the Crossley unit having reached the end of its useful life. Only about two dozen were made in all.

In 1933, Lagonda had come out with the 16/80 model, which used the 2-litre Crossley engine, arrangements being made, but not implemented, to manufacture the power units at Staines. This was perhaps the least-liked of the Lagonda models, and it did not survive that company's bankruptcy in 1935.

For all Crossley's talk of abandoning private-car manufacture, they made one last effort, with the 'Regis' range of 1935, for which they retained C. F. Beauvais to undertake the styling. Beauvais was one of the most accomplished 'packagers' of the nineteen-thirties: the cheaper British cars may have been devoid of any distinction, but by the time Beauvais had finished with them they could hold their own in *concours d'élegance* with the finest that the Paris *carrossiers* could offer. He had made his name with the famous 'waterfall' motif on the 'Kaye Don' Singers in 1931/2, and followed these up with the 1933 Avon Standards, pausing on the way to transform the undistinguished and spidery Coventry Victor three-wheeler into a smart little runabout. Even the dowdy Lanchester Ten emerged as a *concours* piece when cloaked in a Beauvais-designed Avon coupé body. For Crossley he designed two bodies—a four-door sports saloon and a sports tourer; prototypes were made by New Avon at

Warwick in 1934, but Crossley's own body shops at Gorton handled all production coachwork. For 1935 and subsequent cars, a double-drop frame was used, but the preselector gearbox and Bendix brakes remained as before. In addition to the 'Regis' model 10 h.p. cars, there was a 59 × 90 mm. (1,476 c.c.) 'Regis Six', also with i.o.e. Coventry-Climax engine. It could rev up to 5,000 r.p.m., but 66 m p.h. was its effective limit on a 5·3 : 1 top gear, and, to quote a contemporary road test report, 'the brakes do not come on with full power when the pedal is pressed'! The four-cylinder 'Regis' listed at £335, and the 'Six' at £365.

For all their numerous faults, quite a number of these cars were made; around 2,000 Tens leaving the works between 1932 and 1937, and perhaps 500 'Regis Sixes'. But few came off the lines in 1936, and fewer still in 1937: in the latter year, the *marque* had disappeared from the Motor Show.

Crossley continued with the manufacture of commercial vehicles, but after the second World War they concentrated on buses and trolley-buses alone. The move from Gorton to Errwood Park, Stockport, in 1947, broke the last link with the car-making days, and after 1951, when the firm became part of the A.C.V. group, even the buses lost their individuality, and were no more than A.E.C.s sold under another brand name. The announcement, in 1956, of the impending closure of the Crossley factory as an uneconomic unit passed almost unnoticed.

Crossley frittered away their existence in the nineteen-thirties by marketing a line of cars in direct competition with Riley and Triumph, and, unfortunately, inferior in every respect. Neither Riley nor Triumph came through the uneasy years unscathed, so it is hardly surprising that the Manchester firm gave up the unequal struggle. But if we go further back, we shall find that the big Crossleys never had a chance either, since their makers, like Arrol-Johnston, could not resist the exploration of any interesting avenue, however unprofitable. Their final 'Regis' phase was almost comic, the name itself suggesting some decayed seaside resort trying to arouse business by the evocation of former illustrious patronage. We are bound to accept the firm's own story that they committed deliberate *hara-kiri*, but by 1933 they can have had no choice. Let Cecil Bianchi sum up:

'They lost, in my opinion, through never having a sound sales policy, and their failure to get down to a competitive cost basis. The sales side always wanted to produce a car for each agent's requirements.'

76

CHAPTER 6

Rivets Down the Bonnet:
Invicta and Railton, 1925-50

'The accessory to which we take most exception is an engine revolution indicator, and we now make no provision for driving it. The information that it gives is of no value, except in case of clutch slip. . . . Many motorists seem to have the mistaken idea that a revolution indicator is more to be relied upon than a speedometer. . . . Nothing in the ordinary way is more harmful to a car than "seeing how far she will rev. up on second", and we urge our customers not to lay themselves open to this temptation by fitting an instrument whose indications would appear to be of no value at all.'

Invicta catalogue, 1927

'No expense or ingenuity has been spared in evolving this all-British product into a car which it is confidently believed will place British supremacy on both road and track beyond dispute. At the same time it introduces an innovation in that it is designed as to chassis and engine both as a sports car for use in international Reliability Trials or even touring work, and as a racing vehicle capable of competing on level terms in international Road and Track events, with any foreign car at present produced.'

Invicta 5-litre catalogue, 1932–3

THESE two quotations from the beautifully produced literature of Invicta Cars might in themselves form the Cobham firm's epitaph. The quiet dignity of phrase which stressed in 1927 the maker's intention to produce a touring car combining American flexibility with British design and workmanship was giving way in 1933 to an urge to build sports cars pure and simple. Originally laid down as a top-gear touring car, the Invicta grew more and more complicated, and in the end this complexity killed it. In its time it attracted at least four different sponsors, as well as fathering a whole race of sports-touring cars which sought to pursue the original Invicta ideals at lower first cost. In the hands of such drivers as Violet Cordery, Donald Healey and Raymond Mays, it won more than its share of international laurels, so much so that the famous and rare low-chassis $4\frac{1}{2}$-litre cars are now prized items for any discriminating American collector.

The story of the Invicta is largely the story of Captain (later Sir) Noel Macklin. Sir Noel's motoring career forms the least important part of his life, his major contribution to engineering being undoubtedly his work at Cobham, from 1940 onwards, on Fairmile gunboats, and later on prefabricated houses. But the seeds of both Invicta and Railton were sown in 1918, when he put on the market a small sporting car named the Eric-Campbell, after the second names of its two sponsors, Noel Campbell Macklin and Hugh Eric Orr-Ewing.

There was nothing particularly unconventional about this little vehicle, which had a 66 × 110 mm. (1,505 c.c.) Coventry-Simplex s.v. four-cylinder engine, a three-speed gearbox, and a leather cone clutch, mounted in a 7·1 h.p. Swift chassis frame of pre-war design. Pedal and lever alike operated internal expanding brakes on the rear wheels, and the car's sporting character was emphasized by its disc wheels and polished aluminium two-seater body with bulbous tail. A radiator of unmistakably Rolls-Royce aspect set off its attractive lines, and it listed at £395, though a year later this figure had been inflated to £525. Eric-Campbell production was undertaken for Macklin by Handley Page Ltd. at their aircraft works in Cricklewood, which were lying idle after wartime contracts for the V/1500—Britain's first four-engined bomber—had been cancelled.

The Eric-Campbell was only one of a whole host of 'assembled' light cars which were announced in the immediate post-Armistice years, but its sporting flavour was shared only by two other competitors—Hillman and Calthorpe—and its makers plunged wholeheartedly into a competition programme, which, understandably, had an adverse effect on the financial situation. In 1919, while the new design was as yet scarcely known to the public, two cars were entered in the 60–70 mm. bore class of the Targa Florio, and one, driven by Jack Scales, actually started. Preparations seem to have been of the sketchiest, since Scales had to rebuild his machine in a garage in Palermo just before the race, only to retire with a broken steering gear. One suspects further that the tough and brigand-ridden Sicilian event was selected for the machine's début simply because as yet few events were being run anywhere. The immediate upshot of this abortive venture was that the stroke of the Coventry-Simplex engine was reduced to 109·5 mm. to bring it within the new 1,500 c.c. class—it should be remembered that pre-1914 *voiturettes* ran to some 3 litres capacity, and would be looked upon as big cars nowadays!

By the time the Eric-Campbell design reappeared on the circuits, the competitive side of the business had been entirely divorced from the touring cars, and from the late spring of 1920, Macklin concentrated his efforts elsewhere. The Eric-Campbell, nevertheless, continued to do well in sundry events, 1920 successes including a Gold Medal in the Bath and West of England twenty-four-hour trial, three 'Golds' in the J.C.C.'s London–Manchester Trial, two class wins at Kop hill-climb, and 'Golds' again in both the 'London–Edinburgh' and the 'London–Land's End'. A Miss Kathleen Sprake set off on a 25,000-mile trip through Great Britain, France, Italy, Spain and North Africa, the results of which have eluded me; but in May 1920, one Violet Cordery won a 1,500 c.c. race for lady drivers at Brooklands.

However, financial difficulties occasioned by the earlier racing programme supervened, and in 1921 Wood and Lambert of Stamford Hill, later to be well known as Ford and Lincoln agents, were 'remaindering off' the unsold stock of cars at bargain prices. The Eric-Campbell subsequently passed into the hands of the Vulcan Iron and Metal works of Southall, who continued to make cars of largely similar design until January 1926, when a receiver was appointed. One of the minor mysteries is their possible connexion with Vulcan of Southport, since in 1922 they were marketing a 10 h.p. Vulcan, identical in almost every detail with the contemporary Eric-Campbell, but sporting an unmistakably Vulcan radiator. A special 1,352 c.c. o.h.c. Eric-Campbell was driven by H. J. C. Smith in the 1922 200-Mile Race at Brooklands, but retired; it was a non-starter in 1923. The Eric-Campbell remained quite popular to the end of its days, despite a noisy back axle, F. J. Eric Findon of *The Light Car* being an enthusiastic user.

In the meantime the workshops adjoining ·Macklin's home at Cobham, where the first racing Eric-Campbell had been evolved, had, as a result of the divorce of May 1920, become a separate entity manufacturing the Silver Hawk sports-racing car. It is a mistake, incidentally, to imagine that this little works stood on the site of the subsequent home of Invicta, Railton and the Fairmile patrol boat: 'Glengariff', Macklin's house, lay to the west of Cobham, towards Wisley, whereas the later cars were made on the Fairmile, on the London side of the village. The Silver Hawk was basically an Eric-Campbell, but the tuned 1,498 c.c. Coventry-Simplex engine had lightened con-rods, aluminium pistons and special crank and camshaft. The narrow chassis was crowned by a radiator of unmistakably Invicta shape, but as yet there were no rivets down the bonnet.

The Silver Hawk was evolved by Macklin strictly as a competition car—a brave effort in 1920, but also a sure way of stifling any hope of commercial success. Along with a G.N., the new *marque* represented Great Britain in the 1920 *Coupe Internationale des Voiturettes*: Gedge, René Thomas and Pickering were the drivers, and the first two did well to finish sixth and seventh in the face of opposition from the rapid Bugattis and despite overheating. Silver Hawks also successfully attacked records in the new 1,500 c.c. class at Brooklands, G. M. Harvey taking the standing mile at 61·53 m.p.h. in June 1920, while in October there was a three-cornered struggle for class records between Major Empson's A.V., the Crouch driven by J. Cocker, later of Clyno, and the Silver Hawk of Gedge and Violet Cordery. The Cobham-built car had the last word, and it is of interest to note that this was the first occasion on which a woman driver participated in a record attempt.

For the 1921 season, the 10/35 h.p. Silver Hawk chassis was a catalogued machine at £495, and there is a hint of future trends in the following advertisement:

'For sale, the actual G.P. car that took part in the race, guaranteed speed of over 70 m.p.h. on the road, can be driven from London to Edinburgh in top gear.'

Unfortunately, even the smallest and simplest of car factories cannot be run on a racing programme alone, and despite continuing hill-climb and sprint successes, the Silver Hawk Motor Co. was wound up later in 1921 after perhaps a dozen cars had been made.

In the meantime, the brothers Oliver (later Sir Oliver) and Philip Lyle, friends and neighbours of Macklin, were seeking an ideal motor car. Their great interest was top-gear performance, Oliver Lyle being of the opinion that he had changed gear perhaps a million times during his motoring career, and that 900,000 at least of these changes were unnecessary. As yet, however, he and his brother felt that a steam car was the only possible solution to this problem. So they and Macklin imported one of the very advanced Doble cars, with flash boiler, from America. The Doble went very well—present-day owners talk of 90 m.p.h. and instant starts from cold—but it was fiendishly complicated, and clearly not an economic solution for the ordinary motorist, however tractable it might be in the hands of an expert.

Philip Lyle's wife observed in conversation to Macklin that she was sure she would never be able to change gear again properly. 'Right,' Macklin replied. 'I'll build you a car on which you won't have to change gear.' So the Invicta was born. It is of interest to note

'Step on the pedal gently, my master': a 1926 Jowett short two-seater all set for a weekend in the country

F. W. Hutton-Stott's magnificent collection of Lanchesters.
1919 40 h.p., 1913 38 h.p., 1912 25 h.p., 1910

The spidery sports model Jowett, of which fifteen were turned out in 1928

From left to right: 1929 30 h.p., 1928 21 h.p., 1928 40 h.p.,
28 h.p., 1910 20 h.p., 1908 20 h.p., 1903 12 h.p.

The Becquart-Wilkins Jowett Jupiter on its way to achieving the firm's
hat-trick, Le Mans, 1952

Heavy metal: a 1919 Lanchester 40 h.p. saloon. There were only two doors

Military adaptation: a 38 h.p. Lanchester chassis for armoured cars, 1915

that one of the prerequisites was an ability to start on, and to climb, the steep and treacherous Guildford High Street in top gear.

With design assistance from W. G. J. Watson, an experimental vehicle was built up from proprietary parts—a 2-litre six-cylinder Coventry-Simplex engine and gearbox, Marles steering gear, a Moss rear axle, and Alford and Alder front-wheel brakes. These units were mounted in a Bayliss-Thomas frame, and proved highly successful on test.

It is conceivable that this car might have been evolved into the production Invicta, but disaster stepped in. The first batch of six chassis were left out on a cold night without any anti-freeze, and the engines were ruined.

The decision was then made to utilize a more powerful engine in the shape of a $2\frac{1}{2}$-litre (69 $\times$ 120 mm.), o.h.v. push-rod Meadows, which had a very high torque at low speed, and early in 1925 the Invicta was launched on the market at a chassis price of £594.

Throughout its career, the Cobham firm was strictly an assembly plant. Thompsons and later Rubery Owen made the frames, Meadows the engines, gearboxes came from Moss and E.N.V., the front axles from Alford and Alder, while bodywork was never the concern of Invicta. In early days they furnished their customers with a list of recommended coachbuilders, and only in their last years were 'standardized' bodies listed, the principal firms involved being Cadogan, Mulliner, Carbodies and Vanden Plas. Little was made in the factory except finned brake drums, spring brackets and cast aluminium dashboards.

The Invicta might be an assembled car, but it was also highly individualistic, and this individuality extended far beyond the square-cut radiator and the immortal 'rivets down the bonnet' which were to be inherited by the Railton in 1933. These, be it said, drew their inspiration from Rolls-Royce. It was always Invicta's aim to achieve a monopoly of their particular brand of six-cylinder Meadows engine, and this was largely achieved until the nineteen-thirties, since other Vintage users of the 3-litre unit—Whitlock and Hampton, for instance—were obscure, and enjoyed little currency. Close liaison was always maintained between Watson and Macklin at Cobham and Crump, the Meadows designer, and it is fair to say that the 3-litre and $4\frac{1}{2}$-litre engines were evolved by the Wolverhampton firm for Invicta. Lagondas did not start to use the latter unit until the end of 1933, when Invicta were on their last legs, and the subsequent marine and military adaptions did not appear in quantity until the later nineteen-thirties.

It is also worth remembering that J. G. Parry Thomas, who was always intolerant of mediocrity, served as design consultant to the firm until his tragic death in 1927, himself ran a 2½-litre two-seater, raced cars of the make at Brooklands, and was working on plans for a big racing version when he was killed.

There was nothing unconventional about the Invicta, except the manner in which it performed. Its merit is reflected in that the only noteworthy change of specification between its introduction and the adoption of the 4½-litre unit late in 1928 was the boring-out of the Meadows engine to 72·5 mm. in 1926, giving a capacity of 2,973 c.c. and an output of around 75 b.h.p. at 3,500 r.p.m. The sponsors' aims were stated fully in the 1927 catalogue as:

'The flexibility of the good American cars; the speed and road-holding of the best European sports cars; a delicacy of control not found on any other car; an unique top-gear performance; a long-lasting reliability which has in public competition never been equalled; absolutely certain and instantaneous engine starting at all temperatures; a service and guarantee which are the acme of generosity and despatch.'

A pretty tall order, this. In its original form, with stolid tourer body and artillery wheels, the Invicta looked ponderous, and proved capable of no more than 60 m.p.h. in the hands of *The Autocar*, but top gear would take the car from a standing start to 30 m.p.h. in nine seconds (only three seconds slower than the acceleration figure through the gears), while 1-in-6 hills such as Pebblecombe, White Downs and Netherhall Gardens could be negotiated without a downward change. The advantages of a powerful starter motor with adequate battery power were further extolled by the makers, who knew of an owner,

'. . . who ran out of petrol nearly two miles from home at 2 a.m. and who drove the car in on the self-starter in top gear except for a hill of 200 yards of 1 in 8, in which he had to come down to second.'

The rest of the Invicta virtues were demonstrated by the numerous and varied exploits of Miss Violet Cordery, which compensated amply for the lack of press advertising. Her first appearance at the wheel of an Invicta was at the West Kent Club's Brooklands meeting in July 1925, when she beat Oliver Lyle into first place in a half-mile scratch race, an event admirably suited to the Invicta's accelerative powers. 'The remainder of the field,' commented *The Autocar*, 'hardly got going.' The following year she led a team of six drivers who took one of the first 3-litres, with lightweight fabric four-seater body by Newns, to Monza for long-distance record work. They took the World's 10,000-Mile Record at 56·47 m.p.h. and the 15,000-Mile Record at 55·76 m.p.h., although operations had to be suspended for five days while Isotta-Fraschinis sportingly repaired damage incurred when one of the drivers fell asleep at the wheel during the long grind.

Not content with this, Miss Cordery and her team were out at Brooklands in July on a R.A.C.-supervised trial of five thousand miles' duration, completed at an average speed of more than 70 m.p.h. After a false start occasioned by trouble with the universal joints, the Invicta ran the whole distance trouble-free, the total time occupied by adjustments amounting to a fraction over two hours. The car used for these performances had the 'high' axle ratio of 3·6 : 1—the makers recommended 3·9 : 1 or 4·5 : 1 for normal customers—and weighed 19¾ cwt. dry. In recognition of this fact, the R.A.C. awarded Invictas the Dewar Trophy for the most outstanding motoring achievement of the year.

In 1927, the indefatigable Miss Cordery was off again, this time on a world tour in a virtually standard 3-litre tourer, accompanied by a mechanic, a trained nurse and an R.A.C. observer. No major modifications were deemed necessary, though this time a 4·5 : 1 rear axle was used, and the makers permitted an overload of seven cwt. 'beyond the point at which we disallow our guarantee'. A collapsible tent·was attached to the near side of the body, which was executed, as were many of Invicta's prettiest bodies, by Cadogan Motors. In five months the big car covered 10,266 road miles in Europe, Africa, India, Australia, the United States and Canada. The worst incident was an encounter with a runaway tram in Algiers, twenty-four covers and tubes were consumed, and the average running speed was 24·6 m.p.h. At this speed, Invictas were quick to point out, the engine was turning over at a mere 1,200 r.p.m., though it is doubtful if Miss Cordery could have stayed in top gear all the time!

Nor had this exploit exhausted the firm's ingenuity. In 1929, Miss Cordery, this time partnered by her sister Evelyn, brought the Dewar Trophy home to Cobham again by covering 30,000 miles in 30,000 minutes at Brooklands with a standard 4½-litre tourer, the overall average speed being 61.57 m.p.h., or, in Invicta parlance, something over 1,800 r.p.m. on top gear. Five hours were occupied in routine servicing, and the Invicta averaged 18·47 m.p.g. on petrol and 894 m.p.g. on oil, the latter figure excluding two changes. If anyone was still in doubt as to Invicta durability, this should have allayed their fears, while the car's amazing flexibility was demonstrated by a 'freak' performance by the same driver in 1930, when she drove from London to Monte Carlo and back in third gear, from London to John-o'-Groats and back in second, from London to Edinburgh and back in bottom, and eleven times round the eleven-mile R.A.C. traffic route in London on top. Miss Cordery (now Mrs Hindmarsh) recalls that she decided at the last moment not to cap this feat with a projected twenty-five-mile run round Brooklands in reverse. Fuel consumptions on these eccentric voyages ranged between 6 and 11 m.p.g., but the Invicta emerged intact.

Miss Cordery was undoubtedly an expert, but even the inexperienced could cope. A Mrs Connell of Claygate, who bought a 2½-litre coupé in 1926, drove from her home to Maidstone across distinctly hilly terrain in top gear, for a £5 wager. Her only anxious moment was provided by a blind cross-roads half way *down* Westerham Hill!

Invictas offered their customers a wide range of options—wheelbase lengths of 9 ft. 4 in. or 10 ft., large or medium-lock steering, central or right-hand change, a variety of axle ratios, ring or racing wheel-nuts, polished aluminium or black carmaloid instrument panels, and Solex or S.U. carburetters. They also issued firm recommendations, notably in respect of gear-change (they favoured a right-hand layout), the weight of bodywork (a nine-cwt. limit was imposed) and the choice of a gear ratio ('the effective gearing should be as LOW as is compatible with each individual's taste—not as HIGH as possible'). The Invicta handbook, for which Oliver Lyle was responsible, was a masterpiece of good typography and simplicity, its value being tested by setting a novice to undertake a variety of routine maintenance tasks with no aid other than the handsome, leather-bound work.

I have gone into the Invicta background in considerable detail because it is fascinating to look behind the scenes at a specialist manufacturer in the Vintage era, and to witness the personal approach to the customer. Invicta, to the end of their days, sold almost every car direct, and when the client called at Cobham, he met the men behind the car, and not just a sales staff. What is more important, the slightly didactic tone of Invicta sales literature was eminently forgivable, since the writer invariably assumed that the customer took a practical and intelligent interest in what he was buying. Magneto ignition gave way to the dual system in 1927, and Invictas devoted a long paragraph to explaining exactly why. In this year, be it noted, S. C. H. Davis took a 3-litre four-seater through the London–Exeter trial, and found that 70 m.p.h. and 25 m.p.g. were possible, while acceleration was up to the usual Invicta standards. Invictas were also made available with l.h.d. and one or two were shipped to America.

As yet the ideal of superb top-gear motoring was still being pursued, the four-speed gearbox being a concession to tastes shared by Macklin and a portion of the Invicta clientele alike. In the summer of 1928, a new 4½-litre (88·5 × 120 mm.) six-cylinder engine was evolved by Meadows for Invicta. This was very similar in general design to the earlier units, and in standard form, with a four-speed gearbox and 3·5 : 1 top gear, it propelled the car at about 85 m.p.h. A tourer tested in 1928 had the higher (3·6 : 1) ratio, weighed 28½ cwt., and proved capable of over 90, with 75 m.p.h. available on third for those who preferred to use it as a sports car. It toured up Pebblecombe on top, while the brakes 'gave results superior to those which it is theoretically regarded as impossible to attain.' This may sound a trifle dramatic, but the ability to pull up dead from 50 m.p.h. in ninety-seven feet was still a performance not to be sneered at in 1960.

A stiffer and deeper frame with big cross-members was adopted in the summer of 1929, the suspension and front axle also coming in for attention. For 1930 production was centred solely on the 4½-litre model, which also acquired a 'conventional' gear gate, with third and top on the off'side. Chassis price was £1,050, and a massive but well-proportioned tourer cost £1,475. Donald Healey took Violet Cordery's Dewar Trophy car through the 1930 Austrian Alpine Trial and won his class, being beaten in the Josefsberg hill-climb only by an Austro-Daimler, and making fastest time of all on the Arlberg.

Drastic price revisions were the order of the day in 1931, when a Mulliner semi-panelled four-door saloon was standardized on the 4½-litre chassis at only £765. But in the meantime Watson had evolved a very exciting sports car in the shape of the low-chassis '100 m.p.h.' machine. The chassis was underslung at the rear, wheelbase being 9 ft. 10 in. as against the high-chassis car's 10 ft. 6 in. Like the touring version, it had twin S.U.s with an auxiliary starting carburetter, but the 'high-ratio' box was used, a hand-operated pressure feed replaced the Autovac of the standard versions, and the radiator was lowered, the four-seater standing only forty inches from the ground. Chassis price was £750, a tourer costing £875, for which the customer got 95 m.p.h. with the 'ton' available under favourable circumstances.

These cars have now become a part of motoring legend, and remain controversial to this day. It has been said that the low centre of gravity gave excellent cornering only at the price of a sudden and dangerous breakaway, and S. C. H. Davis's heavily publicized accident at the Brooklands Easter Meeting in 1931 did nothing to help sales. Having seen Invictas perform with abandon in the rain at Prescott, I am inclined to wonder if this failing has been exaggerated.

In three brief years, the low-chassis cars accumulated a fine crop of competition successes: Donald Healey won the 1931 Monte Carlo Rally outright, and was placed second in 1932. In both years Invictas ran in the Alpine Trial, bringing home one of the coveted *Coupes des Glaciers* in 1931, while all three cars entered were successful in 1932. In England Raymond Mays, who had been using a similar car to test India tyres, turned in some impressive performances at Shelsley Walsh, Skegness and Brooklands. His best Shelsley performance was a climb in 45·6 seconds in September 1932, when he broke the sports-car record, and this was followed very shortly afterwards by second place in the Brooklands Mountain Championship, behind Sir Malcolm Campbell's 4-litre vee-twelve Sunbeam. It must be admitted that Mays had the full co-operation of Mr Crump and Meadows, and that his engine was giving some 158 b.h.p. at 3,900 r.p.m., but he recalls that the Invicta ran through two seasons with complete reliability. Even today the low-chassis 4½-litre cars are still seen at Vintage events, and J. A. Shutler's coupé has climbed Prescott in just over fifty-two seconds.

The firm's Brooklands efforts were generally less auspicious. Nothing came of the experimental 1925 car with 3-litre o.h.c. F.A.S.T. four-cylinder engine, the Italian unit's lack of low-speed torque rendering it useless in an Invicta, and Froy's 'Bluebird'-styled single-seater 4½-litre crashed in practice for the 1932 500-Mile Race; while the two low-chassis cars entered for the 1933 race also failed. None the less the car's reputation rose out of all proportion to the number built, which has always been somewhat of a mystery.

Previously published estimates have suggested a total production of seventy-seven low-chassis cars, and this figure has been based on the serial numbers issued. One or two serials, however, seem to have been missed out, and, out of a total of about 1,000 Invictas made between 1925 and 1935, only fifty-odd were of the '100 m.p.h.' type. Of these, perhaps thirty were made at Cobham, a dozen were assembled at Chelsea after the reorganization in 1933, and the remainder were assembled under contract by the Beverley-Barnes firm—who were evidently glad to have something to do at a time when work on their own straight-eights had come to a standstill. Donald Monro has identified nearly fifty individual examples, and J. A. Shutler knows of over thirty in existence at the time of writing.

For the 1932 season Invicta, like Crossley, decided to beat the slump by introducing a small car, though in the interests of flexibility they gave it six cylinders. It had a single o.h.c. unit of 57 × 97·9 mm. (1,498 c.c.), the prototype's 52 mm. bore being enlarged in the interests of more brake horsepower. This was mated to a 'silent third' four-speed gearbox. The engine was made at Bookham by Gillett and Stevens, who also handled the series production of Blackburne engines. As the 1½-litre unit's designer was H. J. Hatch of Blackburne, later responsible for the Brough Superior 'Golden Dream' motor cycle, it is hardly surprising that the little Invicta engine is often referred to as a Blackburne. It was good for 5,000 r.p.m., but unfortunately this attractive power plant was mounted in a scaled-down 4½-litre chassis, necessitating a top-gear ratio of 6 : 1. The traditional flexibility was undoubtedly there, but brisk road performance was obtainable only by dint of brutal use of the gearbox. The 'small Invicta' also had a disconcerting thirst for oil after the first 20,000 miles or so. Saloon or tourer models, with coachwork by Carbodies, cost £399; and in 1933 a supercharged variant, the '12/90', joined the range. This would comfortably exceed 70 m.p.h. and about half a dozen were made. The Wilson preselector gearbox was standard on this model, the saloon was priced at £575, and the unblown 12/45 cars were also available with preselection in place of the normal central-change box for £15 extra.

For the 1933 season, also, a last attempt was made to produce three exciting super-sports models with twin-overhead camshaft supercharged six-cylinder engines, five-speed Wilson preselector gearboxes and hydraulic brakes, but despite financial negotiations between Humphrey Cook, Raymond Mays and the Invicta management, these came to naught. Neither the 5-litre Meadows-engined car, which featured in the 1933 catalogue at £2,250, nor the 1,660 c.c. 14/120 based on the 12/45 was ever built, but a polished chassis of the 1½-litre 12/100, complete with raked radiator *à la* Maserati, was on the Invicta stand at the 1932 Show. It never ran in its original form, and when it took the road two years later, it was registered as an F.M., was powered by a supercharged 2-litre Lagonda engine, and was cloaked with a foursome drophead coupé body. This chassis still exists, but the last known engine was a Mercury V-8.

Invictas were nearly through. Macklin's interest in competitions, plus the adverse effect of the slump, had defeated them, and in the summer of 1933 the company was taken over by Earl Fitzwilliam, who for some time had been running the London sales end of the concern. All production ceased at Cobham, but for the next two years a handful of cars, all 4½-litres in high and low-chassis forms, were assembled at the official service station in Chelsea, which also undertook work under contract for the British concessionares of Delage and Hotchkiss cars. Another obituary notice was surely indicated.

Meanwhile, however, the trumpet horns of America had been blowing. The Depression had made heavy inroads into Detroit's home and export sales alike, but it had also spurred transatlantic manufacturers to discard such unpleasantnesses as fixed wooden wheels and grim, tasteless styling. Among the leaders of the new look in America were Hudson Motors, who had done good business in Britain in the nineteen-twenties with their cheap line, the Essex.

While the Hudson 'Super Six' was a car of some performance, particularly in its later form with i.o.e. engine, the Essex was a dreary affair, even if its bilious blue paintwork did add a splash of colour to the breakers' yards of the nineteen-thirties. In 1932, however, Essex had come out with the 2½-litre six-cylinder 'Terraplane'—the name, be it said, was dog-Latin for 'land-flying' and was not intended to convey the impression accorded to passengers! Handling apart, it was fast, light on petrol, and listed at under £300, while its R.A.C. rating of 16·9 h.p. kept the annual tax within reasonable proportions. The companion Hudson model, the 'Pacemaker', was a 4·2 litre s.v. straight-eight and altogether a pleasanter car, which made a considerable impression by winning the premier award in the 1932 Scottish Rally. By 1933, the company was offering three Essex models—the 'Terraplane Six', a 20·7 h.p. 'big six' and a 27·6 'straight-Eight', plus the Hudson 'Pacemaker'.

At Cobham, Macklin and L. A. Cushman found themselves with a factory and nothing to do. The Invicta had failed because it represented too costly a compromise between top-gear performance and the sports-car virtues. The Hudson was cheap, it possessed fine top-gear acceleration, and was established in public favour. Its worst faults, in the eyes of the discriminating motorist, were its unashamedly transatlantic appearance and its unendearing handling qualities. Why not, therefore anglicize the Hudson, and give the Invicta customers all the traditional Invicta characteristics at a fraction of the price, allied to cheap and readily available spares and servicing facilities?

Work on the rehashed Hudson started almost before Invicta production had ceased, and the first car was on the road in July 1933. The modifications were the work of Reid Railton, sometime assistant to J. G. Parry Thomas in his Leyland days and a director of the famous tuning establishment of Thomson and Taylor. Railton had specialized in record-breaking cars, having re-designed Sir Malcolm Campbell's 'Bluebird' in 1932 and built the famous Napier-Railton track car for John Cobb in 1933. His Railton Mobil Special, also evolved for Cobb in 1938, raised the World's Land Speed Record to 394 m.p.h. Railton's modifications to the original Hudson were quite simple, consisting of a lowered frame, the stiffening of the suspension, and the provision of Lucas electrical equipment. Both the six-volt system and the Hudson's splash lubrication were retained, though the rivets on the bonnet commemorated the connexion with Invicta, and a special, 'aircraft-type' radiator was fitted, distinguishable from that of the Invicta by a pronounced vee.

Very little actual work on these cars was done at Cobham. The chassis was delivered, complete but unmodified, by road from the Hudson works near the present-day Chiswick Flyover, body-work was made by outside firms—chiefly R.E.A.L. of Ealing and Coachcraft of Hanwell, the body-building subsidiary of University Motors, the London distributors—while Hudsons undertook all servicing of Railton 'products'. It was rudely said that all the Cobham works did was to knock the rivets in! But the Railton worked—and it sold.

It is not generally realized that the original Railtons did not have the famous Hudson Eight engine. This was not adopted until well into 1934, the first machines having the 4,010 c.c. eight-cylinder Essex engine, hence the clumsy name 'Essex-Railton-Terraplane', to be found in early press releases. Whatever its faults, the Railton out-Invicta'd the Invicta. The sponsors countered the railway companies' publicity by asserting that it was 'quickest by Railton', and S. C. H. Davis informed readers of *The Autocar* that it was 'ten years ahead of its time'. It was strictly a top-gear car, which more than compensated for the unpleasing gear-change. Early cars had a large, nearly vertical lever, while the later machines sported an awkward central remote-control, necessitated by the adoption of

a column shift on the corresponding Hudson model in 1937. But a
tourer turned the scales at little over a ton, and with 113 b.h.p.
available at 3,800 r.p.m. top speeds of 90 m.p.h. were allied to
staggering acceleration figures for the period—as witness the ability
to reach 50 m.p.h. from a standing start in seven seconds recorded
by *The Autocar* in August 1934, on a strictly stock open tourer costing
£535. 'The Scribe', writing in the same journal a year earlier, had
given these impressions of a Railton in London:

'It glides away into the street, accelerates round a lorry, slows to a walking
pace, accelerates to 50, slows to 10, accelerates to 40, slows, stops, gets
away again without effort, accelerates to about 50, slows to 10, sweeps
round a taxi at 40 . . . until London is left behind, all in complete silence,
and without having touched a gear lever—all in top gear.'

. . . and all before the days of the 30 m.p.h. speed limit, too.

I recently tried a rather tired 1938 Railton to see whether it was
really as exciting as all that. The one I handled would not make
an easy getaway in top gear, but after the first few yards direct
drive could be engaged as a matter of course, and the acceleration
gave me a 'kick-in-the-back' feeling I have not often met on a
pre-war car outside the super-sports class. The brakes were conspicuous by their absence, but the amazing flexibility remained,
minus any of those irritating up-and-down jerks which one senses
with all but the best of today's automatic transmissions.

The cornering was surprisingly good.

The Railton was the first of the 'Anglo-American sports bastards'.
I do not propose to join in the controversy as to whether it is a
Post-Vintage Thoroughbred or not, but its success can best be gauged
by the number of imitators it attracted. Of these, the Brough
Superior used the same Hudson engine, though their biggest model
had the twelve-cylinder Lincoln-Zephyr, a unit favoured also by
the all-independently-sprung 4·3-litre Atalanta and some of the
trials-type Allards. Jensen turned out cars with eight-cylinder Ford
and Nash engines, while my cousin, Lord Avebury, broke new
ground by anglicizing the comparatively rare 3½-litre supercharged
Graham 'Cavalier' in 1937. The result, known as a Lammas, was
short-lived and looked like an overgrown Jaguar, but its designer
ran one at Brooklands with quite fair success, and several members
of our family had excellent service out of these cars, one of which
was only sold after twenty years.

Railtons were tested at Brooklands, and did quite well in events
where their standing-start acceleration was at a premium, such as

sprints. S. C. H. Davis drove one in the 1935 Monte Carlo Rally, and versions of the later 'Sandown' saloon were used by the Metropolitan Police, as well as some provincial forces. These were only slightly tuned, I understand, and Scotland Yard's cars were still in service as late as 1948.

In 1935, Hudsons abandoned their 'Axle Flex' independent front suspension in favour of semi-elliptics, and the Railton followed suit, the 4,168 c.c. Hudson unit having been adopted the previous season. Prices ranged from £553 for a tourer to £687 for the luxurious 'University' sports saloon. During the season there also came the fabulous 'Light Sports', a sketchily-bodied four-seater which put even the touring Railton in the shade. The standing-start-to-50 acceleration figure was still seven seconds, but this model would accelerate to 60 in just under ten seconds. Maximum speed was 98·9 m.p.h., a surprising and useful 75 m.p.h. being available on second. The car ascended the Brooklands Test Hill at 29·29 m.p.h., leaping into the air at the summit, though, be it noted, this is not the fastest ascent recorded: R. G. J. Nash took a Frazer-Nash up at 32·44 m.p.h. in 1932. The Railton's speed would be commonplace today, but it is interesting to note that by comparison, two of the fastest cars of 1950–1—the Jaguar XK120 and the Cadillac-powered J.2 Allard—needed 7·3 and 5·9 seconds respectively to reach 50 m.p.h.

Up to the outbreak of war, the Railton remained an above-average performer and excellent value for money. The weight of a standard saloon in 1935 was twenty-five cwt.; the corresponding 'Cobham' model of 1937–38 was two cwt. heavier, and Railtons found it necessary to offer a lighter and cheaper closed style, the 'Sandown' at £538, as against the £688 asked for the razor-edged 'Cobham'. For 1936, Hudson raised their engine output to 124 b.h.p. other improvements this year being the provision of 12-volt electrics and Hudson's 'double-safe' hydraulic brakes in place of the previous Bendix system. There was also a new 'University' limousine on a long (10 ft. 7 in.) chassis at £895; most Railton customers, however, preferred to do their own driving.

No tourers were made after 1937 except to special order, but in the last two pre-war years an attempt was made to widen the range by bringing out Railton variants of other Hudson models. The first step in this direction was taken in 1938 with a 16·9 h.p. (2,723 c.c.) version based on the contemporary Hudson 112. A 'Sandown' saloon cost £399, and a 'Claremont' foursome drop-head coupé was available at £458. Performance was unspectacular.

A 3,255 c.c. six-cylinder 21·6 appeared at the 1938 Earls Court Show, but only a handful of this type was produced before the outbreak of the second World War.

Meanwhile, a 'baby' Railton had been introduced in 1938. It is said that this was designed by Macklin for his daughters, to replace their FIAT 'Topolinos'. These new 10 h.p. cars were miniature versions of the 'Cobham' saloon and 'Fairmile' drophead coupé, mounted on a virtually unmodified Standard 'Flying Ten' chassis, Bendix brakes and all. The price was £299.

With war imminent, Macklin and Cushman decided to switch to marine work, and thus was born the highly successful Fairmile Construction Co. Early in 1940, Railton Cars disposed of the manufacturing rights of the Railton, plus a number of uncompleted chassis, to Hudson Motors Ltd. In the six years preceding the outbreak of war, 1,425 Hudson-Railtons and fifty Standard-based Tens had been turned out.

Invicta, meanwhile, had been creaking painfully on. Most devotees of the *marque* prefer to forget the Chelsea phase from 1933 to 1938, when servicing and spasmodic assembly were carried on at the Alpha Place depot, now occupied by the London Electricity Board. The last true Invicta left the works in 1935, but various rumours concerning the company's future were in circulation. In September 1936, it was reported that Watson was designing a new Invicta, while Delage, for whose concessionaires, J. Smith and Co., Invicta Cars undertook servicing work, were said to be laying plans to build their D.670 six-cylinder model in a works at Slough. Nothing came of this, except that Smiths closed down and University Motors, who were already London distributors for the Railton, took over the Delage agency.

In October 1937, it was announced that 'Invicta Cars have made arrangements to sell, and later build, a range of cars based on a well-known Continental make', and drawings accompanying this report showed side elevations of a vehicle closely akin to the D.670 Delage. Technical specifications, however, revealed an affinity with the Lago-designed Darracq, in 2½-litre and 4-litre six-cylinder forms, with transverse leaf i.f.s. and Bendix brakes, the only deviation being the adoption of a synchromesh box in place of the Darracq's accustomed Wilson-type. As a few days later a Darracq service depot was opened in Kilburn, the situation was more than a little confusing!

The firm met more financial difficulties before any headway was made, and only one car took the road. Michael Sedgwick, former Curator of my Museum, who has seen it, describes it as 'like a Delage with an Invicta Black Prince radiator', but Tom Rotheram, the former manager of the Chelsea works, assures me that it was in fact a 2½-litre Lago-Darracq under the skin. After the failure of the Chelsea Company, Nash Concessionaires Ltd. took over the works and dumped all the surviving stock of Invicta spares in the attic of their main premises in Somers Town, where they reposed until they were sold for scrap in 1951. John Ahern, the well-known Invicta enthusiast, has described the scene to me: heaps of parts all over the floor, crown wheels, pinions, axle shafts, even the illuminated sign that used to adorn the outside of the Alpha place premises. Customers climbed up, nursed the desired part down the rickety ladder, and then negotiated with the custodian, 'large bits' being charged at ten shillings each, and small ones at half the price. Several Invictas owe their survival to this curious Cave of Ali Baba.

In the immediate period of post-war optimism, the Invicta made one last spectacular appearance. It had moved back to Surrey to works at Virginia Water, but there were two links with the past, for Watson was again the designer, and he had retained Sir Oliver Lyle's old ideal of dispensing with needless gear-changes. Watson, in fact, had gone even further and dispensed with a gearbox altogether.

What emerged was a staggering piece of machinery. At first sight it looked to be just another expensive motor car, but under the surface there was practically nothing conventional about it. The engine was a 3-litre (81 × 97 mm.) twin-overhead camshaft six-cylinder of Meadows manufacture, with dual coil ignition, a twelve-plug head and triple S.U. carburetters fed by twin S.U. electric pumps. It developed 120 b.h.p. at 5,000 r.p.m. and probably needed to, thanks to the odd transmission and its consequent power losses. Brakes were Girling hydraulic, Bishop cam steering was used, and all four wheels were independently sprung by torsion bars. A complete car was said to weigh thirty-five cwt., and the chassis incorporated a platform on which the seats were directly mounted. Equipment was comprehensive, and included a built-in trickle charger for the batteries (probably desirable, with twenty-four-volt starting), an electric immersion heater to keep the oil and water at normal running temperatures, a Smiths car heater, built-in jacks and a radio. In lieu of a gearbox there was a Brockhouse 'hydro-kinetic turbo-transmitter', which offered an infinite variety of ratios ranging from 4·27 : 1 to 15 : 1. The sole control for this device was a simple forward-and-reverse switch. In all this mechanical complexity the absence of the traditional rivets passed unnoticed!

The worst snag about all this was that it was dreadfully expensive; even in 1946, while purchase tax was still confined within reasonable bounds, the car listed at £2,939, and the only example of the new 'Black Prince' running was the prototype saloon, KPK 75. Endless difficulties beset the firm: despite the fact that rumours spoke of £100,000 invested in the project, the company was always short of cash; Charlesworth, who were to have made the bodies, closed down; and the pawl operation of the reverse gear seldom worked for long. A coupé was displayed at the 1947 Paris Show, but the first production cars did not appear until July 1948, by which time the imposition of double purchase tax had caused the price to soar into cloud-cuckoo land, at £3,890. Altogether about twenty cars were made; the 'Byfleet' drophead coupé, which was the company's nearest approach to a standard production, was bodied by Airflow Streamlines of Northampton, Jensen being responsible for most of the other coachwork.

In the event it was not Invicta who upheld the traditions of Cobham at Britain's first post-war Motor Show in 1948, but Railton. Hudson Motors had long been toying with the idea of reintroducing this *marque* as a customized version of the Hudson Eight, and fourteen cars had been turned out in the first three years of peace. The last one appeared at Earls Court, tucked away unobtrusively on the stand of University Coachworks. It was basically the 1939 'Fairmile' drophead coupé with the latest 'Powerdome' version of the faithful old 4,168 c.c. engine, and a steering column gear-change. It was unpriced, but I understand that the original owner had to part with £4,750—nearly £1,000 more than was asked for the unsaleable Invicta. The dollar crisis had priced the Railton right out of any possible market for good.

Down at Virginia Water, the Invicta Car Development Co. Ltd. struggled on in the face of schemes of arrangement and moratoria for another twelve months. Watson was already planning the abandonment of the complex Brockhouse turbo-transmitter in favour of a four-speed synchromesh box, but in February 1950, the company was finally wound up. The goodwill and stock of unfinished cars were taken over by A. F. N. Ltd., who found plenty of evidence of unrealistic buying of components, though the handsome 'Black Prince' mascots were conspicuous by their absence. These were evidently bought one by one. Several of the surviving 'Black Princes', be it noted, have since acquired four-speed Jaguar gearboxes; evidently the owners had recognized the need for reverse on occasion!

Lack of capital, purchase tax and the complexities of a revolutionary design killed the 'Black Prince', and the dollar crisis swept the Railton away. Of the personnel of the old companies, Cushman went on to Fairmile Construction, in company with Gladys Starkey (now Mrs Messenger) who had been Macklin's secretary since the earliest Invicta days, and whose financial acumen did more than anything else to assure the survival first of Invictas, and then of the wartime marine venture. Sir Noel himself died shortly after the second World War, but his son Lance carried on the family tradition for high performance motor cars across the Channel with the Facel-Vega, a 140 m.p.h. saloon powered, like the Railton, by an American engine. Watson went to Jaguar, and Reid Railton went to the U.S.A., where, I believe, he had a hand in the design of the revolutionary 'step-down' Hudson of 1948, which kept the Detroit firm going until 1953. And then, by a strange coincidence, Hudson, the progenitor of the Railton, amalgamated with Nash, whose English agents were the final heirs of the old Invicta company.

It is hard to imagine the Invicta surviving today. It was built by a group of individualists for their own amusement, and their infectious enthusiasm communicated itself to a wide circle of friends whose tastes were similar. The Invicta's proud, foursquare bonnet with its rivets, its superb finish, and the dignity with which its sponsors presented it to the world all belong to a period which has gone. The Invicta is a period piece, and as such it should be remembered.

CHAPTER 7

Jowett:
The Clock that Lost its Contentment

'Jowetts never wear out; they are left to the next-of-kin.'
Jowett catalogue, 1934

'Take a good look as it passes you.'
Jowett slogan, 1950

ONE of our more enlightened motoring writers once described the old flat-twin Jowett engine as 'bleating like a contented clock at cruising speed', and the phrase somehow sums up this tough little Northerner—no nonsense, no frills, and almost indestructible. Yet a friend of mine, when recounting the prowess of his over-tuned Continental small car, would boast in the early nineteen-fifties that he had 'held a Javelin from Slough to Chiswick, and the fellow was trying, too'. The Jowett, in fact, went through a sea-change in its long life, from the crudely utilitarian to international leadership in its class. In so doing it killed itself, but it left behind it a long trail of mourners: as I write, it is a good six years since the last new car left the works at Bradford, but still one hears cries of 'Why couldn't they have revived the "Javelin"?' or 'my Bradford would have made mincemeat of the job'. Unlike Lanchester, that pale ghost departing to the music of the fluid flywheel, Lea-Francis, crushed under the burden of purchase tax, or the Wolverhampton brigade sinking in the 1930 Depression, the Jowett died in the full flower of outward success. The mechanical failings that had dogged its post-war productions were conquered, and even after five years on the market, it was still in many ways ahead of its time. Probably alone of all makes, it had transformed itself from a regional eccentricity into the sort of car that was driven by the knowledgeable motorist, and talked about in pubs.

The brothers Benjamin and William Jowett were the sons of an expert on gas engines. They started in a very modest way with a small workshop, eighteen feet square, in Manningham Lane, Bradford, at the turn of the century. Their capital was £90: £30 put up by each brother and the remainder by one of their sisters, and at first they undertook cycle repairs, making a few machines for their friends. In 1901 they built a small water-cooled vee-twin engine designed as a replacement unit for the then-popular 6 h.p. De Dion and 6½ h.p. Aster 'singles', and quite a few found their way into cars. So durable were these engines that the Jowetts were able to report in 1914 that three were still in service: one working a sawmill, one driving garage machinery, and a third operating a potato machine. Three years later they branched out with a three-cylinder in-line 950 c.c. o.h.v. unit, but this was not developed, as in 1906 the manufacture of Alfred Angas Scott's first production batch of two-stroke motor cycles was undertaken.

The Scott-Jowett association was not a particularly happy or easy one, for Scott had the difficult habit of altering designs overnight. To cap everything, he disclaimed all responsibility for the machines as soon as the first half-dozen were completed, leaving the Jowett brothers to dispose of them as best as they could.

The Jowetts meanwhile, had installed their three-cylinder engine in what later publicity called a 'gearboxless car' —it is amusing to note that this unit was still in service in 1939, driving a compressor at the factory. Concurrently with the Scott experiments, the little company was playing with a two-stroke flat-twin of its own. This was not a success, but it did not deter the Jowetts in their objective: the evolution of a small car capable of operating at a penny a mile. From 1906 to 1910 they experimented, the end-product being the basis of the Jowett car as it was known to private motorists of the nineteen-twenties and nineteen-thirties, and to commercial operators right up to 1953; the last survivor from Edwardian days.

The first true Jowett car, made in the brothers' new factory at Grosvenor Road, Bradford, was a side-valve flat-twin with three-speed unit gearbox and central gate-change. Final drive was by worm. The leather cone clutch was conventional wear for the period, rear suspension was three-quarter elliptic, and the fixed wire wheels gave the car a spidery look accentuated by the very short wheelbase of six feet. The engine was good for 2,750 r.p.m., the 4·5 : 1 top gear giving 17½ m.p.h. per thousand revs. An archaic note was struck by the use of side lever steering in the Lanchester style, while the armoured wood frame was also already old-fashioned. An ingenious feature was the use of the fixed, front-mounted starting handle as a crankcase breather, but neither brakes nor steering could be counted among the Jowett's strong suits. The hand lever actuated external-contracting drums on the rear wheels, while the footbrake worked on the transmission. On Edwardian and early Vintage machines, both this latter and the clutch were lined with asbestos string, and the late J. J. Hall, that great motor cyclist, claimed that he could reline the footbrake of his Jowett by the roadside, in a few minutes, at the cost of five shillings! Another unendearing feature was the inaccessibility of the flat-twin engine. Until the adoption of detachable cylinder heads in 1929, the engine was attached to the frame by lugs on the heads, and had to be turned *in situ* before decarbonization could be carried out. The problem of accessibility always dogged Jowett design, the early four-cylinder cars being notorious offenders, though this failing was probably overstressed by the machine's detractors. Some engines, however, were more than a little vulnerable to flood conditions.

The little cars slowly and unobtrusively improved immediately before and during the war years, the price in 1914 being £152 5s. A conventional bevel replaced the worm drive, while in 1916 Sankey steel detachable wheels were introduced. But the Jowett was still a rare sight outside its native Yorkshire, and as late as August 1923, *The Autocar* published the following prize specimen of Southern superciliousness:

'Somewhere about ten years ago there began to filter down to the South strange tales from Bradford of a car of infinitesimally small engine size, but astounding power and longevity.'

Not that this worried the Jowetts, whose advertising department turned the snobbery of London to good account. A typical Olympia-time advertisement would be headed 'Oop for t'Show', and would discourse unself-consciously on the divergences of Northern and Southern accents. It was the kind of advertisement you had to read and it unquestionably helped to sell the cars. While others were secretly ashamed of their provincialism, the Jowett was proud of its background, and there is no doubt that the presence of Yorkshire moorland in the Idle factory's back garden provided the firm with a testing-ground second to none. In 1921, Willie Jowett loaded three people into a standard two-seater and proceeded to ascend the factory test hill, which had a gradient varying between 1 in 2½ and 1 in 4, at an average speed of 18 m.p.h.

The Jowett reappeared on the scene in 1916 form shortly after the war, priced at £395, its first Show appearance being at Glasgow in February 1921. By May of that year, the price was down to £300, and the cars powered by 'The Little Engine with the Big Pull' were beginning to make their mark in trials. At Rosedale Abbey, the following April, a Jowett was second in the car class behind no less than Captain Frazer-Nash himself, in one of his very potent G.N.s,

who supplied Jowett, they were always notorious gasket-blowers, and of the fifteen made, perhaps not all were sold. Curiously enough, these and the other sports Jowetts evolved by Jackson and later by Lovatt have all disappeared, though occasionally one will encounter one of the unfortunately-named 1935 'Weasel' twin-carburetter sports tourers.

By 1929, production was up to eighty-five cars a week despite the onset of the Depression. After years of experimentation by Benjamin Jowett, who had toyed unsuccessfully at one stage with external contracting bands, a system of internal expanding f.w.b. was adopted. Another development was the introduction of the fabric body, which, incidentally, had a longer vogue at Idle than almost anywhere else, short and long fabric saloons still being available in 1933. The Jowetts, with a good eye for colour, used a contrasting shade —either red, green, yellow or brown—for the wheels and carried this embellishment also to the body beading and steering-wheel rims. The cars were also modernized in mechanical specification under the eye of S. C. Poole, formerly of Singer.

Mr Poole made extensive alterations to engine and chassis alike over the next few years. A stiffer and wider frame was used, with a stronger rear axle casing. The new Poole-designed engine had chain-driven timing gear and a new type of camshaft operating the tappets direct, thus eliminating the old bell-crank rockers. The cylinders had deeper water-jackets, and detachable heads were standardized in 1929. The three-speed gearbox acquired a central ball-change in 1930, and twelve-volt electrics were added in 1933, though the vans continued to use six-volt equipment.

In 1929, rumours of a four-cylinder car began to circulate, but were quickly scotched. Nor did Jowett's attempt at a £100 car, in the shape of a one-door short-chassis 'chummy', quite make it, though the price was cut to 105 guineas. Below this the Jowett brothers would not go, refusing to skimp quality, but even then it was cheaper than Clyno's 'Century' model at £112 10s. These ultra-cheap models, incidentally, never did more than boost the sales of the more luxurious variants in the range, and it is very doubtful if the field-grey two-seater with which Morris eventually attained the ideal of the '£100 car' in 1931 ever sold as well as the *de luxe* 'Minors'.

A disastrous fire in September 1930 knocked the works out of action only a month before the Olympia Show. Somehow a few new saloons, which had been saved from the conflagration, were readied for display: this account, by Maurice S. Smith, an old Jowett employee, in *The Veteran and Vintage Magazine*, shows the mixture of devotion and improvisation that seems to have permeated Jowett activity:

'I was told to go over to the finished-car bay and pick out six vehicles which I was asked to make into show cars. Everyone was detailed to give me as much help as was possible, and we took the six cars—all saloons—and solemnly took them to pieces. Mudguards had to be re-enamelled—the stove enamelling plant was still intact—wood fillets and facia boards repolished, fabric bodies retrimmed, practically from scratch, and seats and cushions re-padded. I had personally to clean and polish six power units, without removing them from the frames.'

The brothers won through. By November a trickle of vans was coming off the production line, by the following March the first private cars were put in hand, and that summer, at the depths of the Depression, the resuscitated Jowett plant was turning out sixty cars a week, and experiencing no difficulty in selling them.

It is perhaps kinder to gloss over the early nineteen-thirties. The Jowett was as undistinguished as most cheap cars, though it had one great merit: the little engine's infinite ability to haul vast and cumbersome coachwork around quite unperturbed. A 1932 long saloon required a 5·37 : 1 top gear, but it pulled nearly three times the original weight for which the engine was designed at 50 m.p.h., and could still log an average fuel consumption of 40 m.p.g. in the process. The cars subscribed to the reforms of the period—wire wheels, safety glass, chromium plate, rear-mounted fuel tanks, twelve-volt electrics—and to some of the sillier fads, the *de luxe* 'Kestrel' sports saloon sprouting twin exposed trumpet horns in 1934. As the years went by, the Jowett's slightly inadequate brakes attracted more adverse comment, while as more and more presswork came into the industry, the bodies began to look a little amateurish. Four-speed gearboxes were adopted in 1934, and in 1935 a centrifugal clutch and free wheel were made available. In that year a *de luxe* saloon with full equipment sold at £175, though prices started at £150. The Jowetts eschewed synchromesh, and were not afraid to tell their public why, in 1934:

'Every year there seems to be some particular item or speciality about a car that is, either by mass suggestion or genuine demand, brought into the foreground. . . . This year it appears to be easy-changing gearboxes. Personally, we experience a feeling of well-being in handling a gearbox with skill, that we do not experience when an automatic change is fitted, but we realize there is a demand for easy change, and we have met it. . . .'

They went on to express their view that partial synchromesh, as used by everyone save Alvis, was confusing to a novice. Though they did not reveal as much, incidentally, Jowett were learning all about 'automatic changes' on an interesting four-cylinder car with vertical cylinders and overhead inlet valves with which they were experimenting. This machine went by the code-name of 'La Roche' (Type M), used a chassis similar to the stock 1935–6 models, and two of the three prototypes had Wilson preselector boxes. After a lot of 'cloak and dagger' testing at night, Jowetts went back to horizontally-opposed units.

The firm still had some years of the old régime in front of them, and one or two stunts punctuated the early nineteen-thirties. In April 1933, the Hon. Victor Bruce and his wife averaged 38·54 m.p.h. for seventy-two hours in a 'Kestrel' saloon towing a trailer laden with a hundred gallons of fuel. Refuelling was conducted at a walking pace, and it was a triumph of patience, one feels, rather than mechanical endurance. The previous summer an enthusiast had diverted himself with a saloon by towing a Rice Folding caravan, another Yorkshire product, up and down Porlock Hill, though it is not clear what this was supposed to prove. One of the 1928 sports models, with three-speed gearbox, was used by a Mr A. H. Garland to climb Walna Scar; he was honest enough to admit that he received assistance from a party of motor-cycling enthusiasts he met *en route*, and this was claimed as the first successful climb of this gradient by a car. About the same time, a certain very well-known manufacturer was claiming that his newly introduced Ten had been tested up Walna Scar: an indisputable fact, since he had taken a film unit with him on the attempt!

The signs of revolution were creeping up. Contributory schemes were introduced in the works in 1934, a year after the erection of a canteen in which, in those halcyon days, a two-course meal cost 9d! Jowett Cars Ltd. became a public company in 1935, the profit for that year's working being £46,000—among the customers were Andrews' Liver Salts of Newcastle, who bought twenty-one saloons for their representatives. In 1936, Benjamin Jowett retired. His brother William severed his connexion with the company four years later, devoting himself to the development of the Bristol tractor, a small caterpillar-tracked machine with a Jowett engine.

Nineteen thirty-six saw two interesting developments: Jowetts collaborated with Coventry-Victor in tests with a 1-litre diesel engine, said to give 50 m.p.h. and 60 m.p.g. when installed in one of their light van chassis; and, for the first time since car manufacture started, a choice of two models was offered. The 7 h.p. 'twin' entered its final season unchanged from the previous year, but alongside it was ranged a 63 × 92 mm. (1,166 c.c.) 10 h.p. flat-four with side valves, an aluminium crankcase and two downdraught Zenith carburetters, one bolted direct to each block. Specification was otherwise conventional, though fuel feed was by S.U. electric pump. A four-speed gearbox was standard and the 'Jupiter' saloon was listed at £197 10s. The more luxurious 'Jason' model cost £205. The new engine was much quieter than the Seven and gave no mechanical trouble, though the adoption of a sloping radiator, lying back over the engine, made life awkward for the service engineer, who had to contend with a forest of induction pipes, carburetter controls and choke control wires.

Worse than this, the new 'flat-four' looked wrong, even if it did prove to be good for 60 m.p.h. and close on 35 m.p.g. The rear panel sloped as violently as the radiator, only in the opposite direction, and sales flopped. Jowetts hurriedly replaced the 'Jupiter' and 'Jason' with the JG-type, or 'Plover', which had a more nearly vertical radiator with painted shell, and used a body similar to that of the 7 h.p. *de luxe* saloon. Perforated-disc wheels were fitted. At the same time, a 'Peregrine' model with the old body served to use up unsold stocks of this style.

For 1937, the Jowett went conventional. A new dropped frame, built-in jacking points, easy-clean wheels and painted grilles were standardized, while the old Jowett f.w.b. gave way to the Bendix system, never one of my favourites. One type of body only was offered, a six-light saloon with flush boot, rather reminiscent of the contemporary Hillman 'Minx', and both the Eight—the old Seven enlarged from 907 c.c. to 946 c.c.—and the Ten shared the same chassis and coachwork. Much the same cars were made in 1938 except that a very ugly 'fencer's mask' grille replaced the 1937 version, which was still recognizably Jowett. For 1940, integral boots characterized the bodies, while four-speed synchromesh gearboxes were adopted: perhaps it was now felt at Idle that the novices were getting sophisticated!

Jowetts made their own gearboxes, with eighty-two needle rollers to each box, which complicated assembly somewhat. Worse still, it was discovered, *after* a preliminary batch of demonstration cars had gone out to agents, that a certain movement of the gear-lever would engage two gears at once. As the cure involved removing the gearbox lid and shifting the gears into neutral by hand, this performance could be highly embarrassing in urban traffic. It should be said straight away that this lamentable defect was rectified before any cars reached the general public.

But through the nineteen-thirties, Jowett remained conservative: they had the genesis of an advanced design in the Ten, but in all probability considerations of sentiment as much as anything else dictated the use of a flat-four layout, and in pre-war years about 30 b.h.p. was deemed sufficient. William Jowett had further set his sights at an output of a hundred cars a week, every week, and no overtime worked. In this he succeeded: at Idle few men remembered being on short time, even during the worst years of the Slump, except after the great fire of 1930. With the small works, however, it was not easy to keep production flowing smoothly; after 1936 only two basic bodies, the saloon and the van, were offered, but colour and upholstery options complicated matters, since *de luxe* Tens were available in four different colours and six different upholstery schemes. The old régime at Idle had reached the limit of its development.

Jowetts abandoned private-car production 'for the duration' in March 1940, but the 8 h.p. engine continued in production throughout the war. It had already found successful application as a stationary unit in such devices as cement mixers, and during the war it was built in large quantities for W.D. generators and trailer pumps. All manner of machinery, incidentally, was adapted for the latter purpose, Coventry-Climax making good use of the unsold stock of 8 h.p. 'Cadet' engines left over when Swift of Coventry Ltd. went bankrupt in 1931. They were very successful, too.

After the war, most British manufacturers went back to their 1940 models. A few, like Armstrong-Siddeley, cloaked these offerings in a new and refreshing style, but hardly anyone was prepared to plunge straight into novelty. Jowett, however, had other ideas. The twin-cylinder design was, in the opinion of the directors, far too rough for further private-car use. So an entirely new design was worked out under the direction of Gerald Palmer, who was joined, as production consultant, by F. E. Salter. Salter had been with Standards from 1930 to 1942, and had helped steer the firm to recovery, his greatest contribution being the launching of the Flying Standard range in 1935–6.

Palmer started with an almost clean sheet of paper. It has been said that his inspiration was the Lancia 'Aprilia' of 1937, and certainly he made use of Commendatore Lancia's recipe to the extent that he adopted a unitary structure, a compact, forward-mounted engine and independent front suspension, and laid great stress on good aerodynamic shape and high power-to-weight ratio. But there the resemblance ceased, for Jowett used torsion-bar suspension at front and rear alike, and they adhered to their 'flat-four' where the Italian firm used a narrow-angle vee.

The original project called for two basic models—a 1,200 c.c. (69·55 × 78 mm.) type for the home market, and a 72·5 × 90 mm. (1,489 c.c.) variant for export. Only the latter ever went into production, the smaller model being rendered unnecessary by the abolition of the old tax formula. The first car took the road in August 1944, early prototypes having a divided vee windscreen in place of the curved type found on all production machines, and the British public had its first sight of the design in the Motor Industry Jubilee Cavalcades of 1946. From the start, the 'Javelin' attracted 'rave' notices comparable only with those that attended the Citroën DS. 19 in 1955, or the first Mercédès in 1901. 'The new revolutionary Jowett' was a topic of conversation wherever motorists foregathered, and at least three eminent motoring journalists let it be known that they had placed orders. Unfortunately, there were no production cars to be had—the first one did not roll off the line until November 1947.

The 'Javelin' really was revolutionary. Nowadays it is half forgotten, eclipsed by the arrival of automatic transmissions, disc brakes and the possible imminence of turbine-driven cars—and people are apt to be shocked because the designers did not think fit to incorporate hydraulic brakes until October 1950. Let us, however, consider what other British and foreign factories were offering in the 1½-litre class in 1947. The new Jowett was streets ahead of such cars as the Austin, Singer and Vauxhall Twelves, only the last-mentioned of which boasted i.f.s., while none of them would do much more than 65 m.p.h. It would be kinder not to consider their acceleration figures, and they were *not* designed for fast cornering. A pre-production 'Javelin', tested by *The Motor* in May 1947, recorded 76·3 m.p.h. and 33 m.p.g., and would accelerate from a standing start to 50 m.p.h. in 13·4 seconds. These figures differed little from those obtained on a production car two years later. By contrast, the *mean* 0–50 m.p.h. acceleration figure for 1939 cars of all types was 21·5 seconds! Even in 1949, by which time most of the pre-war machinery had been shunted off Britain's production lines, a typical 1½-litre family saloon—the Morris Oxford—could barely reach 70 m.p.h. and needed almost twenty seconds to reach 50. By the end of the 'Javelin's' career, it was recording two-way maxima of well over 80 m.p.h., and using no more fuel in the process. The car had everything: performance, roadworthiness, economy and compactness—only there were few 'Javelins' to be had, and Jowett were finding the conversion from 'contented clocks' to the mass-production of high performance cars a major headache.

In the old days, production, promotion and sales had been on a safe, limited and predictable scale. Quite suddenly, the company found itself pitchforked into an entirely new world, and confronted with an entirely new type of customer. Agents were jockeying for the Jowett dealerships, and tours undertaken by company executives were producing energetic reactions from France to New Zealand. On paper, they had the world's best all-rounder in the 1½-litre class. The most ironic aspect of the Jowett story is that Yorkshire doggedness won through in the end—too late. By 1953, the 'Javelin' was ready to meet all comers, but Jowetts had spent themselves in the struggle.

The new model's first rally success was in July 1948, when only a handful were to be seen on English roads. S. M. Lawry won a first-class award in the Junior Car Club's Eastbourne Rally, and set in train a whole string of victories. T. C. Wise won the 1,500 c.c. class in the 1949 Monte Carlo Rally, while in 1951 Jowetts were sixth and tenth in General Classification, and first, second, and fourth in their class. In 1952, Marcel Becquart, who had won the Rally outright on a Hotchkiss in 1950, drove a 'Jupiter' sports convertible into fifth place, and put up the best closed-car performance in the R.A.C. British Rally, in which event Jowetts recorded class wins again in 1953 and 1954. Mrs Mitchell and Mrs Leavens won the Ladies' Cup in the 1952 Lisbon Rally, and the Graaf Van Zuylen won the Dutch Tulip Rally outright in 1953. A victory of an entirely different kind was scored in the *News Chronicle*'s National Fuel Economy Run organized by the Cheltenham Car Club in July 1952, when Gordon Wilkins' 'Javelin' put up the best performance on formula, recording 67·9 m.p.g. To this day, the cars are still a formidable proposition in events of this type, though the extension of the upper capacity limit to 1,600 c.c. puts them at a disadvantage to the Porsches and M.G. A-1600s.

The 'Javelin' was even raced—in retrospect this does not seem very alarming, but just contemplate what might have happened had someone entered a Sunbeam-Talbot Ten, say, for Le Mans in 1939. T. H. Wisdom and Anthony Hume, driving a saloon loaned by the manufacturers, won the 2-litre touring class in the 1949 Belgian 24-Hour Race, at an average speed of 65·6 m.p.h. This is rather slow as compared with the 78·7 m.p.h. of the winners,

Chinetti and Lucas, but their car was a 2-litre Ferrari, and the world was startled to find that an ordinary British saloon, standard save for the use of larger carburetters and altered gear ratios, was capable of lapping at 74 m.p.h., and lasting round the clock at an *average* higher than the maximum speed expected normally of such a car. The drivers, when asked to explain just how non-standard the car was, commented regretfully that after consideration they had had to discard the heater and the radio!

Having proved that the standard article could motor, Jowetts had a sports car ready for the 1949 Show. This was the E.R.A.-Javelin, using the mechanical components of the basic 'Javelin' in what we would now call a space-frame. The structure was the work of Prof. Dr Eberan von Eberhorst, late of Auto-Union, and the car was to be made and marketed by E.R.A. Ltd. at their Dunstable works. These negotiations fell through, and by the time the sports car was ready for the public view—it missed Geneva in 1950, despite a formal Jowett lunch in its honour, and was not seen until the New York Importers' Exhibition in March—it was rather heavier and less aerodynamic in appearance than had been hoped. Jowett's talked of a kerb weight of $13\frac{1}{2}$ cwt., but the production car road-tested by both *The Autocar* and *The Motor* later in the year came out at $5\frac{1}{2}$ cwt. more, even though this gave a maximum speed of 85–90 m.p.h. The 'Jupiter' also suffered from a steering-column gear-change and farcical luggage accommodation, but it would out-perform any other genuinely stock $1\frac{1}{2}$-litre car on the market. The chassis attracted some lovely bodies from Continental coachbuilders, notably Farina and Worblaufen, and some unmentionable atrocities from this country, mainly for owners in quest of stowage space for baggage or offspring!

With the advent of the 'Jupiter', Jowetts plunged wholeheartedly into competition work under the management of C. B. Grandfield and A. H. Grimley. Grimley remembers with pride the success of the Jowett pit-work, first time out at Spa, and 1950 saw some lengthy development tests of the 'Jupiter', one car being driven 3,000 miles all over Britain and France at an average running speed of 54 m.p.h., an overall average of 46 m.p.h., and consuming fuel at the rate of 31 m.p.g. This year also the firm started the issue of their *Competition Tuning Notes* for private owners.

The stock 'Jupiters' were too heavy and cumbersome for racing, in spite of which Wisdom and Wise managed a class win and seventeenth place in general classification at Le Mans in 1950, beating the 1,500 c.c. record for the total distance run, which had been held by Aston Martin since 1935. In the 1,500 c.c. class of the Production Car Race at Silverstone, Grimley finished fifth in his class in a closely contested event; his average was 68·89 m.p.h. as against the winning H.R.G.'s 71·78 m.p.h., in spite of spinning off at Becketts. 'That was how I learnt not to race with the production job', Grimley comments.

Jowetts, however, came back in 1951 with a special, narrow, lightened two-seater, which ran along with a brace of standard cars. On an 8·5 : 1 compression ratio the engine gave 65 b.h.p., but it was left to one of the 'touring' machines (Becquart/Wilkins) to pull off the class victory at Le Mans. Two improved cars, on which the chief visible differences were exposed cylinder-heads and wing-mounted headlamps instead of bomb-nacelles, ran in 1952. The Becquart-Wilkins partnership was the sole survivor in the 1,500 c.c. class, and Jowetts had their hat-trick. Despite a class win in the same year's Watkins Glen Race in America, the Jowett victories were fairly empty, for there was precious little competition in the 1,500 c.c. class, with Riley and Singer out of racing, Aston Martin translated to a bigger category altogether, and Amédée Gordini concentrating on Formula work; but for the Jowetts to have performed so consistently stands to the credit of the hard-working development team at Idle. Racing was abandoned when all the necessary lessons had been learnt, though the high cost, and the difficulty of either lightening the space-frame further or extracting many more brake horsepower from the Jowett engine had quite a lot to do with its discontinuation.

The 'Javelin' had also proved a mechanical nightmare, and many owners will remember the long and painful trail of bearing and gasket trouble. Some cars leaked. These failings were accentuated because the car was basically so good that people took the trouble to air their grievances, and Jowetts were willing to listen to customers. The bearing trouble looked like oil starvation, but was finally traced to aeration of oil, caused by the spill-off from the relief valve. Subsequent to this, no further trouble was experienced, though oil coolers were always recommended on export models, since the constant high cruising speeds attainable under *Autobahn* conditions resulted in dangerously high oil temperatures. The use of a gearbox of pre-war design had its consequences in the tiresome 'Javelin' habit of disengaging third gear, due, to quote Mr Grimley's own words, to:

'Lack of positioning of the top and third hub in neutral after riding the ring gear through into top or third. The hub was free to float and could "kiss" the cone of the opposite gear to that engaged, and the differential speed generated dangerous heat which fired off the lubricant of the adjacent main shaft bushes. This was corrected by the introduction of a simple interlock which engaged after riding through synchromesh into either gear.'

A short sentence which summarizes the result of months of painstaking research and hard driving. Mr Grimley and his staff were for ever out on the road. He remembers solo drives across Northern France in winter in experimental machines, with only a smattering of school French for communication in the event of trouble; daily drives at high speed from Annecy to Geneva for a fortnight while preparing Marcel Becquart's car for Monte Carlo; and the final punishing M.I.R.A. test in November 1952, when three 'Javelins' and three 'Jupiters' circulated round the old perimeter track for twenty-four hours a day at an average of over 60 m.p.h., pit-stops included. This operation continued for three weeks, and the drivers, volunteers from Idle, had to be discouraged from 'dicing'. Three lorry-loads of tyres went the way of all rubber, but no mechanical trouble whatever was encountered. The object of the exercise had been to restore public confidence in the Jowett engine, and that it did.

Unfortunately, Jowetts were running into trouble through overrapid expansion. By 1953, they had an excellent programme in the shape of a reliable 'Javelin' and the Mk. I.A 'Jupiter' with room in the boot for more than the proverbial toothbrush, while the rough and tough twin-cylinder Bradford van was due to be replaced by a more modern vehicle. They had had to extend their premises by the purchase of the Oak Mills works in 1947, and they had to raise a further £350,000 capital in November 1950. They also had to adapt themselves to new production methods. One could not build 'Javelins' on the same assembly lines that had carried the Eights and Tens, and the Jowett body shops could not contend with the 'Javelin' structure. Very wisely, the Jowett management never intended that they should. This work was farmed out to Briggs Motor Bodies of Dagenham, who purchased premises at Doncaster. They then delivered the whole structure, painted and trimmed, to Bradford, where it was offered up to the mechanical components by the ingenious method of inverting it in a revolving jig and dropping the 'works' in from above. This assembly method was highly successful, but the fatal disadvantage of farming out one's structural work to a firm of the size and capacity of Briggs is that an economic price must depend on the volume of vehicles produced, and large press-working firms can only work two ways: 'flat out' or not at all.

Rare specimen: Not even the makers can say if this 1921 Lea-Francis
two-seater is an 11·9 h.p. or a 13·9 h.p.

Kaye Don in the 1928 T.T., which he won in this 'Hyper Sports' Lea-Francis

The 1929 Leyland-Thomas, built up from surviving Leyland Eight
parts by Thomson and Taylor. *Below:* Under the bonnet

One of Group-Captain A. F. Scroggs' Trojans turns in its regular trials performance

Testing the 1929 Trojan six-wheeler on the Sussex Downs
(photo: Trojan Ltd. and *The Autocar*)

Pandora's Box: the curious machinery that lived in the boot of the RE-type Trojan

It is a favourite argument of economists that if one makes enough articles the cost per copy will drop steadily. This is true, as long as one possesses the machinery for distribution, and the ability to sell the end-product. The horrors of purchase tax hit Jowett hard—the 'Javelin' customer paid £943 in February 1949 and £957 at the end of production in 1953, while a 'Jupiter' in 1953 set the customer back £1,284—but the company had no difficulty in selling its products, some 30,000 'Javelins' alone being made in six years. Nor was there any 'remaindering off' at the end, people being willing to pay premiums for a new saloon early in 1954, when there still seemed to be a hope that production might be resumed. What they could not do was to administer the flood of structures pouring into Idle from Doncaster, and in fact *Briggs had ceased delivery before their plant was purchased by Ford;* quite simply because the Idle works and all additional rented premises were hopelessly overcrowded with body units awaiting engines and transmissions. It is therefore not strictly correct to say that the acquisition of the Dagenham factory killed the 'Javelin'; though when Briggs were asked to resume production at a lower rate; they quoted a higher price, understandably enough, and that was that.

The public knew little of this; the ups and downs of Jowett finances, and of the Jowett board, were not unexpected in the tricky economic circumstances of the late nineteen-forties and early nineteen-fifties. One cannot in fact blame Jowetts for all their financial vicissitudes; shortage of materials, for instance, caused the abandonment of hydraulic tappets on the 'Javelin', while periodic adverse financial returns might well be blamed on import restrictions imposed by some of the more valuable overseas customers. Be that as it may, Jowett went under just as they had set their technical house in order, and in September 1953, it was announced that the firm had failed to reach agreement with Briggs. 'Javelin' production was therefore suspended, though a *de luxe* saloon appeared on the stand, as a gesture of hope, at Earls Court the following month.

The contented clock had also ceased to bleat. The Bradford's agricultural ways had at last become too uncouth even for its clientele, and the replacement was still on the way, so no commercial vehicles were being turned out at the very moment when they could and would have tided the company over a very difficult period. The 'Jupiter' could still be made, but the sports convertibles catered for a narrow market, as is indicated by the fact that only about 1,200 were made between 1950 and 1954, as against thirty thousand 'Javelins' and the same number of Bradfords.

Under the guidance of Roy Lunn and Donald Bastow, the firm's new chief designer—for Palmer had departed in 1949—an interesting super-sports version of the 'Jupiter', Type R4, was evolved for 1954. It used a 7-ft. wheelbase as against the 7 ft. 9 in. of the standard article, and at fourteen cwt. dry it was a good five cwt. lighter than the Mk. I.A. Bishop cam steering replaced the rack-and-pinion gear of earlier cars, and weight was ingeniously kept down by the use of fibreglass bodywork and an auxiliary electric cooling fan for use in traffic, which allowed the use of a smaller and lighter radiator than hitherto. Overdrive, effective on third and top gears, was an option, and maximum speed was in the region of 100 m.p.h. One or two cars were made, and performed creditably in club events, but the R4 never went into production—nor did the experimental twin-cylinder Bradford van and two-door saloon with i.o.e. engines (Type CD), which proved rougher and thirstier than their competitors.

Though the R4s were sold to enthusiasts who, it was hoped, would attract interest by their competition successes, the neat little sports car was the firm's swan song. Early in 1954, Oak Mills were sold to the British Wool Marketing Board, and in July, the Jowett directorate, who in a Golden Jubilee hand-out of 1951 had talked cheerfully of 'the next fifty years', announced that an offer of 'more than the book value' had been received for Idle from the International Harvester Co.—less any plant and equipment required by Jowetts for the manufacture of spares for existing models. The shareholders were urged to accept this offer, which they did. Jowett Cars Ltd. moved to smaller premises at Batley, where they continued to service cars and make spare parts until 1965, when these activities ceased. At the time of writing, the Jowett Car Club is endeavouring to safeguard the spares situation for the future.

In the early 'Javelin' days Jowetts fell into the error of using their customers as their experimental department, and early cars displayed an interesting assortment of faults. Some customers, however, volunteered their cars as guinea-pigs! The truth behind the Jowett's demise is that the company changed its way of life drastically, and expanded too quickly. For their boldness in deserting the homely path trodden by the Jowett brothers, they paid with their life; but if they had not done so, there would be no 'Javelins' to take a good look at, as they still sometimes pass us.

CHAPTER 8

Lanchester:
The Car of Too Many Firsts

'We feel confident that the care with which our designs have been worked out in every detail will ensure the advantages of the well-known "Lanchester" balanced motor being thoroughly realized. We have no hesitation in claiming for our carriages that they are unsurpassed for safety, comfort, elegance, and, in short, all the many points which go to make a satisfactory and efficient vehicle.'

Catalogue, Lanchester Motor Carriages, April 1900

The Autocar, in what amounted to an epitaph on the old school of Lanchesters in 1933, published a long list of the firm's 'firsts': these included forced lubrication (1904), scraper rings on pistons (1904), crankshaft torsion dampers (1909), harmonic balancers (1911), forward control (1904), direct top gear (1896), epicyclic gearbox (1895), pre-selector change (1901), worm gear (1897), live axle (1897), motor car-type wire wheels (1895), detachable wheels non-integral with brake drums (1901), cantilever suspension (1897) and foot accelerator (1897). An historian might find cause to dispute the accuracy of some of these: indeed the compiler of this formidable summary qualified the Lanchester claim for the first torsion damper by observing that it was fitted, not on Dr Lanchester's own cars, but on the Knight-engined machines built by the Daimler Co., to whom he was design consultant, while he has also omitted the pioneer use of rubber engine mountings in 1904. Nobody, however, could dispute that the Lanchester made between 1895 and 1931 conformed to no set pattern, and derived singularly little from outside influence. Neither F. W. Lanchester nor his brother George, who took over the management in 1912, was influenced by other people's ideas, any more than was Ettore Bugatti. Late in 1908, when the Knight sleeve-valve engine was creating a furore on account of its amazing silence and smoothness, F. W. Lanchester was interviewed, and expressed himself as 'greatly impressed' with the new design. He might well be—he had designed a vibration damper for it—but he stuck obstinately to poppet valves while his more impressionable competitors plunged into an orgy of experimentation.

115

The complete individualism of the Lanchesters was reflected in their attitude to publicity. They seldom bothered about serious competition work, but in the earliest days their cars appeared frequently in reliability trials, and they never imposed any ban on private owners' participation in such events. George Lanchester, in fact, used Brooklands to good effect in the early nineteen-twenties. They never claimed that they made the best car in the world, yet Lanchester advertising radiated a quiet sense of superiority; and the brothers contrived to invest their contributions to the correspondence columns of the motoring press with a dignity signally lacking in certain other motor magnates. Tempers might wax hot in the long-drawn-out controversies of those days, but the Lanchesters generally contrived to have the last word.

F. W. Lanchester was a tireless inventor whose interests ranged far beyond the narrow field of motoring. He started with the Forward Gas Engine Co. in 1889, and some four years later he was experimenting with 'high-speed' engines, capable of 800 r.p.m. In those days his units turned over faster than most, as can be instanced by the fact that in 1903 his horizontally-opposed 4-litre 'twin' was good for 1,200 r.p.m., yet was a paragon of smoothness compared with some of the heavier and slower-running vertical 'fours'. Frederick Lanchester had a river craft running on the Thames in 1894, but even this reflected the family's disregard for convention, since it took the form of a stern-wheeled punt fitted with a $1\frac{1}{2}$ h.p. engine. It worked very well, and early the following year the first car was on the road, powered originally by a 5 h.p. single-cylinder horizontal engine: this was replaced early on by an 8 h.p. flat-twin. Even at this date Lanchester used wire wheels, his engines had mechanically-operated inlet valves at a time when suction operation was universal, ignition was by low-tension magneto and not by hot tube, and the wick carburettor was utilized. Further, the car had the crash-proof Lanchester epicyclic gearbox, and its tiller steering, even then, endowed the car with a controllability superior to the 'old French type used also on some of the American steam cars'—note the scathing tone applied to the Stanleys and Loco-mobiles, a form of contempt which we shall see extended to the Ford in 1910, and to the Essex in the nineteen-twenties. The Lanchester 'hour-glass' worm drive did not appear until the emergence of Lanchester No. 2 in 1897. Curiously enough, the original car acquired wheel steering later on, and appeared in this guise when it was loaned to Edmund Dangerfield's Motor Museum in London in 1912. This machine was destroyed in the Coventry 'blitz' in 1940, but the second Lanchester is still preserved in running order in the Science Museum.

Eighteen ninety-seven also saw the arrival of the balanced twin-crankshaft flat-twin engine; but the brothers were cautious, and no cars were suffered to reach the public until 1900. In the meantime the Lanchester Engine Company with works at Armourer Mills, Montgomery Street, Birmingham, had been formed, among the directors being C. Vernon Pugh (whose brother, John Pugh, was head of Rudge-Whitworth), T. Hamilton Barnsley and F. W. Lanchester. The first six production cars were allocated to the six members of the Board, and car No. 3, an 8 h.p. 'twin' with a two-seater body, won a Gold Medal at the Richmond Show in 1899. Lanchester also entered two cars, the new 10 h.p. and the 1897 8 h.p. phaeton, in the 1,000 Miles Trial of 1900. Their remarkable smoothness and silence came in for very favourable comment, but their cautious sales policy does not seem to have been applied to competitions. 'The Lanchester carriages,' *The Autocar* accused, 'scarcely added to the reputation that they previously possessed.' The new car's entry was a mistake, since it had only been finished the day before the Trial, while an even worse error, in the eyes of Henry Sturmey and his reporters, was to gear the other car down, since its performance on hills was offset by its funereal pace on the level. Quite clearly the moral standards of Victorian times differed from those of the early nineteen-thirties, when Monte Carlo Rally competitors regularly swapped axle ratios between the completion of the road section and the commencement of the tests.

The Lanchester quickly found favour in the eyes of the more discriminating public. Up to 1905, production centred on the twin-cylinder cars, the 1904 range consisting of four models, two of 4-litres capacity (the 10 h.p. with air-cooled engine, and the 12 h.p. with water-cooled cylinders, at £500 and £550 respectively); and two corresponding types of slightly larger capacity, the 16 h.p. at £660 and the 18 h.p. at £720.

The Lanchester of this period had a twin-crankshaft engine with mechanically-operated inlet valves developing about 12 b.h.p. at 1,200 r.p.m., a disc transmission brake, side lever steering, worm drive and a smoothness and silence of progression which masked a comfortable cruising speed of some 30 m.p.h., a good ride being ensured by cantilever springs all round. The side-mounted starting handle was detachable, and a portion of each front wing hinged back to give easy access to the seats. Control was almost entirely by levers, the left foot coping with the accelerator, and the right foot having no function other than the operation of a gong or bulb horn. The right hand was reserved for the 'side steering lever', and everything else was done with the left hand, whose functions were either simple and logical, or fiendishly complicated, according to whether one liked Lanchesters or not. One had *three* gear levers—the 'compound gear trigger' which preselected 'low' or 'intermediate', a second lever engaging the indirect forward gears and reverse, which last ratio served, *à la* Ford, as an auxiliary brake—and a third one which engaged both 'high' gear and the transmission brake. One also had a lever for the hand petrol pump, a pair of governor levers and a vapour regulator for the wick carburettor. Never having handled an early example of the breed for longer than a few minutes, I do not feel qualified to comment further, but I must confess that the lever steering is as good as many wheel layouts for accuracy and naturalness of operation.

The Lanchester Company adopted precision methods from the start. Their cantilever springs were tested by hitting them with heavy weights. Sometimes they were shaken from their jigs by this process and shot through the workshop roof, never to be seen again. After every engine test the units were stripped, washed and re-assembled, while in the interests of accuracy the firm made its own jigs and tools. Production was never large, but a list of early customers reads like a passage from *Who's Who*: the Duke of Portland, the Marquesses of Zetland and Anglesey, Lord Milner, J. M. Barrie, Rudyard Kipling (who immortalized his car in *Steam Tactics*), Anthony Hope, J. Pierpont Morgan, and 'Ranji', the cricketer, who was a faithful repeat customer, the Royal House of Nawanagar even ordering a brace of special DE27 Daimlers with Lanchester radiators as late as the nineteen-forties. Mr Andrew Hunter, the Duke of Portland's engineer, wrote in praise of his master's Lanchester in 1902, expressing vigorous approval of both the steering arrangements and the air cooling, though he conceded that 'in almost any other car but a Lanchester, the wheel is much the better'. Mr Hunter further said that he had covered five thousand miles with only plug changes, while Mr J. A. Holder was boasting of driving 150 to 200 miles a day on his 10 h.p. machine. C. W. Dixon, contributing an article in my father's series *Cars and How to Drive Them*, could find no criticism except that oil was apt to drop on to the hot exhaust pipes, and estimated his running costs as $1\frac{1}{2}$d. a mile—tyres, presumably, were not taken into consideration. He further backed his fancy by undertaking an unofficial 505-mile trial of a 16 h.p. air-cooled car in November 1903, his co-driver being Archibald Millership of Lanchesters. Their average speed on running time alone was 22 m.p.h., petrol being consumed at the rate of 19·4 m.p.g., while only thirty-five minutes were spent on replacing a plug and other minor adjustments. In 1913, Mr Dixon repeated the trial on the same car, now endowed with water-cooled cylinders, and improved his average by 2 m.p.h., fuel consumption falling to a remarkable 28·3 m.p.g. The Lanchester suspension enabled Mr Millership to 'stew beef extract in a spirit canteen in the back'. One wonders how many modern cars would permit of this process without either disorder or discomfort!

While their publicity lacked the flamboyance of Argyll's, the company kept its products before the public eye. In April 1902, ten cars made a run from London to Worthing, only one succumbing to minor tyre trouble. George Lanchester won his class in the Midland Automobile Club's Gorcot Hill Climb, despite the limitations of acceleration resulting from the use of a wick carburettor, and in the following July he was only beaten at Edge Hill by far more powerful machinery. The year 1903 also saw a massed on-slaught on the 1,350-foot Malvern Beacon by six Lanchesters, in dense fog. The firm provided the official course car for the Gordon Bennett Eliminating Trials at Welbeck Abbey, and even sent a demonstration model over to the Isle of Wight for Cowes week. It is not known how the yachting fraternity reacted.

For all the talk evinced by Frederick Simms' 'war motors' and Pennington's odder military projects, to Lanchester must also go the honour of landing one of the first War Office contracts for motor cars, in the shape of six 10 h.p. air-cooled tourers with reversible cape cart hoods which gave the vehicles a pram-like aspect. Trials, under the direction of Major Lindsay Lloyd of Brooklands fame, included non-stop runs of 150 miles and an observed climb of Edge Hill. Lanchesters were already exploring the export market, the first car being shipped to South Africa in September 1902. In 1904, S. H. Adams, writing in *The Autocar*, was expressing the opinion that this unconventional Birmingham production was the best car for South African conditions, because of its high ground clearance, excellent brakes, good suspension and the quickness of the tiller steering, which was less tiring on long runs than the conventional wheel. He claimed that he could put 250 miles into the day on his Lanchester, and could average 25 m.p.g. Lanchester companies were formed in both the U.S.A. and Germany, but they progressed little beyond articles of association.

In the first months of 1904, Millership drove a 12 h.p. car up the steps of the Crystal Palace, in response to a challenge from the Gobron-Brillié agents, while another machine of this type made the ascent of Great Ormes Head. But troubles loomed on the horizon, and in March a Receiver was appointed. This unfortunate incident seems to have stemmed from precipitate action on the part of certain creditors, for late in 1903 the situation looked healthy enough, with a profit of some £8,000, despite a heavy development programme on a new light car, while a journalist who visited the works shortly before Christmas found no fewer than twenty-five engines in course of erection. Air cooling was on its way out, and Lanchesters were advertising their willingness to convert existing cars to water-cooling at the same time modifying them to current specification 'for a very reasonable cost'. The Lanchester attention to detail is reflected in the neat arrangement whereby the tail-lamp illuminated the rear number-plate.

It is of interest to note that right up to the purchase of the company by B.S.A. in 1931, Lanchester maintained a helpful attitude to owners of their older cars. Tucked away at the back of the 1925 catalogue is the following notice:

'The earlier types of Lanchester cars no longer manufactured or listed are as follows:

> 10, 12, 16 and 18 h.p. two-cylinder
> 20 and 25 h.p. four-cylinder
> 28 and 38 h.p. six-cylinder

These types, although obsolete from a manufacturing point of view have been produced in quantities on the interchangeable system, and we still manufacture and stock replacement parts.'

Lanchester's cheap light car project was a reversal of all their principles and one that was stillborn. It was abandoned officially on account of the demand for the bigger cars, but this, rather than 'the lateness of the selling season', probably brought about their temporary financial embarrassment in 1904, and nothing more was heard of this motor car, apart from the announcement that the firm had taken on the Oldsmobile agency in Birmingham and thus provided themselves with something cheap to sell.

The storm was weathered. In October 1904, when a scheme was presented for the reconstruction of the company, it was stated that the value of sales exceeded that of purchases by £10,000 and by February 1905, the re-formed Lanchester Motor Co. Ltd. was in full operation.

For the next nine years, the Lanchester brothers went their own sweet way. No great claims for performance were made, but the basic features, the disc transmission brake, the epicyclic gearbox, the cantilever suspension and the wick carburettor, were retained. Lanchester made but two concessions to convention in Edwardian times: they adopted the vertical engine in 1905, when they introduced an oversquare 101·6 × 76·2 mm. four-cylinder Twenty with horizontal o.h.v. and full pressure lubrication by submerged gear-type pump; and they offered wheel steering for 1909, though the side steering lever remained an option, and was standard on the four-cylinder cars.

The 133 × 143 mm. twin-cylinder Twelve was still listed in 1907, when the range also included the Twenty and a new 28 h.p. 'six' of similar general design, with a seven-bearing crankshaft and dual ignition, prices being £500 for the 'twin', £650 for the 'four' and £750 for the 'six'. The same three cars formed the 1908 programme, Rudge-Whitworth detachable wheels being standardized on the 28 h.p. cars. In 1911 wheel steering, with a hinged wheel to give ease of access, was standardized, and electric lighting was an option —so, incidentally, were non-detachable wheels, for those who could afford hired labour to man the tyre levers. Both the Twenty and the Twenty-eight came in two wheelbase lengths, and the cars were also available in Colonial form with an eleven-inch ground clearance. This gave quite a lot of variations, and the seven-seaters were really roomy thanks to the 'forward control', which placed the engine between the two front seats. Lanchester made great capital out of the commodiousness of their coachwork, the seating of all passengers within the wheelbase, and the superb ride given by the combination of Lanchester cantilever suspension and the special 'sub-chassis' interposed between the frame and the body. Unlike most car manufacturers of that day, the Birmingham firm maintained their own body shops, and built nearly all their own coachwork—even some of the exotic 'one-offs'—right up to the move to Coventry in 1931. Reactions to the make were mixed. While nobody could misconstrue *The Autocar*'s enthusiasm over the prototype six-cylinder car in 1906 'The sensation was as nearly akin to flying as we imagine it is possible to attain with a motor car'— Owen John's comment in 1912 that 'if I were corpulent and middle aged, I would have a Lanchester' may have been a back-handed compliment.

Also in the 1911 range was a 4·9-litre (101·6 × 101·6 mm.) six-cylinder Thirty-eight at £900. In 1912 the old Twenty gave way to a four-cylinder version of this car, the Twenty-five, with cylinders cast in pairs, electric lighting and provision for dual ignition, at

£650. The last pre-war season saw only two models, the Twenty-five and the Thirty-eight, electric lighting being standard, while a Delco electric starter was standard on the six-cylinder car and optional on the Twenty-five. The firm displayed a curvaceous 38 h.p. limousine at the 1913 Show, which anticipated later styling by concealing its spare wheel in the tail.

These years saw few competition appearances. True, a Lanchester 20 h.p. landaulet shared first place in the Smoke Emission Trials of March 1907 with a 32 h.p. Pilgrim, which kept its horizontal engine under the front seat, and this compensated for their failure to beat the Electromobiles in the previous year's Town Motor Carriage Contest. Two 38 h.p. cars won Bronze Medals in the 1914 Swedish Winter Trials, but, after much hemming and hawing, the firm finally decided not to support that year's Austrian Alpine Trial. They argued, quite correctly, that they would have to design an entirely new vehicle, though they omitted to mention that they were in fact doing so. As they were to discover at Brooklands later on, the Lanchester gearbox did not give brisk standing-start acceleration.

Undoubtedly experimental cars were produced, and in 1907 the public were given a brief glimpse behind the scenes, when a 50 h.p. model with wheel steering, sliding-type gearbox and gate change was announced. An engine was exhibited at the Show, *The Autocar* commenting with suitable awe: 'Who but Lanchester would have placed the camshaft below the crankshaft?', but nothing further was heard of this strange piece of machinery, and Lanchester customers had to wait another fifteen years before they were allowed a conventional gearbox.

By 1914 the firm had built up a first-class record for service, and an owner-allegiance that was unrivalled. The cars were by nature suited for formal work, though handling was surprisingly good in spite of the fearsome roll angles resultant from the peculiar suspension. And Lanchester owners kept their cars for ages: of the three Edwardians which Francis Hutton-Stott has loaned me for display at Beaulieu, all were in daily use up to 1939, two of them in the hands of their original purchasers. The old lady who owned the 1908 landaulet may have been stampeded—literally—into selling the chassis after the car ran away with her in Tunbridge Wells, but she kept the body, albeit on an Austin chassis, up to the day of her death.

During the war, they built lorry and armoured car adaptations of their touring chassis, which proved eminently suitable for such tasks.

The famous group under Commander Locker-Lampson, which held up 20,000 Austrians for twenty-one hours, was equipped with Lanchesters. It is interesting to note that a great deal of development work was done on A.F.V.s in the Vintage era, the last cars to leave the old Birmingham works being armoured six-wheelers using the 40 h.p. car unit. Also in 1914 was evolved the 'Sporting Forty', the halfway house between the Edwardian and Vintage schools of thought. This was identical in external appearance to the 40 h.p. overhead-camshaft model of 1919, George Lanchester at last yielding to convention—and his fellow-directors—in mounting his engine under a long and impressive bonnet fronted by the classic Lanchester radiator, complete with glass window. The engine was a 101·6 × 114·3 mm. (5,588 c.c.) side-valve with the cylinders cast in pairs. The sports tourer weighed thirty-three cwt., 78 b.h.p. was developed at 1,800 r.p.m., and dual ignition was featured. The handbrake and gate-change levers were of identical appearance and located close together on the off-side, a characteristic also of the Vintage productions of the company. This confused some drivers, but I personally like it, since it enables very quick stops to be made, even with a heavy car whose two-wheel brakes are not up to modern standards. Ten of these cars were put in hand in 1915, including at least one two-seater and a limousine.

The immediate post-Armistice period revealed a fine crop of large and complex luxury cars, among them the Leyland Eight, the 40/50 Napier and the big Ensign. Lanchester's contribution was the 40 h.p. car, which resembled the 1914 prototype in outward appearance but had a 6,178 c.c. o.h.c. engine with cylinders cast in two blocks of three, the camshaft being driven by Lanchester worm gears. Cantilever suspension was retained at the rear, and the three-speed epicyclic gearbox had, as before, right-hand control. A single-plate clutch was used. Available in two chassis lengths— 11 ft. 9 in. and 12 ft. 6 in.—the Lanchester was listed at around the £2,800 mark, and, thanks to a high top-gear ratio of 3·3 : 1, it was exceptionally fast for those days. At 2,000 r.p.m. 89 b.h.p. was developed, and at peak revs. on top gear—2,400 r.p.m.—speeds of the order of 90 m.p.h. were claimed. This may seem rather improbable, but from driving experience of a towering 1920 saloon limousine I can testify that both performance and handling are of a high order, while the big car's ride over really bad surfaces would show up a lot of modern machinery. The Lanchester, like the contemporary Rolls-Royce, attracted formal body work, though two examples were raced at Brooklands. The first of these, C. A. Bird's

'Winnie Praps Praps', was more or less a standard chassis with a racing body and a cowled radiator: it lapped at over 95 m.p.h., but was rather overshadowed by its contemporary on the track, Tommy Hann's extraordinary modified 1911 25 h.p. car, once a landaulet. In its original form this bore a peculiar tandem-seated aerodynamic saloon body, and was christened 'Holeh-Wayareh-Gointoo', racing with distinction in 1922: but after problems of reverberation had proved insurmountable, it was converted to an open single-seater and dazzle-painted all over. The result, which answered to the name of 'Softly-Catch-Monkey', was raced during the 1923 and 1924 seasons, lapping at well over 80 m.p.h.

More notable was the special single-seater Forty purchased by Lionel Rapson in 1924 for the purpose of testing his tyres. This conformed closely to standard specification, the only alterations being a shortened and centralized steering column, a raised compression ratio of 5·5 : 1, improved manifolding and twin Zenith carburettors, yet in the hands of Parry Thomas, Rapson and Duller, it took a number of world's long-distance records at speeds between 95 and 100 m.p.h. It must have possessed considerable merit to have aroused Thomas's interest.

Only about five hundred Forties were made overall, and remarkably few survive. Some of the disappearances are most mysterious, especially the case of the car which was located in an abandoned breakers' yard in Sussex, lying on its side in a bog. This was apparently spirited away in the night, despite the fact that it would have needed a winch to detach it from twenty years' accumulation of brambles. Few changes were made to the design during its production life, though cars made after 1921 have higher radiators and larger fuel tanks. Rod-operated f.w.b. were added in 1925, and from 1926 onwards the brakes had hydraulic servo assistance.

A determined attempt was made to sell Lanchesters in the U.S.A., and the *marque* was one of the first in Britain to offer left-hand steering as an option. A tourer was displayed at the 1920 New York Show, and quite a few found customers, largely because of the excellent ride the suspension gave on the atrocious American roads of those days. The cars also attracted V.I.P.s from all over the world: H.R.H. the Duke of York was a regular customer, starting with Forties and later patronizing the 'Straight-Eight': he even remained loyal to the make in Daimler days, buying a 15/18 saloon in 1933. The Jam Sahib of Nawanagar was still an indefatigable enthusiast for Lanchesters, and purchased a rather ugly 40 h.p. all-weather, and later two identical 21 h.p. tourers. Prince Chichibu of Japan owned a 40 h.p. limousine, and the Maharajah of Rewa's Forty had a lantern roof, caravan style, and was equipped with purdah-glass windows, a canteen and a writing compendium. But even he was outdone for sheer garish magnificence by the Maharajah of Alwar, whose car was set out as a state carriage, the doorless and screenless body resting upon C-springs. With a lower than standard 3·6 : 1 top gear, maximum speed was said to be 55 m.p.h., but such statistics were of academic interest, the car's sole function being to transport its owner in state procession. By contrast to this, George Bernard Shaw's striking 'Straight-Eight', with polygonal headlamps reminiscent of the sports Jordan and sundry other exotic American offerings of the late Vintage years, seemed very staid. Mr Shaw, incidentally, was another whose loyalty was untrammelled by the change of ownership, for after his death his stable was found to contain a Lanchester Ten.

The post-1918 boom came and went. Rolls-Royce found it necessary to cater for reduced incomes with their Twenty, and at the 1923 Show, Lanchester introduced a 'small' car in direct competition, in the shape of their 21 h.p. model. The Twenty-one had a 74·5 × 114·3 mm. o.h.c. monobloc engine, Lanchester worm drive and suspension and right-hand change—but there the resemblance to previous designs stopped. Four-wheel brakes were standard from the start—and, most revolutionary of all, a four-speed 'crash' box was provided. It was made by Lanchesters except for the tooth profiles, and was in the main an economy measure, since a four-speed box of epicyclic type would have landed them with a formidable expenditure. In performance it was considerably superior to the Rolls-Royce, a limousine road-tested in 1926 recording 66 m.p.h. and proving capable of starting from rest in third gear, with an almost immediate change into top. As was then customary, the car was driven up a bank to demonstrate the well-known qualities of the Lanchester suspension. Some 700 cars were made between 1924 and 1931, and apart from the enlargement of the bore to 78·7 mm. in 1926, giving a capacity of 3·3 litres, very few changes were found necessary.

In the autumn of 1928, the old Lanchester company uttered its swan song, and, true to type, this was an eight-in-line, which made its mark immediately by winning the Corporation Cup at the Southport *concours d'élégance*. The 4½-litre monobloc engine had shaft-driven o.h.c., a one-piece detachable head and a massive ten-bearing crankshaft, and 82 b.h.p. was quoted at the modest speed of 2,800 r.p.m. The chassis specification followed conventional

Lanchester practice, but the Forty's three-speed epicyclic box was replaced by a conventional four-speed sliding-type. A 3·78 : 1 top gear propelled the big car at 80 m.p.h., and G. Geoffrey Smith of *The Autocar*, who drove the works demonstrator up to the Glasgow Show in 1928, observed that it would cruise comfortably at 70 m.p.h., though he considered that the steering was too high-geared. Unlike preceding Lanchesters, the 'Straight-Eight' lent itself to sporting bodywork with its rearwards-sloping radiator, and one of the prettiest specimens was a sports four-seater for Miss Nancy Lanchester, the designer's daughter.

The Lanchester reputation was untarnished. Their cars were superior in performance to those of their competitors, even if they were a little lacking in silence. The financial situation, however, was not particularly happy, and rumours of an impending merger with a bigger concern began to circulate. In August 1929, Hamilton Barnsley found it necessary to tell the public that:

'We shall only be partners to any scheme in which Lanchester cars of high power will continue to be produced, of the same high quality and workmanship for which we have always been noted in the past, and where the interests of Lanchester owners and buyers will be carefully safeguarded in the future.'

Fighting words, indeed! But a year later Barnsley was dead, and the big battalions were moving in.

Lanchester's 1931 programme consisted of the 'Straight-Eight' and the Twenty-one: by this time, of course, it was a Twenty-three, but the old name stuck. Modifications included the use of heat-treated dry cylinder liners, revised manifolding, grouped chassis lubrication and Dewandre vacuum-servo brakes. The 'Straight-Eight', with a very attractive two-door sports saloon body, was listed at £2,025. All to no avail: three months after the last Motor Show of the Vintage decade, the B.S.A. Group purchased the Lanchester Motor Co. Ltd. No immediate changes were forecast, though arrangements were set in hand to transfer Lanchester production to Coventry, and Stratton-Instone Ltd., Daimler's London distributors, took the cars under their wing. It is ironic to note that in 1956, when there ceased to be any Lanchesters to distribute, this firm signed up with Volkswagen. 'In no sense', a Daimler press release read, 'will there by any fusion of the Daimler and Lanchester cars.''

Nor was there, immediately. The 'Straight-Eight' was continued in small numbers, and Daimlers found themselves, to their pleasure and probably to their surprise as well, the heirs to a design for a smaller, more economical car which George Lanchester already had on the stocks. This, when it emerged, served as the bridge by which Daimler sloughed off the sleeve-valve engine after nearly a quarter of a century's enslavement. The 15/18 Lanchester had, one suspects, been planned as a medium-sized luxury car, but considerations of costing dictated a far cheaper machine, and with its straightforward 2½-litre (69·5 × 110 mm.) o.h.v. push-rod engine, coil ignition and A.C. mechanical fuel pump, it did not differ much from other 1932 offerings of far less illustrious lineage. As might have been expected of a Lanchester, it had hydraulic brakes, and it shares with the contemporary Wolseley 'Hornet' the distinction of having led the way with forward mounting of the engine. One wonders what manner of car it might have been had Lanchesters retained their independence, for the feature which sold it was Daimler's new-fangled fluid flywheel transmission, the lazy driver's dream. The 'Straight-Eight' continued in the range throughout 1932, but the rumours of a supercharged development of this theme died away unfulfilled.

Despite a budget which required it to sell at £565, the first Daimler-Lanchester was quite a good car, over 1,000 being sold during the first season, as a result of which Daimlers were obliged to launch their 1933 model in July 1932. One of these 15/18s, driven by Colonel Loughborough, pulled off the principal award in the R.A.C. Torquay Rally.

Alas, the names of George Lanchester and Laurence Pomeroy, Senior, might be linked with subsequent Lanchester cars, but the *marque* was doomed to fall into a slow decline. The cars degenerated into smaller, cheaper variations on the Daimler theme, proclaiming their presence with the muted-banshee wail of their transmissions. Nineteen thirty-three saw the adoption of Daimler's upward opening bonnet. In 1935 hydraulic brakes gave way to the mechanical type, to bring the cars into line with their costlier sisters, and at the same time a new 2,390 c.c. fixed-head engine displaced the old Lanchester-designed unit. Finally, the unfortunate Eighteen suffered yet another sea change in 1936, as a consequence of which it emerged as a Daimler 'Light Twenty' with a Lanchester grille. In this form it cost £580, the additional snob-value of the senior make being £90.

From 1933 onwards, the firm added a line of small four-cylinder cars associated with the B.S.A. range. Though they sold well among the more impoverished members of the Daimler clientele, they were devoid of any real interest. The original o.h.v. Ten with its 1·2-litre

engine offered all the solid Daimler virtues for only £315, and a
saloon weighing twenty-one cwt. was tested to do 61·64 m.p.h. and
a creditable 33 m.p.g. It was rather cruel, however, to say in 1932
that it ran 'better than some indifferent sixes', as its introduction
coincided with the height of the small-six craze, and the real maso-
chist had a fine choice of horrors at his beck and call. Apart from
a reputation for overheating, the Ten was an inoffensive little car,
and in its later 1·4-litre form, from 1936 onwards, it was quite well
liked. Its companion small-sixes—the 1,378 c.c. 'Light Six' of
1935–6 and the later 'Roadrider Fourteen' of 1937—had the fixed-
head engine, and it would be kinder to pass them by with the
comment that the detachable-head Ten unit fitted both chassis, and
was often substituted by exasperated owners! In 1938, the firm had
second thoughts and brought out a pleasant, if uninteresting 'Roadrider *De Luxe*', with detachable head, styling identical to the contemporary 'New Fifteen' Daimler, and the Daimler's excellent coil-
spring i.f.s. It was not notably fast, but at £330 it attracted quite a
few buyers. It is also interesting to note that Daimlers offered a
synchromesh gearbox as an option on this model: the last time that
any Daimler customer was to be allowed to opt out of the fluid
flywheel for many years to come.

George Lanchester had gone to Alvis to supervise armoured
fighting vehicle development in 1936, and the public were therefore
surprised to hear that more 'Straight-Eights' were being made in
1936. They were not, however, on general sale, nor were they
Lanchesters. Both H.M. King George VI as Duke of York and the
Jam Sahib of Nawanagar were numbered among the customers, but
all they got in return for their loyalty to an illustrious name was a
Daimler 4½-litre with a Lanchester radiator. Be that as it may, the
result was a very handsome carriage, and until recently one was still
in the service of our Royal Family.

Daimlers were among the worst hit of Coventry's factories in the
1940 'blitz', and the B.S.A. car never reappeared. The Lanchester,
however, came up fighting once more, to achieve yet another 'first';
for the post-war Ten was the first car to undergo a full-scale road
test in the hands of *The Motor*.

The new car's 1,287 c.c. engine followed pre-war lines, but it had
acquired independent front suspension, and was cloaked with a
bulky six-light body by Briggs of Dagenham. Its transitional styling
appealed to the conservative ranks of the Lanchester public, who
in 1946 were more than slightly shocked by such *avant-garde* offerings
as Armstrong-Siddeley's 'Lancaster', and were unlikely to be critical

Export trade: the Guy depot in Cape Town, *circa* 1929, showing (left to right) a Star 18/50 h.p. saloon, a Guy lorry, and a Riley Nine

A 1914 15·9 h.p. Star: the sole known survivor of the model

A 1910 10 h.p. twin-cylinder Briton

A convoy of new 10·8 h.p. Cylnos leaves Pelham Street for Maude's of Exeter, the West Country distributors, in 1926

One of the rare Wolverhampton-built A.J.S. *coachbuilt* saloons

A 20 h.p. eight-cylinder Guy tourer in the factory yard, 1920

of the car's depressing acceleration figures—0–50 m.p.h. in twenty-six seconds. When first introduced, it listed at a competitive £595, inflated by purchase tax to £761, but this figure had risen three years later to £927, and I remember being told about this time, when shopping for a new car, that the Lanchester was the only machine in its class for which a reasonably short waiting list obtained. A pleasing gesture was the introduction in 1949 of a version with all-hand controls for disabled drivers, but few disability pensions would have covered the cost of a luxury car by that time.

As if in anticipation of the catastrophe that was to engulf Jowett, Lanchester forsook Briggs in 1950, introducing a new version of the Ten with a four-light coachbuilt body by Barker. Somehow this one misfired aesthetically: it had a tail-heavy look about it.

Lanchester's last serious production car was the Fourteen which appeared at the 1950 Show, but took a painfully long time to go into production. The 76·2 × 107·95 mm. (1,968 c.c.) o.h.v. push-rod engine was really a four-cylinder version of the later Daimler 'Conquest', and its Barker body was identical in style: the car also represented a breakaway from Daimler traditions, for it had a hypoid rear axle and torsion-bar front suspension. Brakes were hydro-mechanical, and the fluid flywheel again featured. The engine developed 60 b.h.p. giving the car a top speed around the 70 mark. Handling was comparable with its Daimler sisters; in other words, very good.

Two additional styles—a drophead coupé with a power-operated hood, and an all-steel saloon for the export market—were announced for 1952. Great things were expected of this latter car, known as the 'Leda' (Type LJ.201), and the works were said to be capable of turning out 200 a week. The demand, however, did not exist.

Up to now, Lanchesters had concentrated on two types of car: luxury touring vehicles, and cheap Daimlers. They had learnt from hard experience that the former did not pay and the market for the latter was dwindling fast, as the retired classes retrenched under pressure of taxation and resorted to Morris Minors or British Railways. This notwithstanding, they attacked each market once more.

At the 1953 Show, they came up with a vehicle of true Maharajah magnificence. In deference to the spirit of the times, they used a tuned 'Century'-type 2½-litre Daimler engine in a Lanchester Fourteen frame, but there austerity stopped, for this chassis carried a two-door sports saloon of Hooper 'Empress' type, with fully enclosed rear wheels, razor-edged styling and built-in headlamps.

Interior appointments were in the best Hooper tradition, and this formidable machine listed at £2,830 (£4,010 with purchase tax). Considering that the contemporary Daimler roadster with similar mechanical elements was good for over 100 m.p.h., it should have had a respectable performance, but unfortunately Indian independence had spelt *finis* to the princely market, and the oil sheikhs of the Middle East preferred their Cadillacs. I understand, however, that about ten of these LJ.250 'Dauphins' were built and sold, the later ones having the 3½-litre Daimler 'Regency' engine.

Thereafter the firm threw caution to the winds, and a year later they were back with the last Lanchester 'first'. The 'Sprite', which was on show at Earls Court in 1954, was like no Daimler produced before or since. In the interests of low first cost unitary construction of body and chassis was adopted, while the whole bonnet and front wing structure swung upwards, *à la* DB.2 Aston Martin, to give access to the 'works'. Weight was kept down by the use of light alloys for the bonnet, doors and boot lid. A return was made to coil front suspension, while full hydraulic brakes with two leading shoes on the front represented another departure. The engine conformed to contemporary Daimler practice in being a short-stroke o.h.v. unit of 1,622 c.c. capacity, but the really revolutionary feature was the transmission. Gone was the fluid flywheel: in its place was a Hobbs fully automatic gearbox, the first instance of such a system being fitted as standard equipment on a light car. Though the Hobbs transmission had been successfully tested on commercial vehicles, and had in fact been shown, unobtrusively, on an Allard two-seater at the preceding Show, it was as yet comparatively untried. Further, the little Lanchester was an ugly beast with a stunted look, and failed to interest anyone except the technical journalists.

Its sponsors were undaunted. At the 1955 Show, a completely rehashed 'Sprite' was displayed, with a six-light body reminiscent of the old Fourteen, torsion-bar suspension and a normal alligator bonnet. Deliveries were announced for mid-1956, but in the meantime a change of management took place at Daimlers. Under the leadership of the energetic Mr Edward Turner, all the dead wood was ruthlessly pruned away, and among the casualties was the wretched 'Sprite'. It was explained at the time that the cost of tooling for a production of a hundred cars a week would be £500,000 as against the £30,000 it cost to put the original Ten into production in 1932; and it is a matter of opinion whether the market could or would have absorbed 5,000 'Sprites' a year.

That was the end of Lanchester. 'One may view the disappearance of the current type with some degree of equanimity,' observed Laurence Pomeroy in *The Motor*, 'but one should not forget that the name Lanchester was the symbol for advanced thinking for over forty years.' Had Lanchesters passed into Valhalla in 1931, they would have attracted far more mourners than they did.

One may liken the *marque* in its declining years to a semi-invalid, still able to render some service but no longer capable of fulfilling the function for which he was trained. The end itself sprang from sociological reasons, for the people who bought the Tens and Fourteens were retired people, professional men and Colonial servants. After the war their income declined and their taxes went up, and when the time came to replace the cars that had served them faithfully for many years, they lacked the cash to purchase another Lanchester. Lanchester died quite simply for this reason, and because the make was allowed to lose both identity and meaning. It is perhaps significant that when the parent Daimler concern came under Jaguar control in 1960, the Lanchester was not revived. The name had lost all the relevance it had once had.

CHAPTER 9

Nemesis Delayed:
The Lea-Francis Story

'Throughout a long history Lea-Francis have demonstrated by successful participation in motoring events throughout the world, the superiority of their cars both for reliability and high performance.'

Lea-Francis catalogue, 1939

WITH this slightly misleading statement, Lea-Francis of Coventry launched for the third time into car manufacture. The high-minded talk about competition work was not by any means unwarranted, for the firm had behind it an illustrious record both in trials and in sports-car racing and, almost as the new catalogue went to press, Mr Charles Follett, their London distributor, was winning an August Long Handicap at Brooklands in a new 1½-litre sports model at an impressive 90·98 m.p.h. The statement was misleading in that Lea-Francis had made no cars at all between 1907 and 1920, and precious few prior to 1922.

Nonetheless, they faced the autumn of 1938 with high hopes, having made a better recovery than most makers who had perpetrated a real 'clanger'. For Lea-Francis in the near past had produced a resoundingly bad car.

I am going to differ violently with the pundits in my definition of a bad car. We are rapidly learning to despise vehicles because we know they will never qualify, even in the remote future, as Post-Vintage Thoroughbreds or because no right-minded person, in our estimation, would drive them for pleasure. There are a lot of cars which I would never drive from choice, and whose specifications fail to interest me at all. I hope I shall never sink to the level at which I shall *choose* to drive one, but I look upon such machines as cars designed for someone who bears no similarity in temperament or tastes to myself. To my way of thinking, a bad car is one which fails to fulfil its intended rôle with either reliability or efficiency, and under this heading I must regretfully list the 14/40 Lea-Francis.

Lea-Francis did not deserve to die. Alongside this lamentable LFS model, they produced some outstandingly good 'fours', and it is these that are now remembered. And in the last resort, the LFS did not kill them: they recovered from this stunning blow, struggled through a long and stultifying receivership and climbed to their feet, only to be forced out of the industry by circumstances over which they had no control.

The Lea-Francis story started in 1895, when R. H. Lea and G. J. Francis opened a factory in Day's Lane, Coventry, for the manufacture of high-grade cycles under the initial brand-name of 'Lea'. Mr Lea had already served seventeen years with the Singer company, the last seven of them as works manager, and the firm rapidly established itself in this field, later extending their activities to embrace the manufacture of motor cycles.

The firm never did more than toy with four-wheelers in Veteran days. While experiments may have been carried out as early as 1902, we do not hear of any Lea-Francis cars in the metal until the 1904 Crystal Palace Show, when the company exhibited a 15 h.p. car of curious design.

This came from the drawing-board of no less a person than Alex Craig, who seems at that time to have divided his talents between various firms. The hallmarks of Mr Craig's ingenuity were overhead camshafts and underfloor engines: the Maudslay of 1903 had o.h.c.; the contemporary Standard, made by another member of the Maudslay family, had an incredibly short-stroke (152·4 × 76·2 mm.) single-cylinder engine under the floor, while the Singer of 1904 bore a marked resemblance to the Craig-designed Lea-Francis shown at the Crystal Palace. As late as 1922, Mr Craig was working on a 2-litre overhead-camshaft 'six' for Maudslay, but his intriguing 15/80 unfortunately never went into production.

The first 'Leaf' had a horizontal three-cylinder engine of 101·6 × 152·4 mm. mounted under the floor. The mechanically-operated inlet valves were actuated by an overhead camshaft, and the connecting rods were twenty-nine inches long, the object of this remarkable feature being to reduce the friction on the cylinder walls; and both these and the crankshaft were drilled—very advanced practice for 1904. A three-speed gearbox was provided, and students of early motoring technology will doubtless appreciate *The Car Illustrated*'s learned exposition of this:

'Each end of the crankshaft is provided with a flywheel containing a friction clutch. These clutches are mounted on both sides of an extension shaft, on the other end being the chain sprocket pinions. The two clutches give the highest and middle speeds, and drive absolutely direct to the rear axle, and the two speeds are obtained by making the ratio of the chain drive on the one side suitable for the top speed, while the ratio on the other side is designed to give the middle speed.'

By 1905, this machine was listed in the *Buyers' Guide* at £787 10s, and an enthusiastic journalist was observing that 'the spanners fit the nuts'—not such a platitude as it sounds, since in those days of non-standard screw threads and non-interchangeable parts any self-respecting 'motor house' included a screw-cutting lathe in its equipment. It was, however, announced that Mr Craig was responsible for the newly introduced 12 h.p. Singer car—an exciting departure from that company's usual line of 'motor-wheels' and three-wheeled governess carts—which was being made 'under licence from Lea and Francis Limited'; so perhaps the idea was that Singer should continue the development of the design.

Be that as it may, neither Singer nor Lea-Francis was bulking very large in the car world at that date, and by the time the former had found its niche it was making conventional front-engined four-cylinder cars with White and Poppe units, which bore little affinity to anything so far offered by Mr Craig. The Lea-Francis rose in price to £850 in 1906, and disappeared thereafter. It was not until the 1922 Motor Show that the Coventry firm was to put in a reappearance.

They occupied the intervening years in building up a first-class reputation as makers of motor cycles at their new works in Lower Ford Street. One of the gaps that is all too often noticed in my motor-cycle collection at Beaulieu is the absence of one of these models, and the quality and workmanship of their machine was seldom surpassed. By 1922, production was centred round two all-chain models of $3\frac{1}{2}$ h.p. and 5 h.p.: both had i.o.e. vee-twin engines of M.A.G. manufacture, and the bigger type cost £125 as a solo—which was certainly not cheap.

After the first World War, the company decided to enter the car market, but their initial efforts were very half-hearted, and only a handful of vehicles with four-cylinder engines of 11·9 and 13·9 h.p. were turned out. Little is known of these cars, but photographs reveal an uninspired and ponderous-looking machine with a radiator quite unrecognizable as a Lea-Francis. They cannot have been profitable, either, for in 1922 the firm got into financial difficulties.

It is a curious characteristic of the Lost Causes that they came to each other's rescue in emergencies, and Lea-Francis's saviour was Mr C. B. Wardman, the firm's London distributor. Mr Wardman had many connexions with the motor industry. Among the makes he handled were Ruston-Hornsby and Vulcan, and he was managing director of the latter firm. Thus began the curious liaison between

Lea and Francis Ltd. and Vulcan Motors Ltd., which was to last until 1928.

While some controversy exists as to the date of the first Vulcan car, it is certain that the company was turning out inexpensive light machines in 1903 under the control of the Hampson family, who were enthusiastic pioneer motorists and featured prominently in the early Blackpool speed trials, driving, be it noted, not Vulcans but Lanchesters and Mercédès. By 1914, Vulcan were well established both in the private and commercial markets: their bigger private cars were doing well overseas, and they were even dickering with a 20 h.p. vee-eight—'A Car of Supreme Smoothness—Ask The Man Who Owns One.' It is not known whether the Packard Motor Company took steps to restrain Vulcans from using this slogan, but one thing is certain: the eight-cylinder Vulcan disappeared smartly from the market after 1920. Thereafter the company tended to concentrate more and more on trucks, though they continued to make fairly pedestrian motor cars, powered by either Meadows or their own units, until 1928. The Vulcan lorry lasted rather longer, though by the end it had not only changed sponsors twice, but had migrated from Southport to Maidstone, where it disappeared, logically enough, into the Kentish-born Rootes organization, never to emerge. But this is anticipating history.

The Vulcan-Lea-Francis association did not destroy the character of either make, though in the long run, as we shall see, it did Lea-Francis no good. From Vulcan, the Coventry concern got a much-needed shot in the arm, while the established chain of Vulcan dealerships was henceforward shared by the 'Leaf'. Both firms used the Meadows engine, Vulcan being responsible for such units as fell outside the Wolverhampton firm's range. In return, the gearboxes and steering columns for Vulcan cars were made at Coventry by Lea-Francis, who proceeded to set their house in order by scrapping the existing programme lock, stock and barrel.

But not at once. The motor-cycle business, it is true, was rapidly wound up, and in 1924 the remaining stock of unsold machines was offered to the works staff at bargain basement prices; but the firm's car programme was a curious half-way house between the old order and the shape of things to come. The machines offered at the 1922 Motor Show looked to be the fruits of indecision. The 7 h.p. model had a 76 × 76 mm. (690 c.c.) oil-cooled Bradshaw flat-twin engine, in unit with a four-speed gearbox, and was claimed to be the smallest car so equipped. The 8·9 h.p. was a strictly conventional light car with a 60 × 95 mm. s.v. Coventry-Simplex unit and three-speed box, 'dish-pan' disc detachable wheels being used as on the 'twin'; while the 69 × 130 mm. (1,945 c.c.) 11·9 h.p. was a survivor of pre-Vulcan days, with a side-valve fixed-head engine, a separate four-speed gearbox and steel artillery wheels wearing 760 × 90 mm. tyres. The Bradshaw-engined 'twin' listed at £190, the Simplex-engined car at £235 and the old '11·9' at £395. Only the 9 h.p. seems to have been made in any quantity; the 11·9 h.p. was dropped almost immediately, though one was retained at the works for a year or two as a hack vehicle. Only one link with the motor-cycle business remained: G. J. Francis' son had founded the firm of Francis and Barnett Ltd. whose two-stroke motor cycles built up an excellent reputation in the 'twenties and 'thirties, the company ultimately being absorbed into the A.M.C. Group. Curiously enough, though the Francis-Barnett factory was situated in the same street as Lea and Francis Ltd., the two businesses were never connected.

By the summer of 1923, the full effect of the new régime was being felt, and the Coventry-Simplex-engined 'Model C' had given way to a car of similar appearance, with a 63 × 100 mm. (1,247 c.c.) Meadows o.h.v. push-rod unit, developing, in its original form, 19 b.h.p. at 2,000 r.p.m. Thereafter, with one brief and unimportant exception, all four-cylinder Lea-Francis cars made up to the closing of the old factory in 1935 were to have Meadows engines.

This Ten was undoubtedly the model which put Lea-Francis on the motoring map, and it was progressively evolved until 1928, though from 1926 onwards it was eclipsed by the more famous series of 12 h.p. cars. In its original 1923 form (the 'D'-type), it had a three-speed gearbox and B.L.I.C. magneto ignition—Lea-Francis adhered to the magneto right to the end of the old company's life. Front suspension was by semi-elliptic springs, quarter-elliptics being used at the rear. The 'Chummy', a popular style of occasional four-seater, cost £250, the sybarite having the choice of a coupé at £295 or a cabriolet for £30 more. Electric lighting and starting were standard on all models, and in January 1924, *The Autocar* organized a test of three examples—a two-seater, the standard 'Chummy', and a sports model with a boat-decked aluminium body and a four-speed gearbox. This component came in for high praise, having a set of 'real trials ratios', including a close-ratio third and an ultra-low bottom. 'The indirect gears,' commented the tester, 'were not unduly noisy', so evidently the tendency towards rude noises manifested by later Lea-Francis boxes was not yet in evidence, but the peculiar layout of the gate on the three-speed models was duly noted. It is a commentary on the spirit in which test cars were approached in those days that peculiar gate arrangements did not evoke a barrage of criticism: in the 'thirties, the practices of such makers as Panhard and Wolseley, who persisted in putting the two higher ratios on the 'wrong' side, and Minerva, who transposed first and reverse, were to come under fire, and a certain manufacturer who essayed a right-hand steering-column shift in 1946 was to find himself very unpopular indeed. Fuel consumption was quoted at 34 m.p.g.

The 1925 models offered a choice of three or four-speed gearboxes, 'low-pressure' tyres were included in the specification, and the price of the two-seater dropped from £270 to £262 10s. A similar car with the three-speed box could be obtained for only £250, these cars being types 'E' and 'F'. A short-chassis three-speed model with brakes on the rear wheels only was available for a mere £210 in 1926, the long-chassis cars being supplied with four-speed boxes and f.w.b. this year. Even in 1928 it was possible to buy one of these cars with two-wheel brakes and a three-speed gearbox. Most of the later 'Model H' cars, incidentally, had the 12 h.p. engine, which was optional for the payment of an extra £10: thereafter the firm concentrated almost exclusively on the production of 1½-litre cars, wisely avoiding the pitfall of attempting to compete with Morris once their reputation in the light-car field was firmly established.

There was nothing very startling about the 10 h.p. Lea-Francis: in fact, if one forgets the 'Hyper' supercharged models, there is very little of a startling technical nature to be found in any Lea-Francis car made during the Vintage era. The secret of the Lea-Francis designers was the blending of conventional components—Meadows engines and their own transmissions and brake gear—into a vehicle which had a character of its own. What is more, they made no attempt to race their products until the cars were firmly established on the market via the hard school of reliability trials. H. E. Tatlow, the works manager, regularly entered the 10 h.p. cars in these events, and they shot into prominence overnight after Tatlow's own performance in the R.A.C. Small Car Trials of 1924. This event had a tremendous effect on the buying habits of the more enthusiastic light-car owner, and it was not lost on anyone that Lea-Francis carried off the awards for hill climbing, consistent running, and, most important, condition at the finish. Nineteen twenty-five saw five 'Golds' in the 'Exeter', six in the 'Land's End', and no fewer than eleven in the 'Edinburgh'. In the first quarter of 1926, the cars figured prominently in the award lists of the 'Exeter', the Colmore Cup, the Essex Motor Club's trial, the Coventry and Warwickshire Club's Manville Trophy, the Victory Cup and the 'Land's End'. Tatlow's name bulks largest in this period, but among the other notable drivers of Lea-Francis cars were R. T. Horton, later to achieve fame behind the wheel of M G s, and L. T. Delaney, a subsequent managing director of Lea and Francis, who combined the selling and servicing of the Coventry-made cars with the importation of such exotic foreigners as the Delaunay-Belleville and the Velie. Delaney, incidentally, sponsored the 'Hyper's competition appearances after the appointment of a Receiver in 1930. Though the S.M.M.T. ban on works entries in the trials put paid to this overwhelming string of official victories, Lea-Francis continued to be a major force in trials, and even in the nineteen-sixties the few remaining 'classic' trials will see the odd 12/40 earning a first-class award.

The success of the 10 h.p. car had given Lea-Francis their place in the sun. The arrival of the 69 × 100 mm. o.h.v. 4ED Meadows in 1925 served to consolidate the situation. The Meadows is possibly the most famous proprietary four-cylinder unit ever to appear on the British market, and it proved susceptible to tuning in a way that its makers could scarcely have envisaged. From 1929 it was installed in many of Frazer-Nash's 1½-litre cars. The French Derby concern adapted it to drive the front wheels of their 1933 offering, and it found its way under the bonnets of a diversity of other machinery, from the staid Rhodes and Hamptons of the late nineteen-twenties to the ferocious supercharged 1½-litre Bond. The Meadows was used by Lea-Francis to propel the square-rigged 12/22, a strictly family car with no sporting propensities: in a slightly hotter form it powered the 12/40, which was a fast touring car capable of an honest 60 m.p.h. in four-seater form, while in supercharged guise it was installed in the 'Hyper Sports', the first blown car to be produced in series in England. Touring models had wide-ratio gearboxes (4·7, 7·3, 11·2 and 18·8 : 1), but an alternative box with a very close-ratio third was available. It is a mistake, incidentally, to imagine that all four-cylinder Lea-Francis cars with sloping radiators are 'Hypers': from 1929 onwards, a number of the staider versions, notably the 'V'-type fixed-head coupés, were so equipped.

While series production of the 12 h.p. cars did not start until August 1925, a sports 12/40 was announced in January of that year. This car (type 'L') had a machined and balanced crankshaft, full pressure lubrication, tulip valves with duplex valve springs, and aluminium pistons. With its polished aluminium body and cream-painted instrument panel, it had a distinctly sporting appearance, while retardation was taken care of by the adoption of compensated four-wheel brakes of Lea-Francis's own design. Sixty m.p.h. was guaranteed. For the 1926 season, the Meadows engine in 'softer' form, with cast-iron pistons, was applied to the new 12/22. Detachable disc wheels were still standard on all but the sports cars, but during the season a number of cars were made with artillery wheels, which somehow looked out of place on this *marque*—far handsomer were the later 12/40s, with their knock-on hubs revolving with the wire wheels.

For the 1926 season Lea-Francis took their first halting steps towards six-cylinderism with an 18 h.p. (69 × 120 mm., 2,244 c.c.) o.h.v. push-rod model. Twin carburettors were featured, but unusual for a Lea-Francis was the adoption of cantilever rear suspension and overhead worm drive. In appearance it was not unlike the contemporary Vulcan—hardly surprising, since it was designed and built at Southport—while the sporting four-seater body had a look of the early M.G. about it. The catalogued price was £525, but it is doubtful if any examples reached the public.

In August 1926, an 'M'-type 12/40 sports-tourer was road-tested by *The Autocar*: 50 b.h.p. at 4,200 r.p.m. was now claimed from the faithful Meadows; the brakes, assisted by Dewandre vacuum servo, proved capable of bringing the car from 40 m.p.h. to a dead stop in ninety feet, while the presence of the close-ratio box was reflected in maxima of 70 m.p.h. on top and very little less on third. Summing up, the testers observed: 'A high average speed can be maintained without risk or effort, and without alarming the passengers.'

A fairly complicated range was announced for 1927. In addition to the well-established 10 h.p. range, augmented this year by a 'chummy' model with the delightful title of 'Bwlch-y-Groes Wizard' —the nickname, incidentally, bestowed on the victorious car in the 1924 Small Car Trials, and executed in mud on the side of the vehicle's coachwork!—there were the 12/22 and the 12/40. All cars except the three-speed Tens had mechanical screen wipers, driving mirrors and bulb and electric horns. The 'Super Sports' models had shock absorbers all round, twin carburettors, a rev counter and ship-type ventilators (one of these curious badges of sportiness which crop up from time to time, like the 'speed-spray' bonnet motifs of the nineteen-thirties), all for £450. Also, they were now guaranteed to do 70 m.p.h.

In addition, there was the unfortunate 14/40 h.p. 'T'-type. This was designed by Mr A. O. Lord, who had previously been associated with the Albert car and subsequently with the odd Loyd-Lord two-stroke, made in Chiswick in 1923-4. On paper, the 'LFS' engine, as it was known, was an exciting proposition. It had six cylinders of 60 mm. bore and 100 mm. stroke, giving a capacity of 1,696 c.c. The twin overhead camshafts were chain-driven, lubrication was by gear-type pump, the crankshaft was of four-bearing type, machined and balanced, and H-section connecting rods were used. The successful Lea-Francis four-wheel brakes and four-speed gearbox were used on this model. Unlike the previous experimental 18 h.p. car, the 14/40 had bevel final drive, and wire wheels were fitted, as on the sports 12/40. A top-gear ratio of 4·55 : 1 was provided for open cars, but the saloons, in anticipation of the horrid practices of the early 'thirties, were endowed with a 5 : 1 top and an 8·46 : 1 third. The engines for these cars were made at Southport, and Vulcans solemnly put out a very similar 14 h.p. model. Prices of the Lea-Francis were £395 for the tourer and £550 for the saloon. Vulcan versions were priced from £375.

The 'LFS' was a disaster. It all but undid the excellent spadework of the four-cylinder cars, now not far from their zenith. Thanks to the excellence of Lea-Francis chassis design, it handled well, and the depressing ratios did good work in coaxing a saloon weighing a formidable 26½ cwt. up Kirkstone Pass at 25–30 m.p.h. Its great weakness, however, was bearing failure, and the manufacturers made the fatal mistake of entering the model for a R.A.C.-supervised trial at Brooklands in July 1927. Six of these six-cylinder tourers were to run for six hours at 60 m.p.h. To make things even more difficult for themselves, they arranged that each car should be timed separately, instead of aiming at a mean figure for all the vehicles. Only three finished; big-end failure accounted for the remainder, A. O. Lord's car, with poetic justice, going out early on. For some mysterious reason, the lower ratio specified for the saloons was used in these cars, in spite of which one car managed to lap at 64 m.p.h. The model was continued quietly for two more seasons, a free-wheel being made available as an option, but the damage was done, though the lubrication troubles were rectified by fitting twin oil pumps, one feeding to the crankshaft and the other to the rocker gear.

This catastrophic performance rather overshadowed the racing début of the four-cylinder cars. Whereas the six-cylinder programme

seems to have been ineptly managed, a careful scheme of development was followed with the 'fours', and Lea-Francis undoubtedly
succeeded where others failed in producing a reliable touring car,
which was evolved first into a reliable sports car and thence into a
dependable sports-racer. It is also fair to say that the 'Leafs' that
were raced bore a closer resemblance to the articles on sale to the
general public than did their competitors' cars. The $1\frac{1}{2}$-litre Bugatti,
though usable on the road, was never by any stretch of imagination
a touring car, the $1\frac{1}{2}$-litre twin-camshaft six-cylinder Alfa-Romeo
was both complicated and expensive, and there is really little
affinity between the truly excellent 12/50 Alvis and the f.w.d. 12/75
cars which the makers matched against the productions of Lower
Ford Street. True, the Alvis was a catalogued production model,
but it was a creation of diabolical complexity, and it nearly bank-
rupted its makers. By 1929, be it noted, Alvis had abandoned even
this in favour of a formidable miniature straight-eight, against
which the 'Hyper Sports' could still give a good account of itself.
Lea-Francis, as we shall see, faded away into temporary eclipse at
the end of the Vintage era, but Tourist Trophy-type cars, driven
by such enthusiasts as Stocks and Mangoletsi, were still winning
events in the late 'thirties, by which time one seldom encountered
a f.w.d. Alvis in the entry lists.

At the August Meeting at Brooklands in 1926, G. N. Norris
produced the first of the racing 'Leafs' in the shape of a $1\frac{1}{2}$-litre
stripped two-seater, with the famous 'sloper' radiator characteristic
of all the subsequent 'Hyper Sports' models and also of the later
'V' and 'W'-type 12/40s. It was entered for a 75 m.p.h. Short
Handicap, which it won at 82·4 m.p.h. from two other Lost Causes
in the shape of Captain Marendaz' $1\frac{1}{2}$-litre Marendaz Special and
Whale in the old 1921 Calthorpe single-seater track car. It reappeared later in the season for the 200-Mile Race complete with
a Berk supercharger driven from the crankshaft, in which form the
Meadows was said to develop 88 b.h.p. as against 56 b.h.p. in
unblown form. Blower trouble put it out of the race.

During 1927, the 'blower' cars were progressively developed, and
by April of that year the press were publishing pictures of a business-
like long-tailed two-seater with the sloping radiator and a vertical,
front-mounted Cozette supercharger in place of the Berk instrument
of the 1926 car. A hinged front valance over the dumb irons puzzled
some people, who imagined that this concealed the supercharger in
the fashion of later Bentleys and M.G.s, whereas in fact it hid
nothing more exciting than the starting-handle dogs. Hendy and

Sutton were entered for the Essex M.C.'s Six-Hour Race at Brook-lands, but both retired, while in the Junior Car Club's Sporting Car Race in August, the more touring 12/40s were beaten by the Alvis opposition. Lea-Francis's day was to come.

The firm apparently faced 1928 with unclouded horizons, for the range embraced the 10 h.p. cars in three- and four-speed form, with the option of a 12 h.p. engine. The 12/22 now had a wider track, semi-elliptic suspension at the rear in place of the quarter-elliptics previously used, Hardy Spicer universals, a handbrake operating on the rear wheels instead of on the transmission, and an engine for which 28 b.h.p. was now claimed at 3,000 r.p.m. Disc wheels, however, were still standard, and a tourer cost £295. The fabric saloon was a lot more expensive, at £408. The 12/40 with a sports engine and wire wheels was listed from £325, the 1½-litre supercharged 'Hyper Sports' was a catalogued model at £495, and in addition to the 14/40 there was also a companion 16/60 of similar general design at £675. It had the conventional cylinder dimension of 65 × 100 mm. (1,991 c.c.), and a Vulcan counterpart, costlier by £200, was also listed.

This vast diversity of models perhaps constituted an unrealistic policy, but the firm had yet to reap the sad harvest of the 'LFS' engine, and the demand for the cars was such that in 1926 they had taken the startling step of running off some fifty cars ('Model N'), conforming generally to 12/22 specification but with 1½-litre Anzani engines, quite simply because Meadows were unable to keep pace with deliveries of 4ED units.

In the 'Hyper Sports', Lea-Francis had a winner. Apart from the blower there were no unconventional features, and provided care was taken to ensure that the Cozette supercharger was properly lubricated, the cars were reliable. This lubrication was critical, for at full bore the oil requirement rose sharply, and the metering pump on the blower could not always cope, with catastrophic con-sequences to the crankshaft. The 'Hyper', however, was unques-tionably a potent piece of machinery, and was good for 90 m.p.h. in road trim with open body. *The Autocar* tested a fixed-head sports-man's coupé in January 1929. This dreadfully ugly machine was described with uncritical abandon as 'very smart . . . with a com-modious luggage box', but it proved capable of close on 85 m.p.h., could accelerate from 10 to 30 m.p.h. on second in five seconds, and would surmount a gradient of 1 in 6½ at 32 m.p.h. in third gear. Its tractability was remarked upon, but customers had to tolerate a fuel consumption of 20 m.p.g., a Kigass fuel mist injector to aid cold starting was necessary, and the testers considered that noiseless changes of gear could be achieved only by practice. The main point, however, was that all this undoubted performance could be purchased for a mere £525. By contrast, the stock 'Ulster' model 12/40 h.p. saloon tested two months later was a good 25 m.p.h. slower, and required three seconds more to accelerate from 10 to 30 m.p.h.

It is of interest to note in passing that the engines destined for all the supercharged cars were completely rebuilt in the Lea-Francis factory, using needle-bearing crankshafts, low-compression heads and pistons and steel connecting-rods, only the block and sump emerging as supplied by Meadows. Team cars had stronger rear axles, full vacuum-servo brakes, and fifty-two-gallon tanks in their tails. Thus it is fair to say that the superchargers on these cars were not just an afterthought to boost the output.

In the 1928 Ulster T.T. the two great rivals—Alvis and Lea-Francis—met face to face, and the result was incredibly close, Kaye Don's 'Hyper' just beating Cushman's f.w.d. Alvis by averaging 64·06 m.p.h. as against his opponent's 64·02. In addition to collecting the *Daily Mail*'s prize for an outright win, he was also awarded *The Motor* trophy for his victory in the 1,500 c.c. class. 'Lea-Francis,' observed *The Autocar*, 'deserved to win, for the cars were well prepared, and gave no trouble.' Even more meritorious was Don's third place, on the same car, in the J.C.C.'s 200-Mile Race, for he averaged 68·93 m.p.h. and was beaten only by two out-and-out racing cars, Malcolm Campbell's straight-eight Delage and the Eyston brothers' eight-cylinder 'Type 39' Bugatti.

Thenceforward the cars were regularly raced with works support up to the appointment of a Receiver in November 1930. But though the 'sixes' were being quietly played down, the firm was still toying with multi-cylinder engines. In 1928, H. W. Purdy went out after Class E British records at Brooklands in a special car fitted with a 2-litre American Miller straight-eight engine, gearbox and transmission, taking the 'Hour' at 110·63 m.p.h. It is curious that the Miller unit, normally associated with front-wheel drive, should have been fitted in a conventional chassis like the Lea-Francis, and this project was never developed further. It had no connexion, incidentally, with the endeavours made by Captain A. G. Miller to utilize the 14/40 for competition work.

Nineteen twenty-nine was a patchy year from the competition viewpoint, though the growing acceptance of unsupercharged and supercharged four-cylinder cars alike compensated for the misfortunes that attended the 'sixes'. A correspondent writing in

The Autocar in March of that year observed that the blown cars would 'scrap successfully with any car made anywhere, costing up to £1,000', and Lea-Francis certainly turned in two excellent performances; one in the Saorstat Cup at Phoenix Park, where S. C. H. Davis, Green and Shaw finished second, third and fourth after non-stop runs; and the other in the B.R.D.C. '500' where the Pellew/Margets car came in seventh, winning the 1,500 c.c. class at an average of 89·9 m.p.h. Alfas, be it noted, had now gone up to 1¾ litres and thus were not competing directly against the Coventry cars. Lea-Francis also finished seventh and eighth in the 'Double-Twelve', but an entry of no fewer than ten cars in that year's T.T., with aluminium bodies, spare wheels mounted in the tail, quicker-action hoods and wire gauze windscreens availed them nothing, only Ellison finishing, well down the list, though their other drivers included Don, Sutton and Stanley Woods, the famous motor cyclist.

The 1930 range was confined to four-cylinder cars; the 'U'-type 12/22, the 'P'-type 12/40 with vertical radiator, the 'V'- and 'W'-types with closed bodywork and sloping radiator, and the 'S'-type 'Hyper'. Peacock and Newsome's works-entered 'Hyper', with obligatory four-seater body, finished sixth in general classification and fourth in the Rudge-Whitworth Cup at Le Mans, averaging 59 m.p.h., but the cars failed to repeat their successes of 1929 at Phoenix Park. At the 1930 Show, they came out with a new six-cylinder car, the single overhead-camshaft 2-litre 'Ace of Spades', so called because the engine, in elevation, resembled this card inverted. It was designed and built by Lea-Francis, and was installed in a chassis very similar to the 12/40 in unit with a new type of four-speed gearbox known as the 'Duo', which had constant-mesh third and fourth ratios. This box was a great deal quieter than previous Lea-Francis productions, and was also more durable in that it did not tend to grow noisy after a substantial mileage—generally about 40,000—had been covered. Seventy-five m.p.h. was claimed on a 4·7 : 1 top gear, and a six-light saloon listed at £495. Chromium plate and safety glass were standardized throughout the range, but right-hand change was retained. This model was road-tested several times by *The Autocar*, which went into rhapsodies over it. In June 1932 the journal praised many features:

'. . . power and performance, with a high maximum when required, and then . . . good steering, a sensitive gear-change, road-holding that will allow the car to be taken round corners quite fast and yet feel safe, and brakes equal to the speed and capable of standing up to their work. . . .'

The actual figures achieved: a top speed of just under 75 m.p.h.

with 60 available on third, allied to a fuel consumption of 24 m.p.g., do not seem startling to us today, but it should be remembered that the average two-litre saloon of 1931 was hard put to it to hold mile-a-minute speeds, possessed dreadfully undergeared steering, and was blessed with gear ratios calculated to make the V.S.C.C. wince. Lea-Francis had at last produced a good 'six' to match their 'fours'.

Unfortunately, they had done so too late. The appointment of Mr Charles Turner as Receiver was announced in November 1930, and for some seven years the firm went into eclipse, despite sanction for continuing manufacture of the 12/40 and the new 'Ace of Spades'. A small number of cars was turned out, 1932 models having electric fuel pumps in place of the mechanical type, while the 'Duo' gearbox was standardized on all save the supercharged models. In February 1932, a 69 × 100 mm. (2,243 c.c.) Eighteen, virtually a scaled-up 2-litre, was introduced. This car had a radiator very similar to the cars built by the reorganized concern in 1938, but hardly any were made. By 1934, though, when a 12/40 could be bought for £315 and a six-cylinder car for only £395, production was almost at a standstill.

In December of that year, interest was again quickened by the announcement that a Mr Edwin Bott had purchased the company, and that full production would be resumed at an early date. As many people still considered—and not without justification—that the 'Hyper' was the fastest standard car in its class, hopes were raised, but nothing happened. The money was apparently not forthcoming, and Leaf Engineering Limited lasted only a few months. No cars were made after the winter of 1935.

This was not, however, the end, for in 1937, G. H. Leek and R. H. Rose formed a new company, Lea-Francis Engineering (1937) Ltd. The new concern was a complete break with the past. Both the Meadows engine and the Lower Ford Street Works were abandoned, operations being transferred to the former Triumph plant in Much Park Street. As might have been expected, the new Rose-designed engines followed very much upon the lines of the same engineer's four-cylinder Rileys, with twin high-set camshafts and push-rod-operated overhead valves. Otherwise the specification was typical of the period: pump cooling, coil ignition, four-speed synchromesh gearbox with central control, single dry-plate clutch, spiral bevel final drive and semi-elliptic suspension all round. Girling rod-operated brakes were used, and the cars retained the knock-on wire wheels of earlier days. Buyers had the choice of two sizes of engine, a 69 × 100 mm. Twelve and a 72 × 100 mm.

(1,629 c.c.) Fourteen. Stylish bodies by New Avon and Charles-worth, centralized chassis lubrication by the Luvax-Bijur system, and luxurious equipment rounded off what amounted to a strictly touring model, saloons being priced at £395 with the choice of four-light or six-light coachwork. A concession was, however, made to the 'Leaf' tradition by the inclusion of a 1⅓-litre super-sports two-seater with specially tuned engine, higher ratio back axle and Telecontrol shock absorbers, at £475. One of these cars, as we have seen, was successfully raced at Brooklands in stripped form by Charles Follett, the *marque*'s London distributor.

Production started in 1938, and the cars were exhibited at Earls Court that year. The new Lea-Francis cars were just making a reputation for themselves when war broke out. Not that this should have been any kind of catastrophe, for the war brought with it an acute car shortage, and the ensuing sellers' market enabled the specialist producers to build up a backlog of orders which kept them going right into the nineteen-fifties. The specialist car also had the advantage that it dated more slowly, and consequently long pro-duction runs could be contemplated with equanimity. Lea-Francis had a sound car with a first-class designer in Rose, and as it was virtually a new model when production was suspended, they could look forward to several seasons of progressive development. There was but one fly in the ointment—purchase tax.

I do not believe in bringing in politics, but there can be no doubt that the crippling 66⅔ per cent tax imposed on cars with a basic price of over £1,000 served to kill off a lot of the smaller manufacturers. For a long time they hung on, trying to keep the basic figure down to the magic £999 without skimping quality, but, as labour and materials grew more and more expensive, more and more of them crossed their Rubicon and were forced to price their products beyond the reach of their customers. This, and nothing else, killed Lea-Francis. They could not stand the cost of introducing a completely new range as long as they were forced to sell the existing cars at uneconomic prices. The post-war cars were well enough liked, though they were regrettably heavier than their 1939 counterparts.

The Twelve and Fourteen duly reappeared in 1946 without many major changes, though the impending demise of the horsepower tax enabled the bigger car's bore to be increased to 75 mm. giving a capacity of 1,767 c.c. The same chassis were used for both models, and the standard coachwork was a four-light saloon with swept tail and high waistline—to my eyes curiously archaic, though a

Lea-Francis advertisement asserted that it had been 'acclaimed on the Continent as the most elegant of the post-war cars'. Alternative body styles were a fixed-head coupé by Westland Aircraft and a station wagon—the last-mentioned an understandable addition when one remembers that in 1946 this style was exempt from purchase tax, even if it was nominally subject to a 30 m.p.h. speed limit. Price, including the regrettable impost, was £1,214; but this rose to £1,342 by May 1947, and in 1951 customers had to part with £1,380.

Nearly all the standard cars made were Fourteens, and in October 1947, Lea-Francis decided to launch into the sports-car market again with a special sports two-seater. The use of twin S.U. carburetters, special connecting-rods and a ribbed sump pushed the output up from the saloon's 56 b.h.p. to 64 b.h.p. at 5,300 r.p.m.; and by the time that this model was replaced by the 2½-litre in 1950, the engineers at Coventry were extracting no less than 87 b.h.p. The aerodynamic body was controversial in style: I rather liked it, but the humped scuttle of the nineteen-thirties consorted ill with the inbuilt headlamps and faired rear wheels of the nineteen-forties. Despite a determined bid by Lea-Francis in the U.S. market—they shipped two works demonstration cars to the United States in February 1948—it never caught on. Early in the same year, Alvis announced that they had taken up the manufacturing of printing machines, so Lea-Francis were not alone in feeling the cold.

Nonetheless, they maintained the unequal struggle. At the 1948 Show, they displayed an export model of the Fourteen (Mk. VII) with a bulky six-light aerodynamic body made, unlike most Lea-Francis coachwork, in their own factory. It had independent torsion-bar front suspension and Girling hydro-mechanical brakes. A year later they followed this up with a brace of 85 × 100 mm. (2,496 c.c.) Eighteens, a saloon on the lines of the export Fourteen, and a sports model replacing the smaller 1947 car. Suspension and brakes were similar to the Mk. VII, and the car certainly went well, but it had to compete with the 2½-litre Riley, and its price of £1,945 (including tax) hardly compared with the £1,225 asked for the Nuffield production. The Fourteen underwent minor styling changes, the saloon model acquiring torsion bar i.f.s., though 'cart' suspension was retained on the station wagons. For 1951 faired-in headlamps were featured on the smaller cars, at which time the station wagon was brought into line with the other models by the inclusion of i.f.s. In 1953 full hydraulic brakes were standardized.

Financial results fluctuated. Lea-Francis made a profit of something over £8,500 in 1947-8, a resounding loss of £11,000 the following financial year, and came back into the black in 1949-50, though a warning note was sounded by the imposition of purchase tax on station wagons. Always they hoped for some alleviation of this burden. In March 1953 they cut their prices drastically, to keep production flowing while buyers, confronted with a Budget in the following month, dickered and kept away from dealers' showrooms.

But while the Lea-Francis car was slowly forced off the market, the Lea-Francis engine went from strength to strength. The high-camshaft Rose engines, as any study of Riley history will show, were capable of considerable development, and in 1948 Lea-Francis tried to sell their units to America—not for sports cars, but for midget dirt-track racers. A party under Albert Ludgate of the firm's design staff successfully demonstrated a 1,674 c.c. engine developing 120 b.h.p., and a few were sold, but this project never brought the dividends it deserved. The Lea-Francis engine also formed the basis for the engines used in Connaught sports and racing cars, and the original 'L.2' and 'L.3' Connaughts, which were sold in small quantities, had modified Fourteen units giving 100 b.h.p. at 6,000 r.p.m. on an 8·2 : 1 compression ratio. By the time Connaught had progressed to 2½-litre Formula I cars, direct fuel injection and Tony Brooks's famous victory at Syracuse, there was little if any Lea-Francis left in the specification, but the facts are interesting in showing the firm's vital contribution to the genesis of a gallant Grand Prix contender. Turner Sports Cars of Wolverhampton also used the Lea-Francis Fourteen engine in one of their prototypes, though this make was not to appear in any quantity for some time to come, and, when it did, it would be transformed into a B.M.C.-powered 800 c.c. roadster. The sporting cars made at Much Park Street, by contrast, were primarily fast tourers and never figured prominently in competition results, though they had their brief moments of glory in the 1951 Isle of Wight Rally, when a 2½-litre was second in General Classification and post-war 'Leafs' collected two class wins in the ensuing Ventnor hill climb.

Lea-Francis did not exhibit at Earls Court in 1953. A company representative was credited with the observation that 'the founders of the Company, Mr Lea and Mr Francis, would turn in their graves' if they heard of purchase tax, but the hard undramatic facts were that the hire and manning of a stand at the Show cost £3,000 and the firm did not feel that this expenditure would be justified by the number of customers it would attract. Lea-Francis buyers, they said, were not 'the sort of people who take a fancy to one at the Show. . . . They are owners . . . of some years' standing.' Car production was maintained at a token level, in anticipation of some alleviation in the next Budget.

But when tomorrow came, Lea-Francis were again unprepared. True, they had tried. The closing of their service department at Coventry in 1958 was followed two years later by the new management's announcement that they were ready to resume production, and the London Show that autumn revealed the 'Leaf-Lynx' sports roadster, with 2,553 c.c. Ford 'Zephyr' engine and three S.U. carburettors. Front suspension was by wishbones and torsion bars, and disc brakes were fitted all round. The only extras listed were Laycock de Normanville overdrive and radio; heater and screen washers were included in the all-up price of £2,096. Unfortunately the car looked American within and bulbous without, and the manufacturers unwisely elected to finish their Show car in an emetic shade of mauve. It met with a cool reception, *Autosport* being notably outspoken. Their Show editorial commented: 'If the concern really wishes to stage a come-back, the opinion of the majority is that the car itself will have to be completely restyled to make it look a "quality" sports car, rather than a superior sort of "one-off" special'.

The 'Lynx' was abandoned after only three prototypes had been made, and the Italian stylist Fiore was commissioned to design a series of *gran turismo* bodies incorporating the machine's mechanical components. Meanwhile Lea-Francis tried their luck with the 200 c.c. Nobel 'bubble-car' (previously made in Belfast) and with a miniature tractor, the Unihorse. Neither, however, prospered, and in August 1962 a receiver was appointed yet again. With the dying company's purchase by Quinton Hazell Ltd., it was made abundantly clear that the new proprietors saw no future in the manufacture of specialist cars, and the 'Francesca' was shelved. Lea-Francis had gone down for the third, and last, time.

CHAPTER 10

Dignity and Impudence:
The Private Cars of Leyland and Trojan

'The only car which we consider worth while having as a sparring partner to the Leyland Eight is the Rolls-Royce.'
J. G. Parry Thomas, letter to *The Autocar*, June 1921

'When picknicking, the Trojan does not remain at the roadside obstructing the traffic; it carries the party and their impedimenta right to the site. The number of short cuts that are negotiable will surprise you.'
Trojan advertisement, 1923

WHEN the makers of commercial vehicles turn to private-car design, they can be relied upon to produce something interesting. A fifteen-ton lorry has to stand up to stresses unheard-of in the world of private motoring, and one thinks almost in terms of architecture rather than of design when contemplating such monsters. Further, the driver of a 'heavy' is seldom the owner, and consequently the shibboleths of conventional design can be laid aside more easily, always allowing that such short cuts do not impose complicated maintenance schedules. Leyland, for instance, had a gearless bus chassis on the market in 1934, a good four years before General Motors were even thinking of offering 'Hydramatic' to the public. Almost without exception, the private-car offerings of the heavy-vehicle manufacturers have been of absorbing interest. Guy were offering a vee-eight in 1920, and two years later Maudslay were contemplating a return to the private-car field with a twin overhead-camshaft 2-litre 'six'. A more recent example of what a mere builder of lorries can do when he really tries is the fantastic 2½-litre Pegaso of 1951. Nor should we forget that one of the most consistently successful sports cars of the late nineteen-thirties—the 'Type 135' Delahaye—was powered by a tuned version of that firm's standard truck unit. It is therefore hardly surprising that when Leyland Motors decided to cash in on the post-1918 boom, they sponsored a magnificent luxury car in the shape of a 7¼-litre o.h.c. straight-eight.

Leylands had appeared on the scene at Leyland in 1896 as the Lancashire Steam Motor Co. Ltd., and for the first six years of their existence they concentrated on steam wagons, which enjoyed considerable commercial success; so much so that they were made up to 1920, though from 1904 onwards the firm devoted progressively more time to petrol vehicles. One of their earliest efforts was, however, a superbly dangerous device in the shape of a steam lawn-mower, which anticipated the flame-throwers of the first World War by nearly twenty years. Not that Leylands had the monopoly of such diabolical contrivances, for at the turn of the century an American named Coldwell built a similar machine, which was reputedly used to mow the lawns of the Capitol at Washington. The history of their private cars, however, is inextricably bound up with one man—J. G. Parry Thomas.

Thomas's association with Leylands had started some four or five years before the first World War, when the Lancashire firm had provided facilities for the development of an ingenious electric transmission which the young Welsh engineer had designed. He had also been responsible for the design of a number of Leyland-built railcars which were exported to South America.

When he reappeared at Leyland in 1915, however, he was in charge of the firm's wartime aero-engine programme, and was working on an ingenious X-type eight-cylinder water-cooled unit developing 350 b.h.p. It was so cleverly designed that two men could lift it unaided. From 1917 to 1923 he was to be chief designer to the company, leaving it only when the Leyland car was dropped and the firm decided to concentrate its efforts on lorries and the Trojan, a vehicle of which Thomas did not approve, and for which he publicly disclaimed all responsibility in a letter to *The Autocar* written in 1922.

Thomas's original design for Leyland Motors was a vee-twelve, based on the then new Packard 'Twin-Six'. It seems probable that tests were undertaken with a Packard, but Leylands have no record of their own vee-twelve ever taking the road. Thomas, however, had a prototype of the later straight-eight design running in 1918, though it was not until July 1920 that a correspondent in *The Autocar* dared to mention that he had seen a very large sports tourer parked in Worthing, which he suspected to be an eight-in-line.

To Thomas may well go the credit of evolving the first straight-eight to go into series production. While C. G. V., Bellamy, Weigel and Bugatti undoubtedly built and ran special 'one-off' racing straight-eights long before 1918, nobody had yet thought to offer one of these impressively lengthy and smooth-running units for sale to the public; and I frankly do not know for certain who was first. In 1919-20, four manufacturers—Bugatti, Leyland, Isotta-Fraschini and Duesenberg—had touring straight-eights on the road, but of these only Isotta-Fraschini were to make any quantity in the next four years. Later, of course, was to come that weird and wonderful crop of machinery with apparently one purpose only: to make a large car longer.

The Thomas-designed Leyland had a 7,266 c.c. (89 × 146 mm.) engine with cylinders cast *en bloc*. The single overhead camshaft was driven by a triple eccentric and coupling rods from the crankshaft, a system adopted as being quieter than the conventional bevel gear. It certainly succeeded, for even at maximum tune the Brooklands Leyland-Thomas cars were ominously silent. The cylinder head was detachable, ignition was by Delco coil, and oil, which was stored in a tank on the off side of the base chamber, was directed by the flywheel into a trough, whence it was fed by pump to the bearings and up the tubular connecting-rods to the gudgeon pins. A four-speed gearbox was used. An ingenious feature, designed to counter-act the heavy camber of contemporary roads, was the arrangement of the drive shafts to the rear wheels in a wide vee, two separate bevel drives being needed as a result. The massive chassis incor-porated a flexible mounting for the gearbox, which effectively prevented any noise from this component being 'telephoned' through to the car's occupants. Semi-elliptic suspension was used at the front and quarter-elliptics with torsion bars at the rear, an anti-roll bar being provided. It was claimed that a soft ride resulted, the torsion bars being brought into play as the up-and-down move-ments of the wheels increased on bumpy roads.

Unlike the Hispano-Suiza or the Isotta-Fraschini, the Leyland had brakes on the rear wheels only, but with vacuum servo assist-ance—a pioneer application of this. Thomas favoured central change with a visible gate. Forward movement of the lever into a position between bottom and third gears completed the starter circuit (a layout found on the 50/60 FIAT in 1914), and equipment included an engine-driven tyre pump and dimming headlights. The car's appearance was massive rather than beautiful, the front end being cluttered up by an immensely long shaft for the starting-handle, and the vast radiator being reminiscent of that used on the smaller Leyland lorries of the early nineteen-thirties.

As 'The Lion of Olympia', it aroused tremendous excitement when exhibited at the Motor Show in 1920, but the high cost of production, coupled with a steady commercial-vehicle business, resulted in its being quietly withdrawn after 1924; by which time, of course, Thomas had boosted the output of the engine to a good 200 b.h.p. In 1920, 115 b.h.p. were claimed at 2,500 r.p.m., though in twin-carburettor form this was raised to 145 b.h.p. at 3,000 r.p.m. Three chassis lengths, 10 ft. 6 in., 11 ft. 9 in. and 12 ft. 3 in., were available, chassis price being £2,500 in 1920. A year later the price was down to £1,875, a complete tourer selling at £2,700. The cars were shown for the last time at Olympia in 1922. Meanwhile, *The Motor* had found a standard car—not one of Thomas' machines —capable of 90 m.p.h., had noted the eight-cylinder engine's flexibility and freedom from vibration, and praised the suspension, which caused the car to glide over potholes 'like a canoe on a deep, unruffled river'.

Various estimates of Leyland Eight production have been given by different writers, so I feel that it would be apposite to quote from a letter I received from Leyland Motors Ltd. on this subject:

'As far as we can ascertain, fifteen chassis were built, plus an additional one as spares, this going to Thomson and Taylor, and therefore would not count to our output.'

This figure may possibly not take into consideration at least two of the three cars loosely referred to as Leyland-Thomases, but I think I can safely debunk one of the more alluring legends. It has often been alleged, at one time or another, that 'more than half the Leyland Eights made went to India', and enthusiasts have been all but stampeded into taking passage East in quest of one. Only two were actually sold to India, both destined for the Maharajah of Patiala. As Leylands did not deem it necessary to issue a handbook, Thomas's assistant, Reid Railton, went with them to advise His Highness's engineers on maintenance.

Among those who did not buy was my father. The Spurrier family have long been near neighbours of ours at Sowley, and the present head of the company, Sir Henry Spurrier, son of the founder of Leylands, was my father's personal pilot in India in the first World War. Henry Spurrier Sr. personally demonstrated a Leyland Eight tourer to him at Beaulieu, the car touching 80 on the Lymington road—though it is a tribute to the suspension that this did not dislodge Mr Spurrier's bowler hat. He certainly picked the best place for showing off the Leyland's special virtues, for the camber was, and is, distinctly tricky. My father was suitably impressed, but he remarked afterwards to his agent, Captain H. E. R. Widnell, that 'as a Rolls-Royce man, I would consider it an act of traitorism to take any other car'.

Thomas, meanwhile, had persuaded the Leyland directors, against their better judgment, that a high-speed demonstration of the car's capabilities at Brooklands would be a good idea. The directors agreed to this, provided that he used a standard model with full road equipment, but this the resourceful Thomas disregarded, and in fact arrived at the 1922 Easter Meeting in a *stripped* boat-tail two-seater. The clutch gave up on the starting line in the first race for which the car was entered, but later in the day it lapped at 99·21 m.p.h., a creditable performance for a touring car handled by a man with no previous racing experience; who, indeed, had been unable to drive when he first joined Leylands. In passing, it may be noted that A. G. Booth, so I was told, designed the 10·8 Clyno before he learned to drive!

Thereafter Thomas never looked back. Between May 1922 and October 1926, when the eight-cylinder Leyland gave way to 'Babs', the giant chain-driven monster in which he was to meet his death, he won twenty-five first places, twenty-four seconds, and ten thirds on Leylands or the Leyland-Thomases which were evolved from the basic touring-car design, in addition to successful appearances at Saltburn, Boulogne, and Montlhéry. At this last venue the Leyland was run as a 6-litre car with two cylinders inoperative. He also collected over eighty class records. Twice at one meeting, in August 1924, he broke the Lap Record at Brooklands, first at 127·38 m.p.h., and then at 128·36 m.p.h. The following year he raised it to 129·36 m.p.h., while Mrs Wisdom used the second Leyland-Thomas to break the Ladies' Lap Record in 1932 at 121·47 m.p.h.

There is some confusion about the number of Leyland-Thomas cars made, but it is generally accepted that two genuine cars did exist, plus one not-quite-genuine specimen. The original Thomas car, which started as a two-seater and ended up as an aerodynamic single-seater with cowled radiator, ended its days at Brooklands in 1936, when it caught fire while being raced by the late R. J. Munday. The remains were destroyed by enemy action during the second World War. The second car, built by Thomas for his friend Howey, later passed into the hands of the Wisdoms and was broken up in Eastbourne around 1940.

As to the third machine, William Boddy, Editor of *Motor Sport*, has taken me to task for calling it a Leyland-Thomas, since it was built by Thomson and Taylor, Thomas's old firm, two years after his death, to the order of the Hon. David Tennant. It may conceivably have been the 'parts car' Leylands originally supplied to the famous Brooklands establishment. Be that as it may, it is not a standard Leyland (if such a thing may be said to exist), for it has

Perrot-type f.w.b. and no vacuum servo. In chassis form it is said to have lapped Brooklands at 123 m.p.h., and it certainly got round the course in the 1937 M.C.C. High-Speed Trial at 100·61 m.p.h. with full and weighty road equipment, driven by its then owner, Sir Lionel Phillips, Bt., with whom I stayed at his famous home, Vergelegen at the Cape, when a boy. Anyone who has seen the cream two-seater since its magnificent restoration by Leyland's apprentices will testify to the massiveness of the enormous flared wings. It has made several appearances at Prescott, and is said to be capable still of 120 m.p.h., at the price of a 9 m.p.g. thirst which limits its practical value in these days of expensive petrol. Officially, this is the sole survivor of a gallant breed, but I have heard intermittent rumours of two others. They are, however, as elusive as the Indian rope trick.

Leylands never made any more private cars under their own imprint, though half a Leyland Eight engine was later adapted for use in one of their lighter lorries, and in 1927–8 they produced a few 2-litre o.h.c. four-cylinder engines for the Arab, a sports car designed by Reid Railton and made at Letchworth. The Arab was certainly Thomas-inspired, but the camshaft was driven by a single roller chain, and it catered for an entirely different market at £550. Very few were made, and I have never seen one.

Undoubtedly the straight-eights furnished the glamour at Leylands. But in October 1922, just as 'The Lion of Olympia' was making his last bow to the public as a touring car, the uncouth crowings and cacklings of the Trojan were making themselves heard in the land.

Anything more diametrically opposed to Thomas's luxurious saurian cannot be imagined. The Leyland was built regardless of first cost, and regardless of maintenance expense—witness the absence of a handbook—for the man who wanted the best. The Trojan was designed as a multi-purpose poor man's motor car, with simplicity of operation and maintenance as the keynote. The Leyland was an uncommonly fast vehicle: the Trojan was painfully slow, even in an era of slow, overbodied and undergeared cars. The Leyland's silence was uncanny; while the arrival of a Trojan on the scene was heralded by a chorus of cacophony. The big eight-cylinder car was too massive to rank aesthetically with the 37·2 Hispano-Suiza, but the Trojan was plain, downright hideous; while such oddities as chain drive, solid tyres and a horizontal engine under the floorboards provoked ribald laughter even in 1922.

Some people, it is true, looked upon the Trojan as a comic-opera item, as witness the enthusiast who toured Yugoslavia in one in 1935, and was asked, much to his chagrin, if he had made it himself. What the scoffers conveniently forgot was that before 1939 one did not tour the Balkans—except from the safety of a yacht—unless one was compelled to, or was a Monte Carlo Rally competitor, or both.

Leslie Hounsfield, the Trojan designer, however, had plenty of method behind this seeming madness, which stemmed from three prototypes he had made and tested in 1913 and 1914, and a batch of six 'T'-type cars, so called after the index letter of Devonshire, where they were registered and tested in 1921.

These 'T' cars set the pattern for Trojan private-car design up to 1929, and for the layout of most of their vans, as used by the R.A.F., the Territorial Army, Post Office Telephones, Brooke Bond Tea and many others right up to the outbreak of the second World War. The engine was a two-stroke 'square-four'; each pair of cylinders shared a common combustion chamber and a single sparking plug, and in its Vintage form the unit was mounted horizontally, although the 1913 prototype had favoured a vertical position. Bore and stroke were 63·5 mm. and 120·7 mm. respectively, giving a capacity of 1,527 c.c., and 10 b.h.p. was developed almost throughout the rev range, from 400 to 1,200 r.p.m. Hence the unit's fantastic low-speed torque and its ability to climb anything on which the wheels could get a grip. Top gear of the two-speed epicyclic gearbox coped with any gradient up to 1 in 9, an ample compensation for a top speed of only 38 m.p.h. Drive was by a duplex roller chain to a solid rear axle.

All this machinery was mounted in a punt-type frame, and suspension was by long cantilever springs. Retardation was by a handbrake operating on the transmission and a footbrake actuating two internal-expanding shoes in a drum on the near-side rear wheel.

Though the engine lived under the floorboards, there was a conventional bonnet concealing the petrol and water tanks and the carburettor. Three right-hand levers controlled the gearbox, the handbrake and a mechanical starter which enabled the Trojan to be started 'from the seat' without recourse to complex electrical arrangements. Indeed, an electric starter did not become even *optional* equipment on this *marque* until 1931, and was not standardized until a year later. The controls, incidentally, were of the simplest, and when *The Autocar* tried a 'PB' in June 1924, it was observed that the working of the priming device necessitated by the petroil lubrication was the only exercise involved in the car's operation that demanded intelligence. Nonetheless, Trojan's Delco coil ignition and Miller six-volt lighting were well made, and included an ingenious feature whereby a hole was cut in the back panel of the body. The driver could thus see whether he had left his lights on, and Trojans advertised this as a virtue that would commend itself to the absent-minded vicar. It is hardly surprising that they were the only car manufacturers to advertise in *The Church Times*.

Finally, there were the solid tyres. These were a controversial feature. Mr Hounsfield maintained that pneumatics were rendered unnecessary by his cantilever suspension, and there is no doubt that the Trojan rode very smoothly over abominable surfaces. More important, solids were cheap and durable. The cost of a tyre was £2, against £3 to £5 for a comparable pneumatic, and on a light car such as the Trojan they were good for fifteen thousand to twenty thousand miles, whereas anyone who made a high-pressure pneumatic last for more than 8,000 miles was not only lucky; he was an extremely cautious driver. The firm offered pneumatics at £5 extra, but in a contemporary advertisement they commented that they 'didn't think it necessary', and, right up to the introduction of the 'RE' model in 1930, solids continued to be available. On the more conservative vans, they survived even longer.

A 'T'-type Trojan had been submitted to War Office tests in 1921, but had been rejected as being too unorthodox, in spite of coming through with flying colours. Leylands, however, showed considerable interest, and subjected one of these prototypes to further searching trials, including an 'assault course' over railway sleepers bolted to the ground at six-foot intervals. Even this could not break the Trojan, and early in 1923 production was put in hand at the Lancashire firm's branch works at Kingston-upon-Thames. Cars were made by Leyland on a royalty basis, and for the ensuing six years all development work was carried out at Kingston, with Leslie Hounsfield in charge. Production seems to have run at the rate of eighty to a hundred cars a week, and perhaps 15,000 were made in all. The list price, with occasional four-seater 'Utility' body, was £230 in 1922, and the manufacturers estimated running costs at 2*d* per mile, though a year or two later Trojan advertisements carried the dramatic banner headline: 'Can You Afford to Walk?'

Up to the end of 1928, Trojans continued to be made at the Leyland works. The price dropped to £175 for the 1924 season, when a coupé—the 'Utility' with a detachable hardtop—was offered as an alternative style at £215. The Normand Garage, London distributors, were also supplying a special saloon version for commercial travellers, on which they sought the best of both worlds by equipping it with electric and oil lamps. Later in the season the 'Utility' and coupé models were reduced still further to £157 10s and £190 respectively. *The Autocar* tested a 'Utility', commenting that it was eminently suitable for 'country-house work', though they were unable to extract more than 30 m.p.h. over a measured mile. The car ascended Brooklands Test Hill at 6 m.p.h., while in the R.A.C. Small Car Trials Bowden's Trojan won its class. Fifty cars were shipped to Japan that October for use as taxis, their peculiar qualities lending themselves admirably to the tortuous, hilly and ill-surfaced roads of Nippon.

On 1925 models, foot operation was adopted for the primer, and for 1926 the new roller-bearing 'XL' engine replaced the original 'PB' unit with plain bearings. The 'Utility' model with pneumatic tyres was listed at £125, and a three-door full four-seater tourer at £145. The 'XL' engine continued as standard wear for the following three seasons, in the course of which few major changes were made, though a higher axle ratio was introduced for 1927, in which year Leylands issued a 5,000-mile guarantee on all cars. A three-door 'saloon' was listed in 1928 at £170, but this was no more than a standard tourer with detachable hardtop. In the following year, however, the 'Achilles' saloon with folding roof, pneumatic tyres, detachable disc wheels and five-lamp lighting equipment was available for the more sybaritic Trojan owner at £189.

By this time Leyland and Trojan had parted company. Relations terminated in mutual expressions of goodwill, Trojans regaining their independence simply because the growing demand for the parent company's 'heavies' required all the floor space at the Kingston factory. The changeover was gradual: officially, the connexion was severed in May 1928, but Trojans were using up Leyland-made parts for some time after that, and the first entirely Croydon-built Trojan rolled off the lines at Purley Way in January 1930.

Surprisingly enough, Trojans never participated officially in trials, for which their curious little cars were admirably suited, though they were always willing to lend a helping hand to private owners; and in 1927 we find the name of A. F. Scroggs featuring for the first time in awards lists. Group-Captain Scroggs remained faithful to the Trojan until his death in 1965, and no 'Land's End' or 'Exeter' trial was complete without the sight of his immortal RK 9788 grinding its way slowly and inexorably up all the hills. Trojan adaptability displayed itself in other ways: the company's catalogues show pictures of solid-tyred 'Utilities' towing ploughs, and at least one nobleman habitually employed his car to follow the local hunt. Transcontinental motorists did not spurn the Trojan, either. A party of three Indian enthusiasts, led by a Mr Canagasaby, spent fifteen months in driving a second-hand example from Singapore to London—and they made it, with a boiler tube as a front axle; the crew paying their way by working *en route* as lorry drivers, car repairers and postcard sellers! In 1932, four novices had the temerity to purchase a brace of old Trojans for £45 each and drive them from England to Nairobi via the Sahara. Garage proprietors were less appreciative—confronted with bonnets that concealed no engine, dashboards innocent of self-starters and petroil lubrication, they hung out 'No Trojans' notices and turned their backs. I do remember one character, though, who displayed a sign outside his small premises, proclaiming sportingly that he was a 'Jowett and Trojan specialist'.

In 1929, the Croydon firm bid for military contracts with a six-wheeler on an 8 ft. 6 in. wheelbase. The normal Trojan epicyclic box was augmented by an auxiliary two-speed sliding-type box giving a selection of ratios from 4·9 : 1 to 48 : 1. This fearsome device cost £390, but it could carry a twelve-cwt. payload on normal roads and nine cwt. across country, and proved, on test, to be capable of coping with precipitous 1-in-2½ slopes on the Sussex Downs, the tough shingle of Newhaven Beach, and eighteen inches of water. This model, however, did not progress beyond the experimental stage, despite the provision of detachable tracks on the rear wheels as an optional extra. By this time the company evidently felt that something new was indicated, and at the 1929 Show they displayed two attractive and conventional-looking cars, neither of which had yet run on the road. Unfortunately, the new Trojan had sacrificed almost all the old virtues in favour of an appearance designed to attract the Clan Jones, and as a consequence nobody was very enthusiastic.

The 'RE' Trojan retained the two-stroke engine and the epicyclic gearbox, though the latter now offered three forward speeds and a conventional central gate change. The power unit was, however, mounted vertically in a 'boot' at the back, over the rear axle, drive being by chain. Semi-elliptic suspension was used at the rear, with cantilevers at the front, and the otherwise conventional chassis was cloaked with a pretty two-door fabric saloon body whose distinctly sporting aspect was heightened by the use of cycle-type mudguards. The front bonnet was of normal dimensions and provided a useful luggage locker, but there was no starter other than the handle in the cockpit and no front-wheel brakes, either. Initially the frontal radiator, still bearing the proud head of the Trojan Warrior, was a dummy, an elaborate system of 'evaporative cooling' being provided by means of a horizontal cooling surface on top of the engine. This was claimed to give 'a constant temperature a few degrees below boiling point', but evidently it was unsatisfactory, as when the 'RE's started to roll off the production line early in 1931 their vee radiators at the front were found to be the real thing, connected to the engine by a network of pipes. These were said to warm the feet, while an arrangement was also devised whereby the exhaust gases could be by-passed to give still further warmth. This was, in the event, no necessity, for the 'RE' Trojan had an unhappy reputation for boiling on hills. It was certainly quite a lot faster than the Vintage machines, and the *marque*'s repertoire of crude noises was distinctly more subdued, but a timed maximum of 45 m.p.h. could not compensate for a lack of ground clearance which made nonsense of the car's reputation for 'going anywhere'.

In 1931, the 'RE' in standard saloon or tourer form cost £179, a *de luxe* version with electric starter, wire wheels, clock and electric wiper being available for £198. A centrifugal clutch was incorporated in the gearbox for 1932, to avoid that 'creep' which is a tendency in all epicyclic boxes, while 1934 models had the further refinement of a fluid flywheel, and the gear lever was moved to the steering-column. These last 'RE' cars had bodies panelled to the waistline, but the firm was concentrating increasingly on vans.

That post-Vintage eccentricity, the 'RE', was Trojan's principal private-car offering, but they were still prepared to make machines of the old type for keen customers. Group-Captain Scroggs bought one in 1931, and another was made up, to 1929 specifications, for a lady in Gloucestershire as late as 1937. In the autumn of 1932 they were advertising a 'Colonial' model which looked for all the world like the products of the good old days. At the 1933 Motor Show they offered a curious compromise in the shape of the 'Way-farer' tourer at £165. This had a horizontal under-floor engine allied to a worm-driven back axle and the 'RE' radiator and bonnet, but was blessed with the ground clearance lacking in the more expensive rear-engined cars. It never went into production. Intriguingly enough, contemporary catalogues did not find it necessary to mention the chain drive on the 'RE'.

The 'RE' appeared for the last time at Olympia in 1934, and a year later the company showed an extraordinary vehicle whose purpose in life defeats my imagination. It had a 2,232 c.c. two-stroke

C. M. Keiller with the original G.W.K. prototype

The 1925 G.K.W. with all-hand controls for disabled drivers

Lost Causes in competition: a 1923 Unit Ten (*left*) with a Palladium
tourer

A 1927 11/27 h.p. Imperia fabric saloon

The Thing from the Jam Factory: a 1930 Burney decorates a typical Vintage traffic scene in Oxford Street. Around it are an A.E.C. bus, Citroën and Unic taxis, and an Austin Seven

The first Squire, early 1935. The chassis is overslung at the rear, but later cars had a frame underslung at both ends

six-cylinder engine mounted horizontally at the rear, but the traditional Trojan gearbox had given way to a conventional three-speed synchromesh type, operated by a central remote control. The radiator lived at the front, with the fuel tank behind it, the Girling rod-operated brakes worked on all four wheels, and the specification included a 'foot warmer' and built-in jacks. The coachwork was in contemporary style by Ranalah, a four-seater drophead coupé of understandably tail-heavy aspect costing £380. As if embarrassed by this curio, the firm changed the brand name and called it a Mastra. Alas, neither of the two cars on the stand was complete, and, after a long proving trial in Devon, the Mastra was conveniently forgotten. In October 1936, Trojan announced that they had 'decided to put the manufacture of commercial vehicles first', which promise they implemented to good purpose.

No account of the Trojan would be complete without recalling the numerous and engaging side-issues which the firm sponsored. Leslie Hounsfield was a practical and versatile engineer, and his ideas were both ingenious and profitable. In 1929, Trojan Ltd. were making a sprung-frame camp bed at 21s, which was very popular. Two years later, a Trojan marine engine was added to the range, and a light agricultural tractor was displayed at the Smithfield Show in 1936. A subsidiary company, Tor Equipment, marketed the Trojan-built Universal Stretcher Sheet, the Tor Tilter (for artificial respiration), and the St. George's Open Top Oxygen Tent. After the war, there were the 'Mini-Motor' motor aid for cycles, the 'Universal' oil grooving machine, and the 'Airator', an engine-driven transportable blower for drying grass. During the war years, the 'Electrojan', an electric power unit suitable for installation in petrol-driven chassis, was developed, one being fitted 'for the duration' in Trojan's own service van, a 1927 'Travellers' Brougham', while electric delivery vans were made from 1951 to 1956. Since the amalgamation with Lambretta Concessionaires, Trojan have exploited a novel field by manufacturing the 'Tro-Kart', based on the American Clinton Go-Kart design, and a line of chain saws.

Like Leyland, Trojan are still very much alive. The famous two-stroke engine finally gave way to three and four-cylinder diesel power units of Perkins manufacture after 1956, and the nearest approach to a car, the 'Tro-Karts' apart, in 1960 was the twenty-cwt. 'Personnel Carrier', an omnibus in miniature turning the scales at over thirty-three cwt. Despite the change of ownership, the company takes a lively and sympathetic interest in the Trojans of yesteryear, and will still service them, though lately all spares have been transferred to the flourishing Trojan Owners' Club, founded in 1955.

The last Trojan vans were made in 1961 but the company's vehicle interests still extended beyond the Lambretta. 1961 saw the featherweight 'Tro-bike' ('build it yourself for garden or road use'), while by the end of that year they had taken over world manufacturing rights for the 200 c.c. Heinkel 'bubble-car'. Even more ambitious was the Elva GT, a Frank Nichols design which Trojan produced in series. This was available in open and closed versions, with a choice of two power units, the 1,798 c.c. M.G. 'B', or the 1,498 c.c. Ford 'Cortina GT'. As an alternative to the conventionally-sprung Riley 'One-Point-Five' back axle, customers could also have independent rear suspension by Trojan's own 'Tru-Trak' layout with unequal wishbones. These cars were not built in great quantity, but Trojan fared better than Lea-Francis in the realm of the mini-car, and over 10,000 of the '200' models were turned out before it was discontinued in June 1965. The Government's failure to introduce purchase tax concessions for three-wheelers was blamed, and certainly at £390 the little Trojan was hardly cheap.

But the story of Trojan is still a success story. Neither Leyland nor Trojan can be blamed for turning to the production of commercial vehicles, a field which paid better and offered less formidable competition. Leylands always put the manufacture of lorries first: Trojan's private-car production petered out because, as Group-Captain Scroggs says:

'The makers didn't keep up with public requirements. I still think that it was a masterpiece of engineering design, in that it did what it was intended to do extremely efficiently. The fact that it was designed to do what very few people wanted done does not affect the intrinsic technical merit of the design.'

And it is, perhaps, a little sad that the G.P.O., when they christened a new telephone exchange with the great name of Trojan, located it at Norbiton and not at Kingston or Croydon, the former and present homes of the car that made walking an extravagance.

CHAPTER 11

Wolverhampton:
Capital City of the Lost Causes

'When one considers the undoubted value for money offered in Clyno cars ever since their introduction, it is not surprising that their sale during the past season has increased beyond even the most sanguine expectations. In this fact lies the proof of public appreciation of a thoroughly British production.'

Clyno catalogue, 1927

'So exceptional has been the demand for this car that the Star factory has been forced to double-shift working in an attempt to keep production in step with the daily increasing orders coming from all over the country.'

Star advertisement, December 1931

Thus trumpeted two of Wolverhampton's once-famous car manufacturers on the eve of their Waterloo. Not that there is anything in present-day Wolverhampton to link it with any kind of Lost Cause. In the industrial Midlands it ranks in size only below Birmingham, Coventry and the Five Towns of the Potteries, it is considerably less grimy than many of its neighbours, and it has one of the most consistently successful soccer teams in the country. True, it is a jack-of-all trades, unlike Stoke or Coventry, but there is nothing decadent or nostalgic about this bustling town to compare with the Marble Halls of Alexandria or the comic-opera of the Jam Factory.

One encounters pathos only with that unobtrusive signpost which guides the traveller towards the latter-day scene of Wolverhampton's car-making activities. 'Bushbury Cemetery and Crematorium' it reads, and up this road lie Bushbury and its even more mournfully-named neighbour, Fallings Park. Here are the old factories of Clyno and Star, and not far away are the still-lively works which make Guy commercial vehicles, next door to Henry Meadows Ltd., makers of engines for many a Lost Cause and one-time sponsors of the Frisky minicar.

It was not always thus. In 1919, in Fallings Park, Sydney Guy was busily testing what was to become Britain's first production vee-eight, while across the other side of the town Sunbeam and Star were getting back into post-war production with their big side-valve 'fours'. Slightly farther west A.J.S. and Clyno motorcycles were coming off the lines again, and in Villiers Street, Turners were contemplating a return to private-car production.

Twenty years later they had all gone save Guy and Turner, the former making trucks only, and the latter mainly concerned with components; not that Turner's car business had ever been their staple in the Vintage years. They had entered the motor industry in 1902 by building the Miesse steam car with flash boiler, and had supplemented this venture with light petrol cars from 1911 onwards. The company's speciality seems to have been the construction of cars for other people, since they built the 20/25 four-cylinder Seymour-Turner for Seymours of London in 1907, and the Dorman-engined Varley-Woods for H.S. Motors Ltd. of Acton from 1919 to 1921. In 1914 the 10 h.p. Turner was sold in London under the brand-name of 'Universal'. Production of complete cars ceased in 1928. It is interesting to note that there is no connexion between the Turner Manufacturing Co. Ltd. and Turner Sports Cars Ltd. of Pendeford Airport, just outside the town, whose small sporting machines with B.M.C. and Ford engines are made in small numbers to this day.

But let us go back to 1898, when the Star Cycle Co. made its first car in Wolverhampton. The guiding spirit in this concern was Edward Lisle Sr., who had been a partner in Sharratt and Lisle, cycle manufacturers, since 1883: the name was changed to its later style in 1896, initial capital of the reconstituted firm being £120,000. Though no complete vehicles were made in the next two years, the company, it would appear, made the running gear for an odd three-wheeled device designed by T. H. Parker and known as the Bushbury Electric Cart. It was 'highly commended' in the electric vehicle trials sponsored by *The Engineer* at the Crystal Palace in May 1897, despite its steering method by 'ordinary reins'. Nothing further, however, transpired from these early experiments, and Edward Lisle sensibly decided to launch himself in the motor industry by building cars to a well-proven design in the shape of the 3½ h.p. belt-driven Benz. Up to 1901 the firm's production centred round this model. The quality of Star workmanship is reflected in the fact that in 1925 the company was still experiencing a demand for spares—indeed, at least two survive to this day, and one appeared in the Parade of Historic Vehicles at the opening of the Montagu Motor Museum extensions in 1959. Car manufacture was entrusted to a separate company, the Star Motor Co.

It is of interest to note that the first car imported into Auckland, New Zealand, in 1898 was a Star and, by the following October, the little works in Frederick Street were claiming that they could make a Star-Benz from scratch in seven days, and were thus now willing to accept orders. At the Birmingham Show in February 1900, they were making everything at Wolverhampton except the tyres and the Brampton roller chains, and were even supplying carburettors, axles and wheels to other constructors. To the end of its days the Star was strictly a manufactured car, even though up to the middle 'twenties Star operations were crammed into a network of small, cramped factories in a series of back streets off the Dudley Road—Frederick Street, Nelson Street, Stewart Street, Ablow Street and Dobbs Street. Frames, it is true, were imported from Thompsons of Bilston, but everything else, the bodies included, was made in the little warren of engineering shops, Star's foundry in Ablow Street being in operation as late as 1925. Cycle production —and later that of the Starling, Stuart and Briton light cars—was undertaken in Stewart Street. While other makers, notably Clyno, bought their bodywork out, Star never did, and quite a sensation was occasioned when, in 1926, special craftsmen were imported from the Weymann plant at Addlestone to supervise the erection of their first fabric bodies. Though the move out to Bushbury was already in hand at the time of the Star-Guy agreement in 1928, it is against the congested background of Frederick Street that we have to consider Star history. Anyone who has seen even the outside of the works must needs marvel that it could turn out a steady twenty cars a week right up to the final transfer to the Bushbury site in 1928.

In March 1900, the company introduced the 'A'-type, with passenger seats facing forward, instead of in the *vis-à-vis* style. The driver's forward vision was evidently not considered. That April the Star entries attracted favourable mention in the 1,000 Miles Trial, *The Autocar* observing that they were 'possessed of good speed both on the level and uphill, and making a particularly good showing in the Birkhill climb.'

That June, a Star-Benz made a successful ascent of Birdlip Hill after being driven down from Wolverhampton for the attempt, while the enterprising Mr Jecock, Captain of the Gainsborough Fire Brigade, bought a car of this type for his official duties and proceeded to drive it from Gainsborough to Banbury—a good long run for so primitive a vehicle. In 1901, he sent his machine back to Frederick Street to have side doors fitted. This was typical of Star's progressive spirit as regards coach-work. Their chassis might be unoriginal in the extreme, but their bodies were not only advanced in design, but meticulously executed. In 1903 they catalogued a light delivery van with removable seating and glass side windows, which anticipated the modern station wagon by a good thirty years. By 1905 they were building bodies with curved sections fabricated from laminated wood. In 1908 they were equipping their touring cars with detachable canvas wind-shields in front of the driver. Any style, however bizarre, was tackled. In 1905 they came out with a fantastic taxicab, which followed conventional 'tonneau' styling but had a hansom-cab structure perched over the rear axle. Even in 1927, the firm built eight six-cylinder cars and harem wagons for King Ibn Saud, one of the conditions of the order being that no male worker should enter the bodies of the latter during their construction!

Star policy during the next few years consisted of applying the Lisle family's high standards of material and workmanship to other people's designs. The Star-Benz was still displayed at the National Show in 1901, but also available was a rear-engined model in De Dion style, while on the stand were 6 h.p. and 7 h.p. chain-driven cars with De Dion engines. The range was augmented in January 1902 by an 8 h.p., 88·9 × 127 mm. a.i.v.* vertical-twin. One cannot dispute the makers' assertion that it was 'British-built throughout', but it is an equally indisputable fact that anyone would have found it hard to distinguish it from a contemporary Panhard. Later in the year it was joined by larger crypto-Panhards; a 10 h.p. 'twin', and 'fours' of 15 h.p. and 20 h.p. Unoriginal they may have been, but they certainly gave good service; in 1902 the Automobile Club of Great Britain and Ireland bought one 'for the training of automobile servants', and the forty-five tyros who learnt on it during the first twelve months failed to inflict any damage. The 14 h.p. model which replaced it in 1906 was still going strong four years and 318 certificates later.

Right up to 1914 the Star range remained one of formidable complexity, and reflected contemporary fashion, Mercédès influence gradually replacing that of Panhard. In 1904, for instance, they offered a 6 h.p. (101·6 × 101·6 mm.) 'single' with De Dion engine, chain drive and Mercédès-type radiator, and a two-cylinder (101·6 × 114·2 mm.) 7 h.p. with coil ignition, belt-driven lubricator and armoured wood frame this listed at £220, and was billed as 'The World's Best Two-seater'. *The Car Illustrated* did not apparently agree with this sentiment, as its reporter commented: 'The arrangement of the gears is not too well designed, but may be sufficient for the purpose.'

* Automatic inlet valve.

In addition there was a 12 h.p. four-cylinder 'miniature Mercédès' at £500, a lighter version of this at £420, an 18 h.p. at £550 and a 24 h.p. at £650, not to mention a very large 70 h.p. car based on the Gordon Bennett model, of which more anon. With a flash of unconscious irony, the firm chose 'Stargazing' as their telegraphic address.

Star never supported competitions as enthusiastically as did Sunbeam, though two of Edward Lisle's sons, Richard and Joseph, frequently drove their father's cars in speed events. There is something rather comic about the glimpse *The Autocar* vouchsafes us of a 7 h.p. Star competing in the 1905 Sunrising Hill-Climb:

'Mr Lisle had to hold down the pedal brake, so that he could not press the accelerator pedal, and he had to borrow a walking-stick, which he passed between the spokes of the steering-wheel and pressed down with his hand.'

Star cars were entered for the British Gordon Bennett eliminating trials of 1903 and 1905, but both efforts ended in failure. In 1903, their entry was found to be thirty-four lb. overweight, and had to be pared down at the last moment, the same trouble being encountered in 1905. Nonetheless, two cars faced the starter in the Isle of Man that year, driven by the brothers F. R. and H. G. Goodwin. They were Chinese copies of the Mercédès Sixty, even down to the use of a stellar emblem on the radiator, and were noticeably slower than the Napiers, the Wolseleys and even the Weir-Darracq.

1905 offerings were the 7 h.p. single-cylinder 'Little Star' at £175, the 12 h.p. four-cylinder at £450 and the 20 h.p. at £550, plus an interesting new model in the shape of a 76·2 × 101·6 mm. 10 h.p., one of the first genuine small 'fours' to be made in this country at a competitive price. Its technical origins were apparent from the use of overhead inlet valves, chain drive and low-tension magneto ignition, but it was excellent value at £300. As though to compensate for this simplified range, the Star Cycle Co. re-entered the field of car manufacture, after confining its powered-vehicle activities to motor cycles and a few tricars. Their new contribution was a spidery little *voiturette* with fixed wire wheels, a transversely-mounted 6 h.p. De Dion single-cylinder engine with the usual coil ignition, a two-speed Panhard-type gearbox, and an armoured wood frame. It was known as the Starling, and sold at 95 guineas.

A new 18 h.p. four-cylinder model was introduced for 1906, and Joseph Lisle ran one in the 'fuel consumption' T.T. of that year. Unlike some of the other entries, it was absolutely standard, but retired when Lisle ran out of fuel. The firm entered a brace of

L-head four-cylinder cars the following year, but neither lasted the course. Star were equally unsuccessful when the T.T. was revived in 1914.

No less than seven models under three *marque* names made up Star's 1907 programme, which was complicated further by two new contributions from the Star Cycle Co., the 7 h.p. Starling and the similarly rated Stuart. The Stuart was a four-seater tonneau, was said to do 30 m.p.h. as against the Starling's 20 m.p.h., and had shaft drive, whereas the Starling adhered to chains. At the top end of the scale were a pair of big 'fours', the shaft-driven 105 × 127 mm. Eighteen and the chain-driven 127 × 152 mm. Thirty, at £500 and £650 respectively, and an 89 × 127 mm. 'six' with cylinders cast in pairs. It looked very like a Mercédès.

Thereafter models followed thick and fast. In 1908 the customer had a choice ranging from the 8 h.p. single-cylinder Starling at £150, through the 9 h.p. twin-cylinder Star and 10 h.p. Starling (formerly Stuart) and three Star 'fours' rated at 12, 16, and 20 h.p. respectively, to a large 108 × 127 mm. 6-cylinder car at £600. This was not a notably complex range by the standards of those days, but it took a little sorting-out, since the twin-cylinder Star and Starling models differed only in that the former had chain drive and mechanical lubrication and cost £20 more. On the bigger models, four-speed gearboxes with a geared-up top were standard, and buyers were given the option of shaft or chain drive. 1909 saw the introduction of Star's most successful Edwardian model in the shape of the Fifteen, with shaft drive and dual ignition, at £325. Original engine dimensions were 89 × 114 mm., and in an official R.A.C. trial in August of that year, it lapped Brooklands in standard trim at 50·97 m.p.h. and averaged 22·8 m.p.g. over 105 miles on the road.

In 1909, the Star Cycle Co. Ltd. changed its name to the Briton Motor Co. Ltd., and thereafter pursued a more or less independent existence under the direction of Edward Lisle Jr. In 1913, this concern moved to Walsall Street, on the site of the present-day Ever Ready factory. The Briton cars were cheaper and lighter variations on the Star theme, and a 1,743 c.c. Ten could be bought for a mere £183 in 1914. The move to Walsall Street was to prove a boon to the parent concern, for Britons had only just vacated the Stewart Street works in June 1913 when the Star body shops in Dobbs Street caught fire and were demolished. There was little disruption, for Stars simply resumed operations across the road in the empty Briton plant.

Six models were offered for 1910, the Fifteen's stroke being lengthened to 140 mm., while the manufacturers took the interesting step of offering this engine in either monobloc or bi-bloc form. The larger models had dual ignition as standard equipment, and in the following year shaft drive was standardized throughout the range, options on 1911 models including a direct top gear and Rudge-Whitworth detachable wheels. 1912 saw a 68 × 120 mm. Ten, rather like a small Benz in appearance, which represented excellent value in the light-car market at £250, and a six-cylinder model reappeared in the range in the shape of an 80 × 120 mm. Twenty with overhead worm drive at £475. Rounded radiators were adopted for 1913, and detachable wheels were standardized in 1914, by which time there were three basic models, all with four cylinders: the 80 × 120 mm. (2,409 c.c.) 12/15 at £350, the long-stroke 3,012 c.c. 15·9 at £400, and the 90 × 150 mm. (3,817 c.c.) 20·1 at £460. A 66 × 130 mm. four-cylinder light car with monobloc engine and both brakes acting on the rear wheels was announced in 1915, just before private-car production ceased for the duration of the war.

Star and Briton alike did quite well in competitions in the later Edwardian years, despite a defeat in the challenge match at Brooklands against Hancock's potent Vauxhall 'KN' in 1909. In that year, incidentally, Richard Lisle made several appearances with a very sporting-looking 15 h.p. two-seater of pronouncedly Mercedes aspect. The engine was said to be good for 4,000 r.p.m.—a sensational rate of rotation in 1909—and on a 2·6 : 1 top gear it should have been very fast indeed. With this machine he made best performance on formula at Shelsley Walsh in 1910, and 1911 saw the *marque* taking first and third places in the R.A.C.'s Standard Car Race at Brooklands. They were subsequently disqualified and the prize awarded to Tysoe's Singer, whereupon Lisle proceeded to vindicate himself by taking the twelve-hour class record on a stripped standard chassis at 67 m.p.h. In November 1913, a 20·1 h.p. car with a streamlined single-seater body collected nine more class records at Brooklands, 500 miles being covered at 78·8 m.p.h. The records in this case were wrested from a 'Coupe de *l'Auto*' Sunbeam—if my machine of this type is anything to go by, that Star must have had quite a performance!

By 1914, Star was one of England's 'Big Six'. Among their customers were the Marconi Company, who used six-cylinder chassis to tow portable radio generators, and the Roumanian War Office, who bought twenty 10/12 h.p. tourers in 1913. During the war they made lorries in quantity, while they also worked on the abortive A.B.C. 'Dragonfly' radial aero-engine; not that this was their first encounter with aeronautics, for the company built an unsuccessful aeroplane in 1907. Britons, having no cars to sell, took on the agency for the American Scripps-Booth light car, but as its looks were its strongest suit, they derived little good from this venture. Financial difficulties, incidentally, caused the liquidation of this concern in 1922, whereupon it was purchased by Mr C. A. Weight, who resumed production of the four-cylinder light car. Some 1,000 Britons were made between 1922 and 1929: the post-war article was a conventional 63 × 110 mm. side-valve 'four' of no particular interest, and production was discontinued when Mr Weight started making Wild Cat parts suitable for Caterpillar tractors. As Tractor Spares Ltd. the firm still flourishes at Willen-hall, just outside Wolverhampton.

Star reappeared on the market in 1919 with a brace of strictly Edwardian models, the 15·9 and the 20·1 with engines mounted on sub-frames, cylinders cast in pairs, cone clutches and foot trans-mission brakes. For the 1920 season, flat radiators and disc clutches were adopted, but post-war inflation was reflected in the £765 asked for a 20·1 h.p. tourer.

The full force of Lisle conservatism was now being felt. Joseph Lisle was often heard to observe that he would 'rather build one good car a day' than commit himself to mass-production, and though his little works was making some twenty machines a week, each vehicle was looked upon as an individual order. As a former Star executive put it to me, 'If you had a complaint you saw the service manager, and not just anyone in a white coat.' Engines were conservatively rated, and even in 1921 the makers claimed a mere 32 b.h.p. at 1,800 r.p.m. from the 15·9, which cost a fearsome £800.

A new 1·8-litre (69 × 120 mm.) 11·9 with a s.v. monobloc engine was brought out in 1922, new departures being the use of a unit construction gearbox, semi-elliptic rear suspension (Stars had hitherto preferred three-quarter-elliptic), a detachable cylinder head, central change and 'dimming headlights'—in actual practice the sidelamps provided the 'dipped beam'. It was a good, solid little car, which *The Autocar* summed up as:

'Quiet, but purposeful: lively but innately tractable: fast, but not tiring to drive, excellently sprung, well-braked, and with featherweight steering.'

Unfortunately, fewer and fewer people were prepared to pay

£545 for an 11·9, especially with Clyno turning out a 10·8 in nearby Pelham Street at £265!

For 1923, Star came out with a 69 × 130 mm. six cylinder Eighteen. This had its cylinders cast *en bloc*, but the heads were in pairs, after the fashion of the later i.o.e. Coventry-Climax units, and it looked uncommonly like a Sunbeam. With semi-elliptic suspension all round, a tourer was good value at £675. Curiously enough, there does not seem to have been any connexion other than a friendly rivalry between Star and Sunbeam, though throughout the nineteen-twenties respective six-cylinder offerings displayed a marked similarity.

In 1927 Mrs Diana Strickland made a 6,000-mile trip from Dakar to Khartoum in a special 14/30 tourer, and her 'Star of the Desert' gave little trouble, though the owner was beset in turn by appalling weather conditions, the incursions of robbers and the illness of her mechanic. The Star 'Flyer' range of six-cylinder commercial vehicles enjoyed considerable popularity, the Selfridge group using a fleet of these for years. In the nineteen-forties, the remnants of these were used for refuse disposal by the Buckinghamshire County Council.

The 11·9 became a 12/25 with 130 mm. stroke in 1924, while Rubury front-wheel brakes became an optional extra on the 18/40, which was enlarged to 3·3 litres in 1925 as the 20/50. Prices ranged from £650 to £875, body styles available including the two-seater, five-seater, coupé, saloon coupé, saloon, three-quarter landaulet and saloon landaulet. Also in the 1925 range were a side-valve 2-litre 14/30 at £500 and an overhead-valve sports 12/40 with f.w.b., with one of which Sir Malcolm Campbell won a Short Handicap at Brooklands in 1925. He retained his fondness for the Wolverhampton *marque*, incidentally, using a Bluebird-blue 'Comet' sports saloon as late as 1932. The 12/40 was later to feature in a delectably Irish interlude in the correspondence columns of *The Autocar* in August 1928, when the manufacturers alleged that a standard model had achieved 63·9 m.p.h. up a 1-in-6 hill on top gear; in the Emerald Isle, of course. A whole horde of amateur boffins proceeded to dissect this statement, proclaiming that nothing short of seven litres of supercharged Mercedes-Benz would suffice for such an ascent, but the whole affair fizzled out in anti-climax when someone saw fit to consult an Ordnance Survey Map. The worst gradient on the 'hill' was 1 in 8·95, and this was only over seventy-four yards!

Star publicity advertised 'quiet, smooth power for closed carriage work' but the market for this was dwindling. They came out with o.h.v. 14/40 and 20/60 models, both with f.w.b., in 1926, while in 1927 cellulose finish and a simplified form of brake adjustment were among the season's improvements. Central change was now standard, though side change could be had for £15 extra. An ugly but solid o.h.v. 69 × 110 mm. 18/50 h.p. 'Light Six' at £615 was announced for 1928, and for 1929 only this and the 20/60 were offered, all the four-cylinder cars being dropped. The clanks which had emanated from Star's aluminium pistons were at last disposed of by the use of harder-wearing metals for the cylinder bores.

In the meantime, a new name had come upon the scene, Sydney Guy, to whom the Lisles had sold out in 1928. Mr Guy had once been works manager at Sunbeam, but in 1914 he had set up on his own in Fallings Park, manufacturing commercial vehicles with his inclined side-valve engines on three-point flexible mountings. In 1919, he had startled the British motor industry by launching a luxury vee-eight touring car. Its 72 × 125 mm. (4,072 c.c.) engine featured the Guy inclined side valves, which were claimed to be as efficient as o.h.v. and easier to maintain. More interesting still, the Guy had not only full pressure engine lubrication, but also automatic lubrication for the chassis, which came into operation every time the steering was put on full right lock. Fuel feed was by Autovac, and the Guy guarantee included free inspection by the makers during the first two years of the car's life. Deliveries started in May 1920, but by the time the car was in production, there was little demand for a 4-litre touring car costing £1,475. This was the first British-designed and built vee-eight to go into series production, and no other British engine of this type was to appear again until 1936, when Riley came out with the none-too-successful 8/90 model.

Guy also toyed with a variety of four-cylinder cars powered by inclined s.v. engines, ranging from a 1,676 c.c. Twelve to a 16.9 'Colonial' model. According to Sydney Guy, none of these attained production status, though a 2-litre 13/36 saloon costing £650 was shown at Olympia in 1923. Some 130 private cars were made at Fallings Park between 1920 and 1925, but they were never a profitable proposition, and in the latter year they were quietly discontinued. Their only remaining sally into the private-car field, aside from their association with Star, was the manufacture of fibreglass bodies for the Frisky in 1957, while this vehicle was still under Meadows control.

The immediate result of the Star-Guy association was the sale of the Frederick Street works and the transfer of all operations to the Bushbury plant, which already housed the firm's body shop. Commercial vehicle manufacture was abandoned, while Guy's free inspection service was extended to Star. The cars lost none of the quality associated with the Lisle days, and the 1930 18/50 h.p. at £595 was a pretty and well-appointed car with wire wheels, chromium plating and a sliding roof, at a time when many British manufacturers adopted that abomination, the folding head.

During the last two years of their existence, Star introduced the 'Comet' and 'Planet', restyled versions of their earlier six-cylinder cars with silent-third gearboxes, twin-plate clutches, Bendix brakes and styling which was undoubtedly among the most attractive of the early 'thirties. Equipment was comprehensive: one-shot chassis lubrication, thermostatically-controlled radiator shutters, dual wipers, stop and reversing lights, Jackall built-in jacks and folding tables. The 18 h.p. 'Comet' retailed at £495 and the 21 h.p. 'Planet' at £695, irrespective of body type. For 1932 a 2·1-litre 'Comet Fourteen' at £345, including all the gimmickry, was added to the range, which also embraced the 'Comet Eighteen' at £495, the 'Comet Twenty-One' at £525, and the 'Planet Twenty-Four' at £695. Late in 1931, Stars were advertising that the Bushbury works had gone on to double shifts to cope with the flood of orders.

The new Stars were as good as their predecessors. An 18 h.p. sports saloon tested by *The Autocar* in June 1931, 'concealed beneath a gay appearance a strong individuality'. It recorded 70 m.p.h. on top and a commendable 57 m.p.h. on third. According to Norman Creed, who was in Star's sales department at the time, most of the bigger cars were good for 75–80 m.p.h. Unfortunately, while the move to Bushbury had given Star some much-needed room to breathe, they lacked the capital to re-equip the factory with up-to-date machinery, and the consequence was that each car was made at a loss. The burden of gimmickry might not affect the performance, but it wiped out any possibility of a profit margin, and so the Star went down. In March 1932, the blow fell. Norman Creed had been working late into the night preparing a 'Comet' for a press demonstration when he was hailed out of the darkness by a representative of the newly-appointed Receiver. The car was not allowed out on test.

David Rosenfield Ltd., the Manchester firm of motor traders, purchased the unsold stock of cars, McKenzie and Denley of Birmingham took over the manufacturing rights, and the Star lingered on in the *Buyers' Guide* until 1935. The Bushbury plant lay untenanted until October 1932, when it was put up for auction: as a small boy, Mr Ronald Ridge, Guy's P.R.O., remembers playing within the deserted walls in offices where piles of old photographs still lay around.

When the axe fell upon Star its works manager was Frank Smith, who only three years before had seen his own company, Clyno, go to the wall. While Star had survived unobtrusively through some thirty years of sound engineering and limited production, Clyno had enjoyed a mere seven years of meteoric existence before collapsing with a bang. But to pick up the threads of the Clyno story we have to go back to 1909, when Frank Smith and his cousin founded the Clyno Engineering Co. Ltd. with works in Pelham Street, in the centre of the town. Clyno started on motor cycles—in fact, they made nothing else until 1922. Unlike their later four-wheelers, the Clyno 'bikes' were manufactured rather than assembled machines, and they attained a high measure of success, both with the 5/6 h.p. combination and with the little 2¾ h.p. two-speed two-stroke. The bigger machine was widely used as a machine-gun carrier by the Allied forces in the first World War.

Though a prototype light car was running before 1914, the firm resumed production of both its basic motor-cycle types in 1919, and continued to make them until it ran into financial difficulties in 1921. But when Frank Smith re-formed the company as The Clyno Engineering Co. (1922) Ltd., it was announced that henceforward they would concentrate on cars. 'Jimmy' Cocker, well known for his exploits on Singer motor cycles, was appointed sales manager.

Shortly before the 1922 Motor Show, the new Clyno car was unveiled. It was entirely conventional in design, and was powered by the well-known 66 × 100 mm. (1,368 c.c.) Coventry-Climax s.v. four-cylinder engine. A three-speed separate gearbox of Clyno manufacture was used, with central ball change. Electric lighting and starting were standard, quarter-elliptic springs were used all round, and a solid, differential-less back axle featured on the first cars. A two-seater cost £265.

This was the car that was to challenge Morris and sell some 50,000 in the next six years. Apart from the gearbox, brakes and steering gear, it was an 'assembled job', and the works at Pelham Street, although ample for the limited production of two-wheelers, were far too cramped to allow for large-scale assembly, let alone full production. All the same, the Clyno was a good, if uninspired little car. It came from the drawing-board of A. G. Booth, who was later to design the Singer 'Le Mans' and Rootes Group cars from 1935 until his retirement; its brakes were adequate, and it possessed excellent steering, of which *The Times* was moved to comment in 1926: 'it is sufficiently steady, delightfully light at all times, and has a wide lock'.

The car's sponsors were fortunate enough in securing the Rootes brothers as their home and overseas distributors, and the workmen at the little factory were as happy and loyal a crowd as those at Star, which was the last factory in Wolverhampton to come out during the General Strike of 1926, and then only two days before the end.

Had Frank Smith and his co-directors been content to make a small quality car, it is likely that they would have stayed in business. As it was, they set their sights on beating W. R. Morris, and the consequence was inevitable. It was said that the reconstituted firm came into being on a bank overdraft, and there is no doubt whatsoever that Clyno were grossly under-capitalized. The suppliers—Moss Gear, Coventry-Climax, Willenhall Radiators, and Taylors (and later Haywards) who made the bodies, had to be paid, and the cash was seldom there. It was a standing joke that the Clyno programme for the coming year was never announced until Morris showed his hand, whereupon the team at Pelham Street launched upon a frantic spree of cost-cutting. The result was that next year's improvements were incorporated on the production line 'as and how'. There is no doubt that customers could, and did, buy 1927 Morrises in October 1926, but it would probably be January 1927 before a 'full 1927' Clyno was available. Funnily enough, the Clyno seems to have appealed to a higher income bracket than the Morris-Cowley.

Clynos, largely driven by 'Jimmy' Cocker, did well in trials: the firm's indefatigable sales manager won a Silver Medal in the 1923 Scottish Six Days, and 'Golds' in the 'Edinburgh' and the 'Land's End', and he repeated his performance in the latter event in 1924. Clutch trouble put the Clyno entry out of the R.A.C. Small Car Trials that year. A tourer at £255 joined the two-seater in 1923. *The Autocar* praised the steering, the accessibility, the ease of brake adjustment ('there is no need to get dirty'), and the central gear lever which 'fell readily to hand'. The absence of a speedometer was also noticed.

For 1924, Clyno came out with a 13 h.p. (69 × 100 mm., 1,496 c.c.) model with their own s.v. engine at £275, while the Eleven, now with a differential, a chain-driven dynamo and a wheelbase two inches longer, cost a mere £198 as a two-seater. A coupé was available for £315, and in July a saloon joined the range. This was an exceedingly ugly vehicle with a prominent rear overhang, but Clyno had a winner. Three thousand cars were made and sold in the first six months of 1924, and by December 1925, as many cars were being made in a week as were turned out in the whole of 1923. Production ran at an average of 150 a week, but at the peak of the boom—1925 and 1926—this figure rose on occasions to 350.

For the 1925 season, the firm concentrated on the Eleven, which was given a larger fuel tank, modified bearings, right-hand change and other detail improvements. The 'De Luxe' models had wider bodies and balloon tyres, while the 'Royals' had more comprehensive instrumentation, leather upholstery, a windscreen wiper and an electric horn. A two-seater in the 'Popular' style cost £175, a 'De Luxe' £20 more, and a 'Royal' £225, while a 'Royal' coachbuilt four-door saloon was available at £345—a lot of money, but it should be remembered that the Morris-Cowley saloon still had only two doors. In February 1925, an angular 'Regent' saloon could be had for only £285, and Frank Hallam was operating a fleet of 11 h.p. landaulets in Birmingham, at the same hire rates as the then fashionable sidecar-taxis.

In 1925, *The Autocar* announced that a sports model Clyno good for 70 m.p.h., with four-wheel brakes and four-speed gearbox, was on the way, but C. J. Lloyd-Davies, the firm's then sales manager, tells me that series production of such a car was not planned, though 'Jimmy' Cocker tried out a tuned Eleven with these features at Brooklands. Nineteen twenty-six saw the adoption of very efficient rod-operated f.w.b. on the 'Royal Eleven' and Thirteen, while the Eleven acquired semi-elliptic rear suspension in place of the quarter-elliptics previously used. An 11 h.p. 'Popular' two-seater with rear-wheel brakes only cost £162 10s; the same price as the Morris. Clyno were still keeping pace.

An 11 h.p. two-seater appeared at the 1926 New York Show, but it was only a miniature designed to demonstrate the Stevenson four-wheel jacking system. Rootes reported a boom in Clyno sales to South Africa, and opened their new showrooms in Devonshire House, Piccadilly, where Clynos were prominently displayed. The Clyno front-wheel brakes were further improved for 1927, and were standardized throughout the range, a two-seater 'Popular' being available for £160, though Cowley had the last word by offering a simplified r.w.b. model at £148 10s. On saloons, Clyno emerged the victors, their four-door style costing £199 10s as against £195 for the Cowley two-door model. The dome-roofed 'Royal' saloon came in for high praise at Olympia, equipment including a 'wireless

The special Brooklands Squire built for Luis Fontes. Behind it is the
late A. M. Squire

A 1920 Marseel tourer

A line-up of 13/70 h.p. Marendaz sports tourers. This is not the Jam Factory

S. F. Edge mends a puncture on the 8 h.p. Napier in the 1,000 Miles Trial
(photo: *The Autocar*)

Miss Ellaline Terriss on a 16 h.p. Napier tonneau, 1903
(photo: *The Autocar*)

The Hon. Patrick Lindsay's 1914 15 h.p. Napier 'Gentleman's Estate Carriage' was one of the entrants in the Napier Commemoration Tally in 1958

electric cigarette lighter'. One wonders if it worked—I have yet to meet a car on which this device does. The 13 h.p. was continued as the 12/28, with prices from £215. Clyno did not follow Morris into the light van market, though they compromised by offering a commercial traveller's saloon on the 11 h.p. chassis, with removable sample shelves, at £210.

While they were by no means competitive in price, it is interesting to compare *The Autocar*'s test reports in this year on the 12/28 Clyno saloon, and the slightly bigger, but much cheaper Morris-Cowley saloon. Fuel consumption was much the same at 30–35 m.p.g., and both cars were good for around the 50 mark, but 10–30 m.p.h. acceleration figures differ widely, the Morris requiring 14·6 seconds against the Clyno's 9·8 sec., while the Morris could not come anywhere near the Clyno's stopping distance of ninety-eight feet from 40 m.p.h.

Nineteen twenty-eight was the last year in which Clyno used the Coventry-Climax engine, and it also marked the parting of ways with Rootes. It would seem that the real reason was that the Clyno directors favoured the division of representation into smaller ter-ritories, but there is no doubt that this divorce did nothing to inspire public confidence at a time when Clyno most needed it. Finance was fast running short, Pelham Street was quite incapable of coping with the demand for Clynos on an economic basis, and the Eleven at £152 10s was £10 more expensive than the corresponding Morris model. The 12/28 emerged as the 1,593 c.c. 12/35, the coachbuilt saloon listing at £250; exactly the same price as the much larger 14/28 Morris-Oxford. The adoption of Hayward fabric bodies, a new radiator and oval instrument boards were the principal changes.

In the meanwhile, a new and expensive works at Bushbury, not far from the Star and Guy factories, had been completed, and all assembly and engine manufacture was transferred thereto. Pelham Street now housed the Service Department, as well as making gear-boxes as before. At this new factory, Booth evolved a 9 h.p. car.

The Nine was a conventional enough machine, with a 58 × 90 mm. (951 c.c.) side-valve engine, a three-speed gearbox and quarter-elliptic rear suspension. Cooling was by thermo-syphon, but coil ignition was a novelty for Clyno. A neat little fabric saloon was listed at £160. In March 1928, the first production car rolled off the lines.

Unfortunately, someone had let slip the word that Morris contemplated introducing a £100 baby car. So he did, but the happy event was not due to take place for some three years. This news created a panic among the struggling team at Bushbury. When the news reached them, they had as yet only one prototype 9 h.p. chassis on their hands, and that as yet untested, but they were not slow to work out an answer, and in July 1928 it was unveiled.

All they had done was to take the basic Nine chassis and cloak it in a cheap fabric tourer body, while costs were further pruned by the use of a three-lamp lighting set. The 'Century' was its name, and its price was £112 10s. Wolverhampton called it the 'Cemetery', and this was exactly what it proved to be for its makers, though some three hundred were made and sold. This time, cost-cutting had gone too far. Only the Nine and Twelve were offered for 1929, but even drastic price reductions could not help much, and the overhead-camshaft Morris 'Minor' at £125 attracted more buyers than its bigger Clyno counterpart at £130. Clyno were through. A Receiver was appointed, and production ceased in March 1929, though Frank Smith managed to keep the factory open until August, when Alfred Herbert Ltd., the machine-tool firm, took over at Bushbury. Up to the very end Mr Smith was hoping to find more capital, while 'Jimmy' Cocker was engaged on road-testing the only potential 1930 model that the dying firm could offer. As might be expected, it was a 22 h.p. side-valve straight-eight of conventional design.

So Clyno died, to the purr of eight cylinders in line. Colliers of Birmingham took over the supply of spare parts; their present head, C. P. Hamilton Adams, who was then an apprentice, bought the straight-eight prototype, and Frank Smith went down the hill to Star as works manager. When that concern gave up, he founded the Dome Garage at Ealing on the Great West Road. Singers were fortunate enough to acquire Booth's services. The creditors got five shillings in the pound, but one of them still hoped for more.

The firm of A. J. Stevens and Co. were highly respected motor-cycle manufacturers of some thirty years standing. They had resisted the temptation to build cyclecars, though round about 1914 a couple of curious 'one-offs' had been made at the Graiseley works. Both were hand-controlled three-wheelers based on the big-twin motor cycles, and the original 'Sociable' was tiller-steered. Bodywork consisted of a double-width sidecar.

In the later nineteen-twenties, however, A.J.S. had entered the commercial vehicle field with the 'Pilot' and 'Commodore' chassis, while their subsidiary company, Hayward Motor Bodies, had built the coachwork for the Clyno Nine. In an attempt to recoup their losses on these operations, A.J.S. decided to launch a small private car based on the little Clyno.

The result, the A.J.S. Nine, was announced in March 1930 and displayed at Olympia the following October. It was a conventional and well-made little car, following the general design layout of its predecessor, though it was extensively restyled. The bore was increased to 60 mm., giving a capacity of 1,018 c.c., and semi-elliptic rear suspension was adopted in place of the Clyno's quarter-elliptics. Coventry-Climax made the engines, while a curious legacy of motor-cycle practice was the horizontal mounting of the ignition and throttle levers underneath the steering wheel, one each side of the column. With 57 m.p.h. available on top gear and 40 m.p.h. on second, not to mention the finger-light steering inherited from the Clyno, the little A.J.S. looked an attractive proposition, and would have been one but for the prices—£210 for a coachbuilt two-seater, £230 for a fabric saloon and £240 for a coachbuilt saloon. It was also said to be hard on half-shafts, though as this reputation only started to circulate in the nineteen-fifties, by which time the few surviving cars were period pieces, this is perhaps an unfair aspersion. In February 1931, prices were cut by £11 all round and a new 'Richmond' utility fabric saloon was introduced at £197, but the A.J.S. company was tottering. In October of that year the firm went into liquidation, after some three thousand Nines had been made—quite an impressive effort, bearing in mind the car's short production life.

In November, A.J.S. was sold up, Matchless buying the motor-cycle interests; though the Plumstead firm had made a two-cylinder cyclecar in the nineteen-twenties, they knew better than to dabble further in cars. Consequently the rights of the Nine went to the unhappy house of Willys-Overland Crossley Ltd., who made about three hundred more in 1932 at their Stockport works. These differed from the Wolverhampton-built machines in having coachbuilt bodies with fabric tops (only about ten coachbuilt saloons were made at Graiseley), four-speed 'silent third' gearboxes, André shock-absorbers and S.U. 'Petrolift' electric pumps. The price was £229, later reduced to £189, while a Birmingham firm offered a tuned sports variant known as the Chamberlain Special. Experiments were carried out with an i.o.e. engine in this model, but it never went into production.

Nor was much likely to come of the A.J.S. revival, for its new sponsors were competing against themselves, and only the drastic price cut of May 1932 removed the Nine from cut-throat competition with the Crossley Ten. At the 1932 Show, Willys-Overland Crossley made a làst effort with the 1½-litre Model 'C', a stylish if unattractive saloon reminiscent of the Crossley, complete with synchromesh gearbox and free-wheel, but it failed to draw the crowds at £375, and that was that. The Stockport company went into liquidation a year later.

It is hard to find two firms in such antithesis as Star and Clyno. The former refused to compromise one inch, and went down with their reputation untarnished and their sales figures hardly affected to the end, defeated simply by the changing economic tide, while Clyno sought to take on the big battalions with an inadequate armoury of weapons and cut their costs until their reputation went the way of their bank balance. The A.J.S. became a Lost Cause through no fault of its own, while it is hardly fair to bracket the Guy with any of them, since the firm merely disencumbered itself of unprofitable deadweight.

But why did all these Lost Causes hail from Wolverhampton? Is there anything in the Wulfrunian make-up to account for them? The answer must be No, for Wolverhampton still supplies components, especially tyres and radiators, for Britain's motor industry, as well as making Guy lorries and Turner sports cars. The location is pure coincidence. John Lloyd-Davies, Clyno's former sales manager, summed it all up very succinctly for me: 'Perhaps it's as well,' he said, 'that Wolverhampton gave up making cars—otherwise we'd have been bombed, like Coventry.'

CHAPTER 12

'... But Never Jam Today':
Cordwallis Works, Maidenhead

'A gear for every gradient.'

G.W.K. slogan

'Maidenhead is quite a famous place, and all the best people visit it at some time or other.'

Marendaz advertisement, 1936

ONE of the hazards of the run up A.4 from the West to London is the crowded and narrow High Street of Maidenhead. There was talk of a by-pass in my father's day: gargantuan earthworks started in 1937, only to be interrupted by the war, and only now at long last is the town bypassed by the M.4 motorway. Yet still Maidenhead remains a traffic hazard, as it was when one wore 'whites' on the river, and the town was the alleged home of some one hundred and fifty night clubs of all types and denominations.

If you turn sharp left at the traffic lights by the Town Hall and proceed up the Cookham Road, past the garage which fathered the prototype Heybourn cyclecar, you will find yourself in a medley of administrative offices, modern housing and a few red-brick survivals of Victorian days.

There is little evidence of industrialization, for the industrial emphasis of the town has shifted south across the railway to the Boyn Valley and Cox Green, but if you persevere you will come upon a wide gateway, flanked with red-brick pillars, on the left-hand side of the road. Large notices will advise you that this is the home of St. Martin's Chunky Marmalade, but will remain silent on the subject of cars. Tread respectfully, for you are in the presence of the Jam Factory, most legendary of all the homes of the Lost Causes.

Unlike the manufacturers of Birmingham and Coventry, who succumbed to cut-throat competition rather than to the snares of heterodoxy, the Jam Factory tried everything: friction drive, rear engines, straight-eights, slide valves, electrics and petrol-electrics all emerged from this dreary conglomeration of sheds. Between the end of 1914 and the summer of 1936, well over a thousand cars, from 7 h.p. miniatures to formidable luxury vehicles, drove out of the gates and nosed their way into the streets of Maidenhead, on their way up the Bath Road to London and the markets.

The intriguing aspect of the Maidenhead saga is that Cordwallis Works seemed to exercise a hoodoo on the manufacture of cars. Firms either saw the Cookham Road and died, or saw the red light and went elsewhere. Both Marendaz and G.W.K. attained their successes in other works before translating themselves to Maidenhead and the Official Receiver. The Imperia, which had sold quite briskly for an imported car before the first World War, languished and died a slow death there. Auto Electrics moved to Guildford and abandoned all their interest in car manufacture; while Sir Dennis Burney, recognizing the limitations of Cordwallis Works as anything more than an experimental workshop, arranged for the limited series production of his designs elsewhere. You can still spot exciting cars outside Maidenhead's hotels, especially in the summer, but the odds are heavily against their being the products of Maidonian labour. Only in the little pubs of North Town, Summerleaze and Cox Green will you hear nostalgic talk of the old G.W.K. days.

It is unlikely, however, that these sombre thoughts crossed the minds of Arthur Grice, J. Talfourd Wood and C. M. Keiller as they planned a new light car together in their experimental workshops at Beckenham in 1910. Grice had conceived the idea that a friction gear he had seen used for grinding optical lenses could be applied to a light car. He had succeeded in interesting Wood in this project, and on the strength of a·rough sketch on the back of an envelope they had gone to work, joined by Keiller, who had met Wood while they had been training together in the Great Western Railway workshops at Swindon.

Both their plans and the facilities at their disposal were limited in the extreme. They rented a small stable at Beckenham, while Grice, who at that time handled the London end of Messrs. George Anderson, crane manufacturers of Carnoustie, had an office in Victoria Street through which he was able to conduct the business of the partnership. Plans to use Chater-Lea frames—then proprietary components with a wide currency—were frustrated, since the Chater-Lea concern was not interested in such a small contract, but eventually two Coventry-Simplex twin-cylinder marine engines, a pair of old De Dion-type tubular radiators, a set of Chater-Lea wire wheels of non-detachable type and a Chater-Lea front axle were procured; the rest they made themselves.

The principles of the friction transmission were simple. The flywheel of the engine served as a driving disc, which engaged with a driven disc shod with a 'tyre' in the form of a ring faced with fibre or cork. The second disc was mounted at right angles to the flywheel so that it could be slid across it, engaging at four different points. This action was controlled by notches selected by a thumb-operated plunger on the 'gear lever'. The clutch mechanism engaged one end of the driven-disc shaft. At the other end the shaft was universally-jointed, the drive thereafter being by shaft to a differential. De-clutching moved the driven disc out of contact with the driving disc, while full depression of the clutch pedal actuated a transmission brake. In other respects the car was conventional, though the engine lived below and behind the seats and the radiator was mounted in front. The rear-mounted engine, incidentally, contributed very largely to the success of the early cars, as unquestionably the whip encountered in the long drive shafts of the later four-cylinder machines rendered the transmissions less reliable.

By 1911, a company had been formed and operations had been transferred from the stables at Beckenham to Home Works, Datchet, not far from Windsor. Their landlord here, be it said, was my father, for Datchet was part of the family estates until 1917, and I am still Lord of the Manor of Datchet. Here series production was under-taken, using the 86 × 90 mm. vertical-twin Coventry-Simplex engine. Apart from the provision of detachable wheels in 1912, no major alterations were carried out to the basic specification, and 1,069 cars, mainly the very similar Models 'A' and 'B', were turned out between the establishment of the Datchet works and the dis-continuation of private car manufacture in favour of Admiralty contracts in 1915.

Grice, Wood and Keiller were early in the light-car field. Captain Wood is still most insistent that the G.W.K. was never a cyclecar, which name he associates with the belt-drive and plywood brigade such as the Tamplin and Carden, while the presence of conventional driving controls helped to allay any misgivings the public might entertain on the subject of friction drive. Both Wood and Keiller realized the importance of competition work, the former having been one of only nine finishers in the 1910 Scottish Six Days Motor-cycle Trial, and G.W.K.s were entered in every possible event. The two partners were awarded Gold Medals in the 1912 London–Edinburgh run. Keiller collected another 'Gold' in the 'Six Days', and a stripped touring model won a five-lap race at Brooklands that May, beating an A.C. and a Morgan. Hill-climbs also saw the partners in action, Wood winning the Cyclecar Class at the Streatham and District Club's event at Titsey in September. In

October, the indefatigable Wood was again out after records at Brooklands.

The year 1913 saw Wood and Keiller out again, reinforced by Cyril Wilberforce, the company's Caterham agent and, on occasions, Rex Mundy, later to be associated with K.L.G. sparking plugs. Competition was fiercer now, for H. F. S. Morgan—also a former Swindon apprentice—was pitting his three-wheelers against the more substantial G.W.K.s, and the name of G.N. was making itself felt. A Morgan won the Cyclecar Race at Brooklands that March, though only after the opposition from Datchet had been defeated by tyre trouble, and two months later, in the Herefordshire Cyclecar Trial, the honours again went to Morgan. Nevertheless, both Wood and Keiller won Gold Medals in a Scottish Six Days that included that memorable nastiness, the Pass of the Cattle—and anyone who laughs at the crudities of friction drive should recall the raised eyebrows which accompanied the inclusion of this formidable section in the 1936 Scottish Rally.

With Haywood's tuned Singer Ten entering the lists, the G.W.K.s were now strongly challenged in speed events, but they went on winning. By the end of 1913, *The Motor Cycle* was observing that 'the G.W.K. has won its spurs and can be purchased without fear of future reprisals', and for 1914 no improvements were deemed necessary beyond the adoption of a stronger timing gear and bevel pinion, and some improvements to a body which was already adequate for most purchasers in the G.W.K. class. The little cars bridged the gap between true cyclecars like the G.N., which demanded a degree of mechanical skill and a spartan attitude to life, and big cars in miniature like the Morris-Oxford, already making its mark and keeping its competitors up to scratch. The Datchet product weighed 6½ cwt. in chassis form, as against 4¾ cwt. for the G.N. and a resounding 8¼ cwt. for the Morris. Not that racing cars were neglected, for Wood was now using a slender streamlined single-seater at Brooklands, and getting round very briskly.

In the New Buyers' Number of *The Light Car and Cyclecar* in March 1914, G.W.K. Ltd. took two full pages in the advertisement columns to plug their successes during the past seasons, giving the lie to dark hints on the advent of an American 'cyclecar armada' said to be on its way. Far more useful to the company, however, was a contribution by Captain Wood in the same issue, entitled 'The Case for Friction Drive'. This combined some sound advice with propaganda, the writer arguing that, on grounds of simplicity and ease of servicing, the system took a lot of beating. Facings for the fibre wheel cost only ten shillings apiece, and could be replaced without undoing anything save twenty bolts which held it to the wheel, while the question of facing material itself (G.W.K. tried all manner of linings, including millboard, Ferodo, and cork) was laughed off with the observation that during a record attempt at Brooklands he had 'found some linoleum lying about, and used it'. Slip could be eliminated by keeping the discs free of grease, while flats in the fibre facing, the great bugbear of friction drive and the cause of transmission slip, resulted from letting the clutch in too slowly, or driving with the handbrake on. 'I do not say,' Captain Wood continued, 'that it must be let in with a bang, though little harm will be done if it is, but it must be let in far more quickly than an ordinary clutch of the cone or plate type.' These instructions may seem elementary to the modern motorist, but it must be remembered that the Edwardians looked upon the gearbox as a means of starting from rest and coping with near-vertical gradients, and that the habit of slipping the clutch to propel oneself over the crest of a hill was almost universal among lay motorists. 'Flats do not prevent the car being driven,' Wood continues consolingly, 'but of course they will set up a disagreeable knocking noise.' No skilled driver, however, need go in fear of 'flats', and fibres were good for 7,000 to 10,000 miles by 1914.

When war broke out, the wind had apparently set fair for G.W.K. Ltd. Their £150 light car had the merits of simplicity and reliability. The standard article was capable of 50 m.p.h.—although the owner of one of the few surviving 'twins' still claims mile-a-minute speeds —while fuel consumptions of the order of 45 m.p.g. were readily obtainable. Captain Wood remembers driving one of the Scottish Six Days cars from Edinburgh to Byfleet in less than thirteen hours. A small but brisk export trade was being built up, cars being shipped to East Africa and Ceylon. The prejudice against friction drive had been overcome, and people were beginning to take it seriously. General Motors in America hurriedly bought up the makers of the Cartercar, a transatlantic apostle of the system: its sales were uninspiring, but the patents had considerable potential value.

Unfortunately, his partners had reckoned without the personality of Arthur Grice. Grice was congenitally incapable of pursuing an idea beyond the prototype stage—no sooner had a system been made to work than he was off chasing some new pipe-dream. He seems to have divided his time between the exploration of other people's ideas for possible patent infringement, and the acquisition of an interest in them with a view to their exploitation by his own companies. Self-destruction by an ultra-keen interest in the patent laws was a characteristic of other Lost Causes, notably Argyll. Grice could not resist experimentation, and he had already all but dropped out of G.W.K. Ltd. to pursue his lifelong diversion of forming companies. In 1912, he had floated Rotary Units Ltd. to develop a pumping engine said to have 'five eccentric cylinders'. The G.W.K. company was asked to make this engine, but it never worked, and the newly founded firm was left in abeyance for another eight years until its progenitor found a new use for it, having in the meanwhile repurchased all the shares at cut rates. A year or so later he joined forces with a Belgian marble merchant, M. A. Van Roggen, to whom he had sold diamond bandsaws while still with George Anderson's. They formed G. & V. R. Ltd., for which concern premises on the Cordwallis Works site at Maidenhead were acquired. A car of sorts was certainly built (or, more probably, imported), but by the outbreak of war nothing concrete had emerged from this project.

Whatever mysterious contrivances were being evolved at Maidenhead, Grice suggested to his partners that the body-shops of the expanding G.W.K. business be shifted from Datchet to Cordwallis Works, and, shortly after the outbreak of war, the rest of the factory followed suit. Wood had joined up, leaving the wartime management of G.W.K. to Grice.

The move to Maidenhead was the turning-point. Neither the finances nor the standard of work were ever the same, and many of the old G.W.K. employees I have met say that the 'family' atmosphere of Datchet was never recaptured. However, Grice's fertile brain had not been idle in the war years, and there was no shortage of ideas for a new car by Armistice time. Unfortunately, they were the wrong ones.

After the unqualified success of Models 'A' and 'B', it might have been expected that production of these types would be resumed by the reorganized company, G.W.K. (1919) Ltd. So it was, for a short time in 1919, when a hold-up in the supply of four-cylinder engines forced the company to run off about a hundred cars of pre-war type, using units left over from pre-war stocks. Grice, however, had set his heart on a four-cylinder car. Already a prototype had been made, and had been running since 1915, but this was simply a twin-cylinder chassis fitted with a side-valve M.A.G. engine mounted at the rear and retaining the original 'Model A' layout. Wood held the view that the company's only hope was to produce a redesigned twin-cylinder machine with conventional transmission, but Grice had a *fait accompli* in the shape of 'Model F' by the summer of 1918. This looked just like a conventional car, and had a front-mounted 66 × 100 mm. (1,368 c.c.) Coventry-Simplex side-valve engine, quarter-elliptic suspension and electric lighting. It was an altogether bigger and heavier vehicle, chassis weight being 10½ cwt. and the wheelbase 9 ft. 8 in.

From the start, this vehicle proved a headache. Wood and Keiller laboured hard to overcome its numerous failings, which included wheel-shedding, transmission whip and unpleasant ringing noises from the driven disc, which last aroused adverse comment in the contemporary motoring press. By the end of 1921, they had transformed it into a reliable motor car, Wood winning 'Golds' in the 'Edinburgh' and the Scottish Six Days in 1920, while in the 1921 'Land's End' G. W. K. again featured extensively in the awards list. Unfortunately they had to contend not only with labour troubles, but with Grice's brilliant plan for collecting a Post Office contract for light vans based on the new 'Model F' chassis. But, with the new car still suffering teething troubles, the result can be imagined. The vans were unreliable, the Post Office drivers found friction drive beyond them, and the trial contract merely served to dislocate private-car production further. The protracted moulders' strike of 1920–21 held up deliveries of parts, and even the departure of Grice to resuscitate Rotary Units Ltd. in 1920 could not save the company.

In 1922, G.W.K. (1919) Ltd. went into liquidation, Wood and Keiller resigned, and the story of a gallant little car really came to an end. Unfortunately for the firm's reputation, though, the projects continued, and for the next eight or nine years floods of directors came and went. The Academy of Projectors were given full rein and they had a wonderful time.

Grice, meanwhile, was operating at the foot of Holtspur Hill, Wooburn Green, under the style of Rotary Units Ltd. This impressive title covered no more than a pair of large Army huts which had once formed part of the wartime hospital on Lord Astor's nearby estate of Cliveden, and had been transported to Wooburn by Grice. Here he reverted to a twin-cylinder rear-engined machine resembling the original G.W.K. very closely in appearance. The engine was said to be a product of Rotary Units Ltd., but was actually a side-valve 998 c.c. vee-twin Bovier. The drive from the flywheel to the driven disc was taken by a Hardy universal joint, and a central chain took the drive to the back axle. The finished article sold for £275—the same price as the four-cylinder G.W.K.—complete with oil side-lamps, but *sans* starter. Such deviations as there were from the specification of the Maidenhead cars were undoubtedly due to the need to avoid litigation.

Rotary Units struggled on until 1923, during which period about fifty cars of various types were made. In the company's short life, it produced the original rear-engined car, a front-engined 'twin' (£280, or £297 with water cooling), a four-cylinder s.v. car with a 63 × 100 mm. (1,247 c.c.) engine (£268), a similar type with conventional three-speed box and shaft drive (£297), a third variation on the same theme retaining the friction transmission without the chain, and, finally, a 'Service Model' with unitary construction of chassis and body, which was displayed at the 1922 Show. The standard colour was khaki, with electric lighting, and it cost a mere £186. There seems to have been no standard form of Unit No. 1, and the make featured little in contemporary competitions, though one F. Salter won a Silver Medal in the 1921 Land's End Trial. Mr Leonard P. Lee, for many years head of Coventry-Climax Engines Ltd., served part of his apprenticeship at the Wooburn works.

In the meantime the G.W.K. directors, who had a saleable car on their hands, set about getting advice as to how to market it. Their chosen vessel was Percy Richardson, late of Daimler and Sheffield-Simplex, who was appointed managing director in February 1922. But despite the successes of the *marque* in trials, especially in the hands of Pope and Jackson, little headway was made. Nineteen-twenty-two, however, saw a reversion to a rear-engined lay out with Model 'J'. This retained the frontal radiator, and, owing to the use of a fairly long bonnet, was not readily distinguishable from 'Model H', the 'conventional' car which had been evolved by Wood from the unreliable 'F'. It was unsuccessful, though it will crop up again in the G.W.K. story.

In 1923, Jackson and Pope pulled off their accustomed Gold Medals in the 'London–Edinburgh', while the standard 'Model H' two-seater was reduced in price from £285 to £210 in an attempt to attract customers. More important, however, A. G. Grice tired of Rotary Units Ltd. and returned to the fold, while his associate M. A. Van Roggen also joined the Board.

The picture of the last few years of G.W.K. is a sad one. There were stocks of parts on hand sufficient to assemble as many cars as the market would take, and it was the company's practice to keep a few chassis in readiness for any orders that might come in. There was little production as such, and certainly the company's past policy of over-buying enabled it to keep ticking over feebly in fits and starts until 1931. But the writing was on the wall. Serious competition work stopped after 1924, and activities were confined to the assembly of the odd G.W.K., to sundry Grice experiments including the Grice three-wheeler of 1925–6, which had friction drive and a single wheel in front, and to research work on two other oddities, the French Lafitte and the London-built Waverley.

The former had a three-cylinder radial engine, friction-and-chain drive and a dashboard gear lever after the manner of the f.w.d. Citroën, and suffered the indignity of conversion into a service van after Grice lost interest. The latter had a 75 × 102 mm. rear-mounted flat-twin engine, and actually appeared at the 1926 Show as a £100 car. Its arrival at Cordwallis Works was variously ascribed to Grice's ambition to produce it there, and to his determination to prevent Waverley Cars from infringing his patents by producing it anywhere. The latter is almost certainly the truth.

Half-hearted evolution of the G.W.K. design continued. For 1924, a 1½-litre (69 × 100 mm.) engine was offered as an alternative power unit, while *de luxe* models were at last given a starter as standard equipment. Front-wheel brakes of Stevenson design were available at £10 10*s* extra. In 1925, the firm offered an all hand-controlled car, aimed at disabled drivers. This had no pedals at all, clutch and 'footbrake' being operated by downward movement of the steering column into a slot below. Full depression gave the effect of a clutch. One or two of these hand-controlled G.W.K.s were sold, though R. G. Jackson, the then sales manager, says they were horrible to drive. In 1926, the firm tried to cash in on the low-priced market with a fabric-bodied 'Chummy', intended to sell at £100. The list price was actually £159. At the 1926 Show, the G.W.K. appeared for the last time, a fabric-bodied 'Drophead Saloon' being priced at £335.

Meanwhile, a new development had arisen. Van Roggen persuaded Grice to interest himself and the ailing G.W.K. concern in a Belgian car, the Imperia.

The Imperia was a ready-made Lost Cause. In pre-1914 days, this Belgian *marque* had enjoyed quite a fair success on the British market; indeed, a Miss Edith Paterson had leapt to fame by putting fifty-three miles into the hour at Brooklands on a 16 h.p. Imperia in 1908, at a time when women were not permitted to compete in ordinary races. But in Edwardian days the Imperia had possessed no markedly eccentric features. Nor, outwardly, did it possess them in 1924, being a solidly-built small car resembling nothing so much as a slightly down-at-heel Panhard-Levassor in miniature. It boasted a conventional four-speed and reverse gearbox and four-wheel brakes, but under the bonnet there was one of those weird and wonderful power units devised by those determined people who sought to give the poppet valve premature burial. The Imperia engine was, in fact, a slide valve, in which the slides were located on either side of the cylinder wall, moving vertically and covering and uncovering double ports.

Not that the Imperia was a bad car. Van Roggen won the small-car class in the 1926 Monte Carlo Rally on one of the 11 h.p (66 × 80 mm.) models, and a tourer tested by *The Autocar* in 1924 was quite good value at £375, giving a top speed of 46 m.p.h. and a fuel consumption of 32 m.p.g.; this in spite of the fact that the weight was something of the order of seventeen cwt. The whole vehicle was solidly built for an '1100', necessitating a depressing 5·1 : 1 top gear. A saloon was submitted for road test in 1926, and was found to be undergeared as well as much noisier than a conventional sleeve-valve. At the same time it was announced that 'the car is to be manufactured in this country at the G.W.K. works'.

In the event, it never was. The G.W.K. company underwent one of its periodic reconstructions at the beginning of 1927, and emerged as Imperia Motors Ltd. But the new company did not make, nor even assemble, Imperias, and it made precious few G.W.K.s either, having recourse to general repair work in order to keep going. A few experiments were carried out with a 'plastic' form of body construction, the principal ingredients of which seem to have been hair and plaster of Paris, but the sum total of the Imperia operations amounted to perhaps four dozen cars imported in four years. These were sold initially through the London firm of W. G. Nicholl Ltd., Mr Nicholl being a director of the Maidenhead concern. A 66 × 80 mm. 'six' of similar design arrived on the scene in 1929, but very few were sold in England. The main interest of the Imperia venture was the advent of Mr Alfred Dougill.

A. W. Dougill dominated the company's later years. His main concern was the development of Cordwallis Works into a Trading Estate, and by the time of his death in 1941 he had achieved this. None the less, it is likely that Grice was attracted not so much by Dougill's business acumen as by his connexions with his pet hobby-horse, friction drive.

Mr Dougill's father had built a series of experimental cars in Leeds between 1896 and 1898, and in 1899 acquired the British sales agency for the friction-drive cars designed by Ludwig Maurer of Nuremberg. He was also, incidentally, responsible for the assembly in 1899 of that curiosity, the Lawson motor-wheel, a true 'mechanical horse' which was mounted between the shafts of a trap. From 1902 to 1906 the younger Dougill assisted his father in the manufacture of a small number of cars and trucks, using a double-disc system of friction drive, under the trade-name 'Frick', and the elder Dougill patented these designs in the latter year. In 1907 the son joined Wolseley, remaining with them until the company was wound up at the end of 1926, by which time he was their works manager. In the course of his career at Adderley Park, he had been closely connected both with Count Schilowsky's famous gyro-car and with the Brennan gyroscopic mono-railcar, which had a Wolseley petrol engine and was made at the company's Crayford works. Such a man would surely appeal to Grice.

By 1930, the G.W.K. was no more than an entry in the *Buyers' Guide*, while Imperia operations were only on a token scale. They exhibited at the 1930 Show, but that was all. No G.W.K.s were displayed on this occasion. Nevertheless, Grice was having his final fling, in the form of yet another rear-engined four-cylinder car. The old Coventry-Climax engine was retained—there were still quite a few lying around at Cordwallis Works—but this time it was mounted well over the axle, driving forward. A punt-type chassis reminiscent of the early Trojan was used, and indeed the finished article looked uncommonly like a punt on wheels, this effect being heightened by the use of a convertible 'roll-top' with rigid sides, styled on the lines of the camping punts so popular on the Thames. The price was £165; a simplified version, to be priced 'in the neighbourhood of £100', was hinted at, but never materialized.

In the meanwhile a Mr Murphy had started a firm by the name of Auto Electric on the Cordwallis Estate. This concern made two experimental vehicles in the 1928–30 period, the first a little battery-electric car with a motor 'at each corner', four-wheel drive and four-wheel independent suspension, and the second a petrol-electric device, using yet another unwanted Coventry-Climax engine—presumably because it was there! This latter was never completed, and both ventures were abandoned when the firm moved to Guildford.

1930, however, saw a far more interesting arrival in the form of Sir Dennis Burney, the designer of the airship R.100. Burney aimed to produce a car with optimum weight distribution, efficient suspension and a true aerodynamic form. Streamline Cars Ltd. never interested themselves in series production: Sir Dennis told me that Cordwallis Works were totally unsuited for anything other than prototype work, which is hardly surprising in view of the fact that in 1930 one large shed housed the remnants of the G.W.K. project, Imperia Motors Ltd. and the Burney experimental shop. The partitions between each section were of beaverboard, and one shudders to think what might have happened had they collapsed.

Burney started with a clean sheet of paper. His car had its engine mounted over the rear axle, and had independent suspension to all four wheels, transverse cantilever springs being used at the rear. His first experimental car was produced at the airship station at Howden in 1928, and consisted of a 12/75 f.w.d. Alvis chassis turned back to front, with the steering locked and the dead rear axle of the original Alvis design replaced by a conventional steering axle. Unlike Grice, Burney did not feel himself bound by any aesthetic conventions, and the original design had a short nose falling away immediately in front of the driver, the radiators being mounted in the logical position at the rear, one each side of the engine. The 'aeroplane-fuselage' effect of the body was rather spoilt by the use of conventional, cycle-type front mudguards, turning with the wheels. The gearbox was of four-speed 'crash' type, with central remote control. One small concession was made to the diehards in that buyers had the choice of an alternative body style, with a vestigial bonnet housing a petrol tank in front of the driver. All cars had exhaust gas heaters to front and rear compartments.

Sir Dennis, however, conformed to the fashions of the later Vintage years in fitting his cars with a straight-eight engine, a true Lost Cause in the form of a 3-litre (66 × 108 mm.) Beverley-Barnes. This unit had twin overhead camshafts and bore a superficial resemblance to an Alfa-Romeo, the employment of Marelli coil ignition heightening the similarity. It is hard to know why this obscure power plant was chosen, but it was fairly potent, giving 80 b.h.p., sufficient to propel the heavy Burney at a sustained 70 m.p.h. In any case, the depression had hit Beverleys hard, and their very small sales were dwindling away to nothing, so it is scarcely surprising that they were seeking to invade the proprietary engine market. In standard form the Burney listed at £1,500, which was a high price even for seekers after the bizarre.

The Burney created a sensation, especially when it was announced at the end of 1930 that H.R.H. The Prince of Wales had ordered one. 1932 models boasted a dummy vee-radiator, and the designer took one of these to America on a lecture tour, where it was favourably received. Despite the fact that on this occasion a Lycoming

'Six' engine, as used in the contemporary Auburn, was installed, nothing happened, and the American public had to wait another twenty-seven years for a rear-engined car at a popular price.

Altogether twelve cars were made between 1930 and 1933, nine of them with the twin-cam Beverleys, which proved unreliable. Apart from the Lycoming unit in the car which went to America, the last two had o.h.v. Armstrong-Siddeley Twenty engines. Streamline Cars Ltd. remained in existence for some time after the closure of the Maidenhead factory in the spring of 1933, but only design work was undertaken, and the 2-litre Crossleys built under Burney patents in 1934 were made entirely at Manchester. At one stage the presence of a Crossley-Burney prototype at Cordwallis Works brought forth a wild rumour that the whole Trading Estate was to be turned over to the mass-production of rear-engined cars, but this, I am assured, was baseless.

By 1932, Grice had retired to an island in the Thames, where he was selling replacement facings for friction discs, while Dougill kept the Imperia business ticking over. Into this void came the colourful personality of Captain D. M. K. Marendaz. Marendaz had spent most of his life in the motor industry, having served his apprentice-ship at Siddeley-Deasy before fighting in the R.F.C. during the war. Upon demobilization, he went to work with T. G. John at the Holley Bros. factory in Coventry, and was thus connected with the early days of Alvis. A former brother-officer of his, Mr Hulbert, was at this time in partnership with G. P. H. de Freville, a well-known Ford agent. De Freville had designed a 1,500 c.c. side-valve four-cylinder engine of sporting potentialities.

It was Marendaz who suggested that a batch of fifty of these De Freville engines should be laid down at Coventry, and the result was the 10/30 Alvis. He then contracted to build 500 gearboxes for the Emscote cyclecar, an ephemeral of the immediate post-war years sponsored by Marlowe, a former works manager at Standard, and Seelhaft, who had been Marendaz' senior in his apprentice days at Siddeley-Deasy.

Marendaz, having made 260 gearboxes for cars which never materialized, decided to go into partnership with Seelhaft, the result being a little 10·8 h.p. car with Coventry-Simplex side-valve engine known as the Marseel. Apart from the adoption of worm final drive it had no very unusual features, but between the summer of 1920 and the closing of the factory in 1925, it won over 250 trials awards, many of them in the hands of its designer, who raced a blue-and-white example, nicknamed 'Blancmange', at Brooklands.

The Marseal range (the spelling was changed after Seelhaft's retirement in 1923) embraced the usual diversity of models, ranging from a 1,247 c.c. 9/20 to an o.h.v. small 'six'. The 12/40 h.p. car had a polished aluminium body in·the manner of those times, and was said to be good for 75 m.p.h., while in 1922 some experiments were carried out with a four-cylinder in-line oil-cooled engine of 1,018 c.c., rather reminiscent of the Bradshaw-designed units used in a number of contemporary motor cycles and in the Belsize-Bradshaw light car. Despite 6,000 miles of successful road tests, this model never reached the production stage. Altogether, the Marseal made quite an impression, and about 1,200 were built, with bodies by Lawson or Hancock and Warman (the latter subsequently doing much of Riley's bodywork), before the firm went into liquidation. Characteristically enough, the demise of Marseal Motors Ltd. followed closely upon the introduction of the six-cylinder car.

After a brief period on the Stock Exchange, Captain Marendaz took premises in 1926 in the London General Cab Co's. garage at the Camberwell end of the Brixton Road, which building also housed, in addition to the freshly reconstituted cab concern, Ettore Bugatti's London depot and, from 1928 onwards, the British concessionaires for the Graham-Paige. The main activities of D.M.K. Marendaz Ltd. were a garage and tuning establishment. The firm also sold second-hand sports cars, contributing some of the more exciting items, such as Alfa-Romeo or Lea-Francis, to *The Autocar*'s series of Used Car Road Tests. More or less as a sideline, he also constructed—or rather assembled—about twenty Marendaz Specials. Most of these used four-cylinder s.v. Anzani engines, separate gearboxes and cone clutches. The 1½-litre (69 × 100 mm.) car retailed at £495 as the 11/55, or in supercharged chassis form at £750 as the 11/120. A smaller version in the same chassis was the 9/20, with 59 × 100 mm. (1,093 c.c.) o.h.v. engine. The four-wheel brakes were so arranged that the pedal acted on the front wheels and the lever on the rear. With their vee-screens, Bentley-shaped radiators and flared wings, they were exciting-looking little cars, and though limited capital prevented Marendaz from supporting a big racing programme, he was a tireless performer at Montlhéry, cleaning up record after record. The World's Class 'G' 24-Hour Record fell to a stripped 1,100 c.c. two-seater in February 1928, driven by its designer and Douglas Hawkes; this in spite of the fact that a mechanic backed the car into a petrol pump during the proceedings and damaged the rear axle. Marendaz, Forrest and

Hanks also collected the 1,500 c.c. 24-Hour Record at 59 m.p.h. under impossible conditions of fog, while Marendaz also set up a number of long-distance records with the big straight-eight Graham-Paiges, even putting up the fastest lap as yet made at Brooklands in a saloon, at 90·06 m.p.h. Incidentally, his open Graham-Paige was the car which won the very last race ever run at Brooklands, in August 1939.

At the same time, he was experimenting with a small straight-eight of his own, with exhaust-over-inlet valves. This had cylinder dimensions of 52 × 88 mm. (1,495 c.c.), and was catalogued in chassis form at £600, or £750 with supercharger. A special Anzani crankshaft was used, and the block was made specially in Birmingham to Marendaz designs, but this project came to naught, though certainly the engine was completed. This may have been the car which cropped up in 1931 as a 'Miller-Marendaz Special'.

Late in 1931 came a small side-valve 'six', the 13/70, which was of fairly conventional design apart from one or two intriguing features, including the employment of a 2 : 1 reduction gear for both brake and clutch pedals. Brakes were Lockheed hydraulic. The engine's appearance was enhanced by an aluminium cover plate which concealed the plugs. 70 b.h.p. at 4,700 r.p.m. was claimed from the 1,869 c.c. (59 × 112 mm.) unit, which was creditable, though much unkind nonsense was published about the alleged origin of these engines. They were in actual fact assembled by Marendaz, the camshafts and crankshafts being made by Continental Motors Corporation—hence the rumour, no doubt, that they were surplus Erskine engines bought when Studebaker got into financial difficulties. The blocks were produced by Birmid in Birmingham. Dual coil ignition was used, and fuel was fed from the rear tank by an Autopulse electric pump. The car was cloaked with a very pretty four-seater 'International' body which owed its inspiration to Max Millar, *The Autocar*'s artist, and, apart from the stub exhausts which rather spoilt the general effect, the resemblance to a miniature Bentley was very pronounced—so much so, in fact, that in 1933 *The Autocar* found it necessary to deny rumours that Rolls-Royce were bringing out a new small Bentley. The rumour-mongers had clearly spotted a 13/70 Marendaz, and had drawn the obvious conclusions. This model was listed at £375.

Clearly a factory less cramped than the Brixton Road workshops was indicated; so Marendaz took on the lease of one of the buildings at Cordwallis Works. When I met him, incidentally, he was rather hurt at the suggestion that the works of Marendaz Special Cars Ltd.

occupied yet another section of the congested shed in which the G.W.K., Burney and Imperia enterprises were eking out a precarious existence. In actual fact, they were located in a completely separate building, and remained there until the company went into liquidation in the late summer of 1936.

In May 1932, Marendaz Special Cars Ltd. was formed 'to carry on the business of manufacturers of, and dealers in, cars, motor cycles, engines, airships, aeroplanes, etc.'—not so illogical in the light of subsequent events. Capital was only £5,000, but this did not deter Marendaz from making quite an impression during his tenancy of Cordwallis Works. In September of that year, Mrs E. B. Norris, Mayoress of Maidenhead, christened the first 13/70 to leave the newly commissioned works, though it is to be regretted that by this time the locals were becoming cynical on the subject of the native motor industry, and *The Maidenhead Advertiser* gave far more publicity to the launching, two years later, of the first *traction avant* Citroën to roll off the lines at Slough.

Three basic models of Marendaz were offered: the 13/70, the bigger 2·6-litre 17/97 at £475, both with Marendaz engines, and the 15/90 with a 65 × 100 mm. i.o.e. Coventry-Climax six-cylinder engine, which was introduced for the 1935 season and had become the staple product by 1936. Supercharged variants were also marketed, and the cars competed regularly in the National rallies of their day, mainly in the hands of Captain Marendaz and Mr and Mrs A. E. Moss, the parents of Stirling Moss. In 1936, Mrs Moss even had built for her a special short-chassis version of the Coventry-Climax-engined car with an ultra-light two-seater body made of fabric on a light steel frame, which she ran in the R.A.C. and Scottish Rallies that year, gaining a first-class award in the former. An even more noteworthy success was scored by Miss D. Summers, who was the first woman to win a race at Brooklands (in 1936) after the fair sex had been admitted on equal terms with the men. What is more, she did it at the first meeting of the season, and on a standard 15/90 Marendaz tourer! The Coventry-Climax-engined Marendaz proved very successful, and it is only regrettable that it appeared on the scene when the company's fortunes were already at a low ebb. At £425, it represented remarkable value for the enthusiast, and when road-tested by *The Autocar* it recorded nearly 82 m.p.h. on top and 73 m.p.h. on the very close-ratio third.

'Great Britain's Fastest and Safest 2-litre' was soon to succumb to the Maidenhead hoodoo. All the same, the 2-litre car did quite well in the 1935 T.T. in the hands of W. T. McCalla, while a supercharged 17/100 h.p. tourer had the distinction of featuring in the production of 'Man and Superman' at the Cambridge Theatre in August of that year. Bernard Shaw, however, stuck to his Lanchester Ten.

But Marendaz was looking to other fields to redress the adverse balance of the car business. He had shown a marine engine at the 1933 Olympia Show—his only London show appearance since the Marseal days, though a 17/90 (as the 17/97 had been renamed) was displayed at the Kelvin Hall in 1934—and now he prepared designs for a two-seater light aeroplane. All to no avail: the company was wound up in July 1936, the remains being taken over by Colliers of Birmingham, who already owned the remnants of Clyno, Swift and A.J.S., among others.

Thus perished Maidenhead's motor industry. Cordwallis Works passed into the hands of the manufacturers of preserves. As late as 1935, Imperias theoretically were still being imported into Great Britain, while Mr Dougill advertised Imperia Motors Ltd. as a source of spares for the Derby, having taken over the stocks held by Ortons of Cookham, the erstwhile concessionaires. But the Imperia was doomed to lose its identity, and when the make reappeared at Earls Court in 1937, under the aegis of Minerva Automobiles Ltd., the cars were found to be no more than re-styled f.w.d. Adlers. Later on, Imperia took a further step away from individuality by manufacturing Standard 'Vanguards' under licence.

Captain Marendaz' aircraft business in Bedfordshire was just getting under way, and the Cirrus-powered Marendaz Trainer was undergoing trials, when the war intervened. Afterwards he emigrated to South Africa, and when I met him in 1959 he had started a factory in Meyerton, Transvaal, for the manufacture of the first stationary diesel engines to be made anywhere in Africa.

The Maidenhead area also harboured other short-lived ventures, in addition to the products of the Jam Factory and the Heybourn cyclecar. There was the Payze, a conventional light car assembled at Cookham in 1921, but far more interesting was the 1½-litre Squire, which burst upon a startled world in September 1934.

Adrian Squire was a brilliant young draughtsman who had worked for M.G. at Abingdon, and is remembered there as a man who never turned out a crude job, even simple brackets being rendered with delightful precision on his drawing-board. Late in 1934, he formed the Squire Car Manufacturing Co. Ltd at Henley to market a 1½-litre sports machine built to the highest possible standards and regardless of cost, as might be understood from the fact that a two-seater was listed at £1,195.

The engines were specially-built twin overhead-camshaft 69 × 100 mm. Anzanis, a Roots-type supercharger driven from the forward end of the crankshaft being used. This potent engine was mated with an E.N.V. preselector gearbox, and the standard top-gear ratio of 3·0 : 1 gave 100 m.p.h. at only 4,300 r.p.m.; hence the startling performance. Ignition was by coil, and a large S.U. carburettor was used. A massive and low-built frame with extra-wide side-members was combined with long underslung semi-elliptic springs, and the powerful hydraulic brakes had fifteen-inch drums. The bodywork was not skimped, either, being undertaken mainly by Ranalah and Vanden Plas, though the lightweight two-seaters were built by Markhams of Reading.

As the firm had its headquarters in a small garage at the top of Remenham Hill, on the London road, space demanded that a certain amount of machining should be 'bought out', and Stuart Turner, the marine engine firm, undertook some of the work for Squire. Every car was supplied with a guarantee that it had lapped Brooklands at over 100 m.p.h.

Unfortunately, there were snags. The production of such a design needed more resources than the company possessed, and even the ranks of the connoisseurs included few purchasers in 1935 who were prepared to expend four figures on a 1½-litre car, however superb the workmanship. Even a steady reduction of prices could not save the day, though by mid-1936 a Squire two-seater could be bought for a mere £795. Also, the brakes were almost too powerful, and at least one car had to have a flitch-plate welded on to the frame. Luis Fontes' racing model retired from the 1935 B.R.D.C. 500-Mile Race with a cracked rear dumb-iron. The lighter cars also suffered from axle patter.

None the less, the Squire deserved a better fate. Apart from Fontes' abortive Brooklands appearance, the late Duke of Grafton raced a stripped lightweight two-seater once or twice at Donington.

A production batch of twelve chassis was laid down, and when the company was wound up in July 1936, eight cars had been made —five short-chassis, two long-chassis, and one special racing car for Fontes. Also on the stocks was a 1,500 c.c. o.h.c. six-cylinder racing car, which Squire had designed with the intention of beating Frank Lockhart's 1½-litre Flying Mile record of 164 m.p.h. Only a few engine parts had been made at the time of liquidation, and it was allowed to die with the company. Adrian Squire went to work for the Bristol Aeroplane Co. Ltd., and was killed in an air raid in 1941.

Yet this was not the end of the story. Mr Val Zethrin of Chisle-hurst had bought a Squire in 1935, and was so impressed with its potential that he purchased the name, goodwill and spares a year later. He went further than that, and between 1937 and the out-break of war completed two further Squires, a short-chassis Corsica drophead coupé and an open car which he bodied himself. After the war, the late Robert Arbuthnot planned to finance limited pro-duction of the *marque*, but this scheme fell through.

Undeterred, Mr Zethrin made up yet another short-chassis Squire, and as I write he is working on the twelfth car, 'but as I am designer, draughtsman, welder, turner and fitter, it takes time, and it goes so quickly," he comments ruefully. There seems little doubt, though, that there will be a ready market across the Atlantic for as many Squires as Mr Zethrin can make, for in 1959 I heard of one of these fantastic thoroughbreds—one of three, incidentally, in America—changing hands for $8,000. I had a run in the ex-Duke of Grafton car in Cape Town in the winter of 1959, incidentally. Squire's departure from Henley coincided with the end of Marendaz Special Cars Ltd. But the last word, curiously enough, was left to Reichsmarschall Göring. Maidenhead, despite its proximity to London and the wartime importance of Air Transport Auxiliary's airfield at White Waltham, survived the war unscathed—save for one minor incident. On 1 July 1944, the peace of the riverside town was disturbed by one flying-bomb, which descended upon a con-verted Victorian mansion backing on to Cordwallis Works. Four families were rendered homeless, but Britain's jam ration remained intact. While we all know that no great measure of control over the V.1 was ever possible, it is hard to dismiss this as a coincidence. Had some boffin in the Wilhelmstrasse fallen behindhand with his intelligence, and conceived a violent fear of the design potential of the Jam Factory?

CHAPTER 13

The First to Wear the Green:
S. F. Edge and the Napier

'When asked by the editor to contribute an article . . . I rather demurred at first, as it seemed to me that, as I am interested financially in the success of the Napier car, anything in its favour, however innocently stated by me, must read too much like an advertisement.'

S. F. Edge, *Cars and How to Drive Them*, August, 1902

'The works are open to the fullest inspection to enable anyone to see the wonderful care and skill employed on their construction.'

ibid.

It was February 1960, and I stood in the grounds of H. H. The Kabaka of Buganda's royal palace staring at the remains of a once lordly limousine. Nothing was left of the tyres, and termites and vandals had reduced the coachwork to a mere husk. The engine, however, had escaped almost intact, and the proud 'water tower' still crowned the big radiator. The sight was infinitely pathetic, and brought home poignantly how complete has been the eclipse of the Napier car.

Nowadays the name of Napier is associated with the world of marine and aeronautical engineering. As part of the big English Electric combine, they are still a name to conjure with, and the firm's 150th anniversary, celebrated in 1958, attracted much press comment. But until a Napier Rally was held in Regent's Park that summer it is unlikely that many people realized that as late as 1910 the Acton firm's name, linked with that of Selwyn Francis Edge, symbolized the British motor industry at its best. Unlike many of the Lost Causes, D. Napier and Son Ltd. opted out of the car business and did not wait to be forcibly ejected by slumps and the onset of mass production.

The story of Napier cars from 1899 to 1924 is the saga of two men, Montague Napier and Selwyn Francis Edge. Without an engineer of Napier's calibre and foresight at the helm, the company might never have emerged from the role of a relatively insignificant workshop in Lambeth, engaged on the production of a few complex machines for the world's mints and arsenals: and without Edge's genius for publicity, the Napier car might have gone the way of such vehicles as the Star, which never skimped quality, yet never made the headlines because of its makers' inherent conservatism in sales policy and design alike.

It is too easy to dismiss Edge as a mere bombast. Bombastic he undoubtedly was, as this passage from the correspondence columns of *The Autocar* as late as 1921, will show:

'S. F. Edge, and S. F. Edge Ltd., pushed forward the merits of the six-cylinder, and made the world accept it.'

by which time, be it said, Edge was no longer concerning himself with Napiers at all. He was forever setting up Aunt Sallies and knocking them down with floods of vituperative prose, in which no holds were barred, and he expended this energy over the best part of two decades on a determined attempt to prove to the world that he invented the six-cylinder engine. True, he was not alone in using the correspondence columns of the motoring press as free display advertisement space, and he never waxed quite as abusive as D. M. Weigel, for instance. Nor were his claims as improbable as those of the Hillman Motor Car Co. Ltd., who just before the first World War engaged Rolls-Royce in single combat and challenged the Olympian directorate at Derby to explain in what respects the 'Silver Ghost' was better than their own 9 h.p. light car! The fact is that Edge overplayed his hand. He may not have been the first to build a six-cylinder car engine, but he certainly sponsored the first unit of this type to make any international impression: he was one of the earliest car manufacturers to realize the value of publicity: many of his long-distance runs and odd experiments, though cloaked in bombast, possessed much practical merit and, above all, he put Britain, and Napier, on the international competition map by the racing programme he pursued, in the face of sundry frustrations, from 1900 to 1908. Anthony Heal, the historian of Napier's racing years, describes the *marque* as 'The first to wear the green', but even this is an understatement—for British Racing Green is but the descendant of that colour which still features in paint manufacturers' catalogues as 'Napier green'—and this shade first saw the light of day in 1903, when Edge was defending the Gordon Bennett Cup on the Athy Circuit in Ireland.

Montague Napier, in 1899, had for three years been the head of the old-established family engineering firm in Vine Street, Lambeth; founded in 1808, D. Napier and Son had built up a solid reputation as makers of printing presses, balances, and other complex devices demanding a high standard of accuracy. J. M. Napier, Montague's father, had lost interest in his declining years, and the business had been going gently downhill when his son fell victim to the growing cult of the motor car. His own design, however, was discarded in 1899 when his fellow-cyclist S. F. Edge, already a well-known member of the Bath Road Club, asked him to design a replacement engine for an 1896 Paris-Marseilles-type Panhard.

By November 1899, the conversion was complete, and Edge's Panhard was on the road, powered by a vertical twin engine said to be capable of 1,200 r.p.m. It had, of course, automatic inlet valves, but Montague Napier adopted coil ignition from the start, refusing to consider the unreliable tube even as a standby. At the same time, the firm advertised that they were willing to convert any existing vehicle from tiller to wheel steering.

The next step was taken when Edge started the Motor Power Company, and in 1900 there was signed the first of a series of agreements between Edge and Napier, whereby the latter undertook to produce a guaranteed number of cars to be sold by Edge's new concern. This arrangement anticipated, and probably inspired, the contract drawn up four years later by the Hon. C. S. Rolls and Frederick Henry Royce, and was to last until the end of 1912. It had the advantage of relieving Napier from commercial responsibilities, though it also resulted in the virtual identification of the cars with Edge, and in the long run helped to kill the *marque* once divorce proceedings had been instituted. Initially Edge 'padded' his list with agencies such as the Gladiator and the German Windhoff, which he sold under the name of Regent, but after 1907 he concentrated on Napiers to the exclusion of any other make, special emphasis being laid always on the six-cylinder car which formed the subject of most of his polemics in the correspondence columns of the press.

For 1900, a twin-cylinder chain-driven car was built, using the same type of engine that had been fitted in the Panhard. This was entered for the 1,000 Miles Trial by Edward Kennard, and driven by Edge himself. His mechanic was none other than my friend St. John C. Nixon, now a *doyen* among motoring journalists and a Director of my Museum, but then a youth of fourteen. The car had been on the road only a week when the trial started, and the aluminium body—a feature of Napiers from the start—was unfinished, yet it came through with flying colours, and was awarded a bronze medal. Eight years later, Kennard was still a Napier customer, and claimed that the average annual maintenance bill on his cars was a mere £11.

Edge's next step was to do still more to enhance Napier's prestige. Britain had as yet done little in Continental motor-racing, apart from my father's performance in the 1899 Paris–Ostend Race, and no British competitors started in the first of the Gordon Bennett series in 1900. But quite unobtrusively, Edge, with the Hon. C. S. Rolls as mechanic, entered a 16 h.p. Napier for the Paris–Toulouse race.

This was the company's first four-cylinder car, and was described by *The Autocar* as a 'racy, classy-looking road engine'. It followed closely the lines of the twin-cylinder model, its bore and stroke being 101·6 mm. and 152·4 mm. respectively, and the capacity 4·9 litres. This engine had triple automatic inlet valves, coil ignition and chain drive featured as before, and cooling was taken care of by two Loyal tubular radiators. The lubrication was complex, the Dubrulle-type lubricator being assisted by two hand pumps on the dash. A monstrous forty-gallon petrol tank, reminiscent of a bath cistern, lived behind the seats, and the ground clearance was considered to be meagre at twelve inches, in spite of which Edge's unhappy pet dog was killed when he fell from the passenger seat at speed.

Despite the failure of this entry, ascribed variously to troubles with ignition and the water-jacketing of the cylinders, the 16 h.p. and its twin-cylinder stablemate quickly established themselves in the front rank of British-built cars, and early customers included A. J. Balfour, who ordered the first of his many Napiers in February 1902. By contrast, Lord Salisbury preferred a Locomobile steamer. The 16 h.p. was progressively developed, and by March 1902, that most devoted of customers, Mrs Edward Kennard, was rhapsodizing thus:

'. . . the improvements effected by Mr Napier in the short space of eighteen months are simply marvellous. The original 16 h.p. was conspicuous rather for strength and solidity than for that indefinable quality—life. But her successor, whilst retaining all the good attributes of her precursor, possesses remarkable buoyancy. She answers to the change-speed lever as does a high-mettled hunter to a touch of the spur.'

In November 1901, it was announced that hire-purchase facilities were available to customers. A month later one of the first Napier commercial vehicles, a 12 h.p. 'toast-rack' charabanc, was in service at Scarborough, and a small paragraph in the motoring press proclaimed the departure of a 'Mr C. J. Gladden' on a 2,000-mile tour of England and France.

1901, in fact, was to produce two landmarks in Napier history—

the entry of a car for the Gordon Bennett Cup, and the commencement of Charles J. Glidden's seven-year 'slimming tour'. This
indefatigable American set himself the task of driving fifty thousand
miles in fifty countries, and when he retired from the fray in 1908,
four Napiers later, he was still 3,462 miles and eleven countries short
of his target. Nor was he, apparently, any slimmer, for *The Autocar*
commented in January 1906, that as the tour progressed "Thomas,
the mechanic, becomes more travel-stained, Mr Glidden stouter
and Mrs Glidden more handsome'. In mitigation, it must be said
that at that time the Gliddens were in Afghanistan, which is hardly
a recommended touring-ground even now. Their exploits included
a considerable amount of railroad work, for which the Napier was
specially equipped with flanged wheels, and on one occasion Glidden
varied the diet by putting in fifty brisk miles at Brooklands on one of
Edge's stripped touring chassis. Glidden inspired the series of Tours
which bears his name, the first of these long-distance rallies taking
place in 1905. As a result of his efforts, the Napier Motor Co., of
Boston, were turning out 45 h.p. four-cylinder cars by 1906: these
retailed at $6,500, another $3,500 being demanded for the genuine
London-made article!

Napier's first try at the Gordon Bennett was less successful. Aware
that the 16 h.p. car was lacking in power, the firm went to the
other extreme, and produced a $16\frac{1}{2}$-litre, four-cylinder chain-
driven monster weighing approximately two tons. The tubular
radiator and automatic inlet valves were inherited from the 1900
design, and the engine, nominally rated at 50 h.p., was said to develop
103 b.h.p. at 800 r.p.m., giving an alleged maximum speed of
85 m.p.h. and a fuel consumption of 4 m.p.g.—not that this was
of great import, since tankage was provided for fourteen gallons
of water and fifty of petrol. Unfortunately the Gordon Bennett
regulations stipulated that all parts of the cars had to be made in the
entrant's country, and there were no British tyres capable of coping
with this behemoth. The Napier had therefore to content itself with
the 'open' race from Paris to Bordeaux, run concurrently with the
Gordon Bennett Cup. Clutch trouble put it out of this event,
and it also retired in that year's 'Paris–Berlin', though Edge had the
consolation of a class win at the Gaillon hill climb. The catalogue
price (surely of academic interest only?) was quoted as £1,500, and
it is characteristic that Edge, having claimed in his pre-race releases
that Napiers had made the whole car apart from the tyres and chains
firmly disclaimed any responsibility for the clutch after that component gave way on the road to Bordeaux.

This gargantuan machine, however, taught Edge and Napier some valuable lessons, and for 1902 they were back with a far more compact 30 h.p. car of 6·4 litres (127 × 127 mm.), weighing only 16¾ cwt. A throttle was now fitted—engine control on the 1900 car had been limited to an advance-and-retard—and while coil ignition and automatic inlet valves were retained, Napier used shaft drive, an innovation in the field of big car racing. It is now history that Edge, in spite of troubles with cylinder heads, and all-night work on the gearbox up to the moment of the start, brought the Gordon Bennett Cup home to England, and thus forced the world to take this country's motor industry seriously. A hollow victory it may have been—for once De Knyff's Panhard was out of the race, Edge only had to finish to win—but nonetheless, the courage and determination of driver and designer alike had paid off.

At the subsequent banquet, Edge missed no opportunity of trumpeting the Napier virtues, and gently disparaging his rivals—the big Panhards were 'marvellous carriages when going, but whenever they slowed up, they began to steam', while the pressure fuel feed on the Mercédès also came in for criticism. Not that this sniping was entirely unjustified, for Panhards, unlike Napiers, were still pursuing the policy of brute force. Many years later, Edge revealed the economics of the 1902 race. The total cost of the car, fares and expenses for himself and his cousin Cecil, who acted as his mechanic, entry fees, and tyres, came to £1,418, of which £1,200 was recovered by the sale of the Napier after the event. Modern competition departments would blanch at the thought of winning any international Grand Prix for an outlay of £218!

As it happened, Napiers never bulked so large again in inter-national racing, though they contested the three remaining races in the Gordon Bennett series, and contrived to outshine their rivals in the British Eliminating Trials which preceded the races proper. In 1903, as a result of Edge's victory, the race was held on the Athy Circuit in Ireland, the three British contenders being a brace of 7·7-litre cars based on the 1902 machines, and a 165 × 152 mm. (13-litre) 80 h.p. car which Edge himself drove. Jarrott and Stocks, on the smaller cars, retired, while Edge finished last, only to be disqualified for receiving a push-start from spectators. Only Edge on an 80 h.p. car competed in the 1904 race, held in Germany, and he retired after making the second fastest lap; while despite the arrival of the legendary six-cylinder L48 with its Rudge-Whitworth wheels and enormous tubular radiators in time for the 1905 event, Edge could manage no better than ninth place.

The cars were growing up, and by 1903 a 12 h.p. four-cylinder car was on the market with the modern-style Clarkson radiator in place of the old tubular Loyal. Edge was likewise widening the scope of his interests, and began the development of a series of successful racing motor-boats, sniping at the makers of steam launches *en route*:

'It is just as useless . . . to try and oppose the success of the motor car engine on the water as it was to try and prevent its success on the road.'

Edge's victories at Monaco were so frequent that in 1906 the Prince awarded him the Order of St. Charles, but less was heard of Napier's aeronautical ventures. In 1901 a powered dirigible was catalogued at £950, and as late as July 1909, Edge was offering to build an airship, and run an air service from London to Manchester, if other backers would find £12,000 'for out-of-pocket expenses'. He might argue that the Austrian Government had just authorized the expenditure of £60,000 towards a similar end, but the Graf von Zeppelin remained unchallenged. More successful, if less spectacular, was the Napier luggage trailer, which Edge put on the market in 1904.

In October 1903, there came a momentous announcement: Napiers were to make a six-cylinder car for the coming season. Curiously enough, Edge's statement contained more sound thinking than ballyhoo. He was clearly anxious to save weight, and cited the example of the firm's four-cylinder engines. In 1900, a unit weighing 340 lb. had developed only 24 b.h.p., whereas by 1903 80 b.h.p. was obtainable from an engine turning the scales at 183 lb. Perhaps the dramatic effect of the new 'six' was a little spoilt by the simultaneous appearance of the four-wheel-drive six-cylinder Spyker, and the publication, in the same issue of *The Autocar* that had carried Edge's announcement, of a photograph of a launch powered by a vertical 'six' of Brooke manufacture.

Be that as it may, the result of Napier's move from Lambeth to Acton that summer was an ambitious range, embracing not only the new 'six' at a chassis price of £1,050, but chain-driven 'fours' of 15 h.p. and 24 h.p., and a shaft-driven 127 × 127 mm. four-cylinder car based on the Gordon Bennett design and listed at £1,200.

The new six-cylinder car adhered to chain drive and coil ignition, but the automatic inlet valve gear had given way to mechanically operated overhead inlet and side exhaust valves. As yet, however, the four-speed gearbox of earlier Napiers was retained, though Edge was in years to come to deride the provision of more than three forward ratios. A separate lever was provided for reverse, 'single-lever control' being optional. It was claimed that a standard car could climb Reigate Hill on top. The 1904 Napier catalogue also mentions two more four-cylinder cars, rated at 45 h.p. and 65 h.p., and a big 90 h.p. 'six', but adds that these are 'not designed for use in the United Kingdom'.

Edge in later years claimed with ever-increasing bombast that he originated the six-cylinder engine. As one Fernand Forest had such a unit running in 1889, this assertion must be disallowed, but even if we accept the claims of such makers as Spyker, Sunbeam, and Brooke, we must concede that none of these three firms made much impression. Edge's attitude to Spyker's claims undoubtedly mellowed in the early nineteen-twenties, when he took over the agency for this famous Dutch *marque*, and used a six-cylinder example to attack long-distance records at Brooklands, but nevertheless the best-known Edwardian products of the firm had four cylinders. The original 16 h.p. Sunbeam 'six' scarcely progressed beyond the prototype stage, while Brooke, though they made quite a number of 'sixes' before abandoning cars for marine engines in 1913, never made a great impact on the motor industry. By the 1907 season, over twenty British manufacturers, these pioneers apart, were listing six-cylinder models, and they can be said to owe their inspiration to Napier's example. To Napier and Edge, too, must go the credit for producing smooth and flexible 'sixes', rather than adding the extra cylinders, as Laurence Pomeroy puts it, for the purpose of 'making a fast car larger'. There is no comparison between an early Edwardian Napier and the eleven-plus litres of the 1905 50 h.p. Panhard.

Edge still raced his Napiers. L48, the famous six-cylinder car, was a great success in sprints, making f.t.d. at Portmarnock in 1904, and third fastest time at Gaillon the same year. In 1905, Clifford Earp won his class at the Brighton Speed Trials, establishing a new British kilometre record of 97·25 m.p.h., while the enterprising Dorothy Levitt, one of the few women competitors in those days, recorded 78·71 m.p.h. at the same meeting. Earp's f.t.d. at Chateau-Thierry rounded off a successful year. In 1906 a Napier took second place at Gaillon, and the following season Glentworth, later Napier's American representative, made the fastest ascent. Perhaps the *marque*'s greatest triumph was, however, the 1907 Bexhill Speed Trials, when Napiers swept the board, winning everything, the Appearance Competition included, save for two events, for one of which no existing Napier would have been eligible.

The big six-cylinder car was also sent to Daytona Beach for the

American Automobile Club's trials in 1905 and 1906. The first year Arthur Macdonald did extremely well, taking several records, including a mile at 104·65 m.p.h. and twenty miles at 89·21 m.p.h. On one occasion, he was surprised when preparing for an early morning trial by the armed watchman, who let fly at him with a six-shooter. In 1906 Clifford Earp had a tougher time, being outclassed by both the 200 h.p. vee-eight Darracq and Marriott's Stanley Steamer, and the car's best performance was a victory in the Minneapolis International Trophy at a speed of 79 m.p.h.

Napiers also supported a diversity of events, including the Herkomer Trophy, the Kaiserpreis (in which their entry did not survive the eliminating trials), Shelsley Walsh (H.C. Tryon made f.t.d. in 1908, with a time of 65·4 sec. but was only fourteenth on formula), and the Town Carriage Competition of 1906. They also entered two 90 × 108 mm. 18 h.p. four-cylinder cars for the 1905 'fuel consumption' T.T., but these did not shine, although Montague Napier reverted to automatic inlet valves in quest of better m.p.g. Edge, however, played to win, and withdrew his entries from the 2,000 Miles Trial of 1908, for instance, as he maintained that they were not ready, and so stood no chance of beating the field on all the observed hills.

The opening of Brooklands Track in 1907 provided Edge with a golden opportunity, and in June he successfully drove a 60 h.p. six-cylinder car 1,582 miles in twenty-four hours, thus becoming the first driver to average a mile a minute 'round the clock'. This tremendous achievement—Edge's rival, Jarrott, had asserted that it was 'not really possible'—was the prelude to two successful seasons on the Track, in the course of which Edge's 'circus' of six cars, mainly stripped touring models, took nine first places and a number of records: these included Tryon's victory in the first heat of the first race—the Marcel Renault Memorial Plate—ever to take place at Brooklands. Edge won £1,760 in prize money in 1907 alone, while L48, now known as 'Samson', had its stroke lengthened to 178 mm., giving a capacity of over twenty litres, and performed splendidly in the hands of Frank Newton. Though Newton lost his famous match race against Nazzaro's FIAT 'Mephistopheles' when the crankshaft broke, he took the 90 h.p. Short Record at a resounding 119·34 m.p.h. in November 1908. This was the Napier's competition swansong.

Meanwhile, 1908 had seen two other competition ventures. The preparation of three 11½-litre six-cylinder cars for the French Grand Prix proved abortive, since Edge adopted Rudge-Whitworth wheels, and the A.C.F. refused to countenance these. The cars, however, were later catalogued as 'sports' models at a list price of £1,600 and one or two were sold. More successful was the Napier entry in the 1908 'Four-Inch' T.T.

The regulations for this event stipulated the use of four-cylinder engines of a bore not exceeding four inches, and the original entry list included a '25·6 h.p. Napier' nominated by Edge. By this time, of course, he had become indelibly associated in the public eye with six-cylinder engines, and felt disinclined to appear to eat his words by sponsoring a 'four'. Thus a nominal sponsor was found in J. E. Hutton, a well-known importer of foreign cars such as Panhard, Mercédès and Berliet, and incidentally a great friend of my family. Hutton's own productions had hitherto progressed little beyond the prototype stage—whatever in fact they were, neither the 20 h.p. of 1904 nor the 10 h.p. of 1905 had anything to do with Napiers, while the odd six-cylinder cars with sprung wheels and Barber infinitely variable transmissions, which he entered for the 1904 Gordon Bennett race, do not seem to have left the drawing-board. True, it was announced shortly after the 1908 T.T. that Hutton had accepted an appointment with Wolseleys and was closing down his retail business, thus being unable to take up his contract for the sale of 'production' T.T. Huttons—but there is no reason to suppose that he was ever expected to do so.

In the event, the three Huttons were unmistakably Napiers, even down to the radiator 'water tower'. Side valves, a four-speed all-indirect gearbox, and detachable wire wheels featured in the specification. Of the three cars, Watson's and Stirling's had a 178 mm. stroke, that of Hutton's own car being lengthened to 204 mm. Watson, though challenged strongly by George's Darracq, won the race at 50·25 m.p.h., and his car is still going strong in the hands of Francis Hutton-Stott, having been rescued from oblivion during the late war by Anthony Heal.

Meanwhile the touring Napiers flourished. Though production was never high—only 4,258 private cars were made between 1906 and 1924, and some 1,800 of these were turned out during the 'boom' period from 1909 to 1911—they enjoyed an as yet unrivalled reputation. By 1906 chain drive was on its way out, and the 'water tower' was firmly established as a trade-mark of the breed. Models listed were the four-cylinder Eighteen and Forty-five, and the six-cylinder Forty and Sixty, the most expensive type costing £1,600. *The Autocar* tried a Sixty in that year and rhapsodized over its ability to start on the switch, and the way it could be driven away in top gear, 'controlled entirely by the manipulation of the 'throttle valve lever'. On this car Arthur Macdonald introduced the press to his pet party trick, comparable to the Lanchester habit of motoring smartly up a bank to demonstrate the qualities of the suspension. The car was allowed to run downhill at about 8 m.p.h., whereupon reverse was engaged, and the car backed smartly back upwards without snatch.

From 1907 to 1911, Napiers pursued a policy of extreme complexity, concentrating on large six-cylinder cars, but also coming out in 1909 with two low-priced offerings, a twin-cylinder 10 h.p. at £375, and a companion 15 h.p. 'four' at £430, both of which were made in some numbers as taxicabs. The 1910 programme embraced ten separate models, ranging from the 10 h.p. to an enormous 156 × 127 mm. six-cylinder Ninety, with a wheelbase of 11 ft. 11 in. for which £1,620 was asked. Only six models were catalogued in 1912, however.

For all Edge's bombast and wild challenges, he was careful also to submit his Napiers to officially-observed trials, from which they emerged creditably. In 1905, Cecil Edge drove a six-cylinder car from Brighton to Edinburgh on top gear, combining a flying kilometre at 46 m.p.h. with a creditably 'freak' hundred yards at 1·33 m.p.h. A Sixty submitted for test in May 1906 proved capable of 5 to 60 m.p.h. on its 3 : 1 top gear, although fuel consumption was a discouraging 8·98 m.p.g. In April 1907, E. A. Paul broke the London–Monte Carlo Record on a similar car with a time of thirty-three hours thirty-four minutes, and in March 1909, one Vivian Lewis knocked nearly three hours off the record for the Melbourne–Adelaide run.

From 1910 onwards, Napiers were regularly submitted for R.A.C. Monthly Trials, and these are of particular interest, since they provide the chance for an accurate assessment of performance which is singularly lacking in the woolly appraisals of contemporary journalists not blessed with modern recording apparatus. In February 1910, a 45 h.p. six-cylinder tourer of 6,840 c.c. weighing 4,063 lb. ready for the road, was timed to do 66·12 m.p.h. at Brooklands. 0–30 m.p.h. acceleration time was 8·75 sec., by contrast with which a typical 1966 1-litre saloon takes only 5·2 sec., but more impressive was a fuel consumption of 19·93 m.p.g. Thanks to modern automatic transmissions, few of today's 7-litre cars could come anywhere near this figure. By contrast, the 30 h.p. Napier was some 15 m.p.h. slower, took nearly two seconds longer to reach 30 m.p.h., and recorded an almost identical fuel consumption, thus illustrating the fact that the enormous and lazy engines of Edwardian days did not have the appalling thirst of their Vintage successors. Incidentally, the 30 h.p. collected the R.A.C.'s Gold Medal for the best performance of the year in a Monthly Trial, while the firm also won the Dewar Trophy for a memorable run on a Sixty from London to Edinburgh in top gear. The driver was Arthur Macdonald, and his fuel consumption of 19 m.p.g. reflects the advantages of a 2·7 : 1 top gear.

Top-gear drives were the order of the day, and a parallel can be found, perhaps, only in Violet Cordery's exploits with her Invictas in the late Vintage years. In September 1911, two firms sought to better the Napier performance—one of these was Sheffield-Simplex, who used one of their 'gearboxless' six-cylinder cars (it actually had two forward speeds), and the other was no less than Rolls-Royce. A 'Silver Ghost' tourer was driven from London to Edinburgh in top gear, recording 24·32 m.p.g., and lapping Brooklands at 78·26 m.p.h. Thus was born the famous 'London–Edinburgh' model.

It is often said that this was Rolls-Royce's final answer to the Napier challenge, and the reason why the admittedly noisier productions of Acton lost out to Derby. Edge, who had but recently made the patronizing comment that the Rolls-Royce was 'certainly quite a nice car', was not however at a loss, and he replied with two remarkable performances in 1912. The first, in June, was an observed long-distance run over the route London–Land's End–John-O' Groat's–Edinburgh–London, in which the 60 h.p. Napier, a far bigger car than the Rolls-Royce, turned in 23·9 m.p.g.; while the second was a top-gear run from London to Edinburgh *and back* at an average speed of 18·7 m.p.h. on which fuel was consumed at the truly astonishing rate of 27·65 m.p.g. One has a feeling that, had the Edge-Napier association continued, Rolls-Royce would have had to have fought harder for supremacy. Alas, a month after the publication of the results of this trial, Edge announced his retirement.

Edge's other activities were multifarious. A Napier hire service was set up in 1910, and he secured a contract for the transport of V.I.P.s at the Coronation of King George V the following year. The Electromobile Co., seeing that the days of their electric broughams were numbered, followed suit and purchased a fleet of Napiers.

Some of Edge's attempts to drum up publicity were, however, strictly stunts, such as the occasion when he and his cousin motored at speed over broken soda water syphons at the Crystal Palace to demonstrate the controllability of Napiers in the face of a tyre-burst.

More diverting still was the demonstration of a 15 h.p. landaulet in 1911. Some pigeons were persuaded to feed within a few feet of the exhaust pipe while the engine was running, and a penny was successfully balanced on the 'water tower'. As Edge explained, for the benefit of the medical profession:

'It is frequently necessary . . . to make notes while travelling from one patient's house to another, and also imperative that a car left with engine running outside a patient's dwelling should be as quiet and inoffensive as possible.'

Other experiments had valuable and practical applications, such as the series of tests carried out at Brooklands in 1907 and 1908. These included trials with a six-cylinder chassis on which was mounted a light steel latticed framework, designed to ascertain the relative wind resistance with bodies of different frontal area: acceleration and braking tests with various weights on the frame: tyre pressure tests which helped to overcome the resistance to the use of low-pressure tyres: and trials with rugs on radiators to ascertain the exact effect of covering the bonnet in winter.

Nor should Edge's contributions to the export trade be forgotten. This astute salesman was not content merely to sell his wares to such illustrious personages as the Nizam of Hyderabad and the King of Siam, but himself carried out a sales tour of South Africa in 1912. The cars were displayed at all the major foreign shows, winning Gold Medals at Paris and Brussels, and turned up at the New York Importers' Salon, the Moscow Exhibition, and the Turin Show. A 15 h.p. car was successfully driven the 450 well-nigh roadless miles from Bahia Blanca to Buenos Aires in August 1910, and a Napier took part in the Russian Army Trials of 1912, though as the account of this ordeal was written by F. A. Coleman, then the British concessionaire for White cars, we do not hear much of its exploits. Napiers were built under licence in Italy from 1906 to 1909 by the San Giorgio company, Macdonald going out to supervise operations. In January 1909, Edge proudly claimed that over £16,000 had been paid out in duties on six cars shipped to the Western Hemisphere in the past month. By the time he retired, the 'Colonial' and 'Extra Strong Colonial' four-cylinder Napiers were well established—these had two inches of extra ground clearance, the hoods could be detached and used as tents, and the seats folded down to form a bed. They were extremely tough—indeed, there is record of a Napier being used to follow a buck-hunt in South Africa. The car was said to be appreciably slower than a springbok, though

THE FIRST TO WEAR THE GREEN

probably a lot brisker than the four-wheel-drive ex-W.D. trucks favoured by present-day trappers.

At the end of 1912, it was announced that Edge and Napier had parted company. Napiers purchased from Edge his holding in S. F. Edge (1907) Ltd., and Edge undertook not to engage in the motor trade for seven years. For some time relations had been strained, owing to Edge's autocratic manner, which applied to partners and customers alike. As an instance of this, Mrs Bolster, the mother of John Bolster, the famous journalist and creator of 'Bloody Mary', had occasion to complain of the quality of the paintwork on her Napier. She returned the car to S. F. Edge Ltd., and requested to see Mr Edge. A note was duly sent up to Edge, who arrived in the workshop, stalked round the car, and retreated to his sanctum without uttering a word. Thence there issued, some time later, a typed note authorizing the disgruntled customer to have the car repainted at the firm's expense by the 'best coach-builders in London'.

Outwardly there were few changes at first: the long series of officially observed trials on the four-cylinder 'Colonial' Napiers continued right up to August 1914. C.A.V. electric lighting, which Edge had distrusted, was adopted for 1914, when a new 4·7-litre worm-drive six-cylinder 30/35 was introduced at £650. The rest of the range comprised the four-cylinder 16/22 and Twenty, and the big Forty-five. The new 'six' was introduced to the public via an officially observed 2,100-mile test in the Austrian Alps. Only the 16/22 and the 30/35 were listed for 1915, but for some time the firm pursued the policy of 'business as usual'.

The war, however, changed Montague Napier's outlook. He saw, rightly, that the future lay in aero-engines, and the return to motor-car production in 1919 was never intended as more than a temporary measure. Indeed, the fact that it lingered on until 1924 was due more than anything else to the production and sales difficulties that dogged Napier's final model, the 40/50 h.p. T75.

This was an impressive vehicle: like several of its contemporaries, it was a curious blend of ancient and modern. Extensive use of aluminium kept the chassis weight down to 24½ cwt., and the 101·6 × 127 mm. (6,178 c.c.) six-cylinder engine featured an overhead camshaft and steel screwed-in liners. The four-speed gearbox had a top-gear ratio of 3·75 : 1 and had central control, while a single-plate clutch was used. The foot transmission brake was a legacy from Edwardian times: this disappeared from the long-chassis cars in 1924, but was retained on the short-chassis models to the end. The price of a tourer was £2,185 in 1920, inflated a year later to £2,735.

In the best Napier traditions, the car was subjected in 1921 to a long-distance R.A.C. observed trial in the Alps, in the course of which it climbed the Simplon, Pordoi and Stelvio passes. The fuel consumption figure of 19 m.p.g. was a lot better than one would expect—the makers only claimed 13 m.p.g. on a weak mixture—but the disadvantages of an 11 ft. 5 in. wheelbase are reflected in the necessity for reversing on twenty-five of the Stelvio's forty-four corners! Such old customers as A. J. Balfour and the King of Siam duly bought the new models, delightfully bodied by Napier's 'house coachbuilder', Cunard, but by the end of 1924 the output of cars was sold, and Napiers went over to aero-engines for good. Cunard, incidentally, became part of the Stewart and Ardern group, and built sporting coachwork for such offerings as the Morris 'Ten-Six Special'.

Actual production of the post-1918 cars was as follows:

T.75 standard model	120 cars	Deliveries start Aug. 1919
T.77 Colonial model	17 cars	Deliveries end July 1922
T.79 l.w.b. model	45 cars	Deliveries end Nov. 1924
T.80 s.w.b. model	5 cars	Deliveries end Dec. 1923

Not that this was the end. Napier never built a car again, but their famous broad-arrow-type 'Lion' engine powered many famous aircraft, as well as a succession of famous record-breaking vehicles, notably Sir Malcolm Campbell's earlier 'Bluebirds', Sir Henry Segrave's 'Golden Arrow' of 1929, John Cobb's immortal Napier-Railton track car of 1933, and his later Railton Mobil Special, which still held the World's Land Speed Record until July 1964. In 1931, a come-back seemed likely, for D. Napier and Son made strenuous attempts to purchase the bankrupt Bentley Company, only to be foiled at the eleventh hour by a higher bid from Rolls-Royce. It was said at the time that fitting shops at Acton had even been cleared for tooling-up on the new Napier-Bentley, so sure were Napiers that their offer would be accepted.

As a successful member of the English Electric Group, Napier can hardly be called a Lost Cause. The firm retains a friendly interest in its cars, preserving a fine T75 limousine at the works, and they were clearly delighted when over two dozen entries turned up for the Commemoration Rally in Regent's Park in June 1958. No one can blame Montague Napier for his astute change of loyalties in 1918, for this step undoubtedly kept the firm on its feet through the lean years of the early thirties. Yet one wonders whether Napier might not have retained the lead had Edge stayed on, and still more one wonders what might have happened had the financial negotiations of 1931 taken a different turn. To quote *The Veteran and Vintage Magazine*, reporting the 1958 Napier Rally:

'What a pity there are no more Napier cars to look forward to—or, as the proud owner of a 4½-litre put it—why couldn't there have been a Napier-Bentley?'

CHAPTER 14

The Reckoning

'It makes gear changing as simple and as noiseless as breathing.'
Unit Ten advertisement, 1922

... AND, we may add, as bankruptcy, too! This is of necessity rather a mournful and nostalgic story, for the Lost Causes are mostly those which failed to make the grade.

Failure, however, is not necessarily ignominious, for it is these earlier efforts which spur later generations to conquer the problems which defeated the under-capitalized experimenters of the past. The sliding-type gearbox is now on its way out, yielding to complex and costly automatic transmissions with dog-Greek names, but G.W.K. had propounded an ingenious if unreliable substitute in 1911, and Lyle and Macklin had all but rendered it redundant on their 1925 Invicta, while Lanchester eschewed it altogether until economic necessity forced them to fall into line with convention. To the Lost Causes we owe not only four-wheel brakes but the concept of disc braking as well.

So it is with competitively-priced machines. In my opinion many of the Lost Causes went to their graves through the impact of three outstanding commercial successes: the Morris-Cowley of the nineteen-twenties, and Hillman 'Minx' in the early nineteen-thirties, and the Jaguar in the later thirties and forties. The less expensive victims—the G.W.K., the Galloway, the Rhode and, most of all, the Clyno—spurred the big firms on, for they were something to compete against, and Invicta and Railton set a very high standard in the specialist field. Competition furthers quality, and the lack of competition today, though it has perhaps not resulted in a general deterioration, has led to a uniformity of design that must be deplored. I personally feel that no one has yet beaten the Jowett 'Javelin' at its own game, but its impact is still being felt, and the standard of handling and fuel economy in 1½-litre family saloons has improved out of all proportion since 1948.

I have often been asked why I have chosen to dig up the past and chronicle the doings of manufacturers whose products were relatively uninteresting. My answer is that they were of absorbing interest; at least four of the *marques* I have recorded are internationally

216

famous—Invicta, Jowett, Lanchester and Lea-Francis, while lesser
lights such as Alldays and Onions, Clyno, Star and Argyll had their
devoted followings. The ingenuity of the pioneers—Johnston, Mead,
Macklin, Frank Smith, and all the others—demands that their
exploits should be set down on paper before they and the teams
that backed them are forgotten; and I would not be my father's
son if I neglected this opportunity of perpetuating their memory.

One-Make Clubs Catering for Lost Causes

THE following clubs are in existence, addresses of secretaries being those ruling on 1 March 1966.

B.S.A. Front Drive Club

Michael Hine,
44 Killieser Avenue,
London, S.W.2.

Clyno Register

J. J. Salt,
Chimley Corner,
High Street,
West Lavington,
Devizes, Wilts.

Crossley Register

C. Thomas,
66 Avenue Road,
London, N.15.

Daimler-Lanchester Owners Club
(for Daimler-built cars)

H. D. Saunders,
Red Bank House,
Hedging Lane,
Wilnecote,
Tamworth,
Staffs.

*Invicta Section of the Vintage Sports
Car Club*

J. E. Jenkins and T. E. Laurie,
91 Main Street,
Cadoxton,
Barry,
Glamorganshire.

Jowett Car Club

N. H. Spawton,
18 Partridge Croft,
Bell Green,
Coventry,
Warwickshire.

Lanchester Register
(for pre-Daimler cars)

F. W. Hutton-Stott,
Speen Place,
Newbury,
Berks.

Railton Owners Club

Alan G. Nichols,
The Mailing House,
London, W.13.

Southern Jowett Car Club

B. W. Street,
3 Elmwood Close,
Wallington,
Surrey.

Star Register

D. E. A. Evans,
3 Blackacre Road,
Dudley,
Worcestershire.

Trojan Owners Club

Mrs. D. Graham,
10 St. Johns',
Earlswood,
Redhill,
Surrey.

In addition, the Veteran Car Club of Great Britain (Secretary, Captain D. C. Morrison, R.N., 14 Fitzhardinge Street, Portman Square, London, W.1) caters for all cars made up to the end of 1916, and cars made up to 31 December 1930 are eligible for the Vintage Sports Car Club (Secretary, T. W. Carson, 3 Kingsclere House Stables, Kingsclere, Newbury, Berks.). The V.S.C.C. also takes under its wing certain cars made between 1931 and the end of 1940, which are classed as Post-Vintage Thoroughbreds. The following Lost Causes are eligible under this head: Invicta, Lea-Francis, Railton (open sports models only), Squire.

Index